FROM PHILANTHROPY

TO SOCIAL WELFARE

FROM PHILANTHROPY

Philip Klein

TO SOCIAL WELFARE

An American Cultural Perspective

Jossey-Bass Inc., Publishers
615 Montgomery Street • San Francisco • 1971

FROM PHILANTHROPY TO SOCIAL WELFARE

An American Cultural Perspective
  by Philip Klein

Copyright © 1968 by Jossey-Bass, Inc., Publishers

Copyright under Pan American and Universal
Copyright Conventions

Jossey-Bass, Inc., Publishers
615 Montgomery Street
San Francisco, California 94111

Library of Congress Catalog Card Number 68-18617

International Standard Book Number ISBN 0-87589-012-1

Printed in the United States of America
by York Composition Company, Inc.
York, Pennsylvania

FIRST PRINTING: *January 1968*

SECOND PRINTING: *September 1968*

THIRD PRINTING: *January 1971*

68011

THE JOSSEY-BASS BEHAVIORAL SCIENCE SERIES

General Editors

WILLIAM E. HENRY, *University of Chicago*
NEVITT SANFORD, *Wright Institute*

Adviser in Social Welfare

MARTIN B. LOEB, *University of Wisconsin*

Dedicated
to the unsung toilers in the
rank and file of
public assistance services
who navigate a precarious course between
the ill-served client and regimented bureaucracy
under the stern eye of the reluctant taxpayer

Foreword

It is not often in the academic and professional world that an occasion arises that so deeply evokes a sense of responsibility, that so challenges the conventional approach, and so relentlessly demands a rethinking of philosophy and commitments as the opportunity to share in the sponsorship of this book. The validity of *From Philanthropy to Social Welfare* rests only partly on the proven scholarship of the author. Because Philip Klein has taken part in the growing sphere of social welfare activities for more than fifty years, this book reflects witnessed events of great historical importance. As teacher and critic, Professor Klein has wielded a sharp scalpel, but it has always been balanced with personal good will toward his fellows, even when differences of opinion and outlook could have occasioned hostility or competition.

We, his professional and academic colleagues, see in this book an unusual combination of values. For the first time, all parts of the social welfare field are presented, comprehensively yet succinctly. Operations, facts, techniques, and philosophies are explained and evaluated with great understanding, but with little patience for the vested interest orientation that in this field—no less than in others—has dimmed the sharp outlines of purpose and dedication.

Unlike so many scholarly analyses, this book puts its chief emphasis on motives and achievements, on purpose rather than on process. It is, in fact, a call for action even more than an analytic exposition. It raises questions concerning the soundness of our "professional stance," and the validity of our academic and curricular structures that threaten to become vested interests. In demanding a re-examination of the "profession" of social work and of institutionalized training programs, the author seeks to integrate that field of service with the larger field of social welfare and with our over-all economy and culture. In the spirit of St. Francis of Assisi (his favorite saint), he calls for reorientation to the affairs of the destitute and the poor. Given this point of view, it is natural that there are pertinent and imaginative suggestions for a novel reorganization of training programs in the academic structure and for a reorientation of professional organization and purpose.

Although we have sometimes been involved in controversial sallies with the author, we have always been aware of the soundness and importance of his basic ideas, and we have—some of us not militantly enough—sought to press for them. We acclaim this book as a most important and timely contribution in our field today. It is controversial and will make many in the profession uncomfortable. But it will not easily be forgotten or disregarded.

Lucille N. Austin
Mitchell I. Ginsberg

The Columbia University   Virginia Bellsmith
School of Social Work   Richard A. Cloward
New York   Carol H. Meyer

Preface

From Philanthropy to Social Welfare is not intended for those seeking greater proficiency in techniques of social welfare operation. My
purpose is rather one of stocktaking: to see in perspective what we
think we are doing and why; whether we are or want to be part of a
large-scale modern enterprise in social engineering for welfare, or
small-scale practitioners and technicians only.

Who is it that should do such stocktaking? The legislator, the
teacher of social sciences, the teacher in schools of social work—and
the man or woman who thinks of himself as a social worker—might
take stock. But so, also, should the board member or director of any

welfare agency, public or voluntary, if he is more concerned with helping the client or potential client than with building status, prestige, or professional recognition. Perhaps the average citizen and voter might also also be interested.

Very few ideas presented here were invented by me. They were created, promoted, and fought for by ethical leaders, social philosophers, dedicated administrators, and rank-and-file workers. In a sense, *From Philanthropy to Social Welfare* reflects what—in the course of more than a half century of practice and teaching in this field—I have tried to learn from leaders in government, politics, the social sciences, and administration.

Philip Klein

Au Sable Forks, New York
December, 1967

Contents

FROM PHILANTHROPY

TO SOCIAL WELFARE

Prologue

This book is deliberately tendentious, even though every attempt is made to present without distortion facts supported by available documentation. It reflects an unconditional conviction that a comprehensive welfare system is essential in the culture and civilization of the United States. It is written in and for this country rather than for the wider world of today. It is concerned with the present and with a foreseeable future. Nevertheless, its justification, and any soundness it may possess, lies in comprehending the past. And the meaning of that past demands sober thought and much soul-searching.

Two different "pasts" concern us here. One is the history over several hundred years of efforts toward some ultimate system of social welfare in keeping with available resources, and of a social philosophy both ethical and practicable. As to these past efforts, we

1

are chiefly the heirs of Britain's history, and such impacts on that history as came from the French Revolution and from scattered European sources. That does not mean simple factual history, for it involves the strifes of class and caste, of power rivalries, of economic and religious groups; it involves inventions, and industrial revolution, and political innovations without number.

The second past is more recent and largely of the United States. It is the history of *social work* as it has developed here since the turn of the century. This particular American history has been chiefly shaped by training schools for social work and the professional organization of social workers. Both have had an enormous growth here and developed some features apparently absent in the latter decades in Britain. Much of this growth came, moreover, during the generation following the great depression. It came with the emergence of public systems of social security, economic assistance, aid to dependent children, unemployment insurance, and the campaign for medical care for the medically indigent. Yet to none of these has training school or professional organization given decisive leadership or even a substantial contribution.

This is a serious indictment. It should not be lightly made. And it must be documented. True, it was foreshadowed, ever so gently, a generation ago by that profound student of professional education, Abraham Flexner. It was suggested obliquely by a leading technician and educator in social work, Porter R. Lee, about the same time (in 1933), when he wistfully observed the tendency of the profession to sidestep concern with economic problems of the destitute.

In the light of these observations these pages must present two separate, though repeatedly coalescing, pictures, moving from the past to the present and to a future to be imagined. One is that of the welfare services of this country, particularly those addressed to the destitute and poverty-stricken, advancing at a crescendo pace, and constituting the particular arena and function of the welfare worker. The other picture is the less well known but nonetheless disturbing one of the inversion of a large body of the service manpower of social work into what might be termed a narcissistic cult, seeking titles, image, and control.

PART ONE

THE WHAT AND WHY OF
SOCIAL WORK OR
"WELFARE"

Chapter I

❧❦

A Vista of "Welfare"

The Constitution of the United States of America begins with these words: *"We, the people of the United States, in order to form a more perfect Union*
Establish Justice
Insure Domestic Tranquillity
Provide for Common Defense
Promote the General Welfare and
Secure the Blessings of Liberty
to ourselves and our posterity, do ordain and establish this constitution . . ."

5

History in this country spells out efforts by its lawmakers,
judges, and executive personnel to carry out that mandate. There
are different degrees of explicit clarity in the several purposes proclaimed. The "common defense" is perhaps the least debatable.
"Domestic tranquillity" is a less independent concept, but the citizen
layman would not quarrel with it. He would also leave the political
scientist and legislator to define what constitutes a "more perfect
union" though he cannot overlook that "states' rights" and a more
perfect union have been at loggerheads for six generations, and not
always for the purpose of "securing the blessings of liberty" for all.
No great effort is required to see that establishment of justice is an
essential. This was true as a bulwark against eighteenth-century
monarchy and is true today against the feudal system that has had
such a lingering death in Europe, the cancerous fascist and Nazi ex-
plosions in this century, and in certain respects the police-state culture of present-day Communism.

In our day political liberty of the individual has been accepted as an undebatable condition of life, and for this country the
Constitution is its exponent and guardian. We take this for granted
as the air we breathe, in happy unawareness of the thousands of
years of history, East and West, of irresponsible domination, en-
slavement, wholesale slaughter, and cruelty, and we have been in-
excusably remiss in making certain that Negroes and some other
minority groups should be assured of that liberty and its accompanying benefits.

The Constitution has two characteristics of immeasurable
importance: one, an organizational blueprint with regulations for
insuring the operations of a government for the purposes set forth;
the other, assurance of the rights of the individual, as defined in its
predecessor Declaration of Independence to "life, liberty, and the
pursuit of happiness." Elaborate entrenchments are provided in the
Constitution, and in successive amendments to it, against abuse of
power. Implicit also in the rights of the individual are the rights of
those dependent on him. But the individual, so assured of his personal liberty, does not, and he thinks he need not, concern himself
with what is termed the "general welfare."

In fact, the "general welfare" would have remained for

John Doe a misty, distant, unreal concept, of concern to legal technicians only, had it not in the past half century been marginally confused with such terms as "public welfare," "social welfare," "Welfare State." The "welfare" component of these terms has, in a way, polarized the John Does into two opposed and almost hostile groups: those who see in it, if but roughly, the flowering of Western democratic culture, so that the blessings of technology, of natural resources, and of economic inventiveness may produce benefits for all men; and those who see individual competition—combining fortunate inheritance with presumed superior endowment—as the philosophically valid foundation of social organization. In a rough sort of way this latter view represents the ethical premises of the "haves" as legitimately enjoying what they have, with whatever reluctant or generous good will toward the "have-nots" which the mores may prescribe. The other philosophy of the democratic culture is not nearly so universally accepted as is the right of the "haves" to what they have.

The meaning of "general welfare," as the term is used in the Constitution, has always been a puzzler to the layman. He has not bothered to decipher it. He has left it to the courts and legislative halls of the land, where it has had a long and colorful history. To most people the term would describe simple things. For example: public health service to prevent epidemics; highway construction and regulation; national, state, and municipal parks, perhaps; licensing physicians, undertakers, plumbers, cab drivers, possibly. He would not be quite certain about tariffs and duties, food and drug inspection. He would hardly think of Federal Reserve Banks and similar institutions as pertaining to general welfare, though he might easily agree that control of currency and of immigration, a national post office, and regulation of air flights were akin to general welfare.

This essay, however, is concerned primarily with what is usually spoken of as "social welfare," sometimes "social work" or "health and welfare"; that is, with the administration of certain services to individuals and families who find it difficult or impossible to maintain themselves and their dependents in material solvency and in health by their own efforts.

As the spectrum of what constitutes material solvency and health has expanded, so has our definition of what services are required. We have developed a better understanding of the hazards of life, of the incidence of need for help, and of the variety of adjustments required to restore a reasonable equilibrium of livelihood and health. We have had to define more carefully, therefore, the term "general" as well as the specific meaning of "welfare" within the fields covered by these services. The needs to be met are "general" in that they occur in a large proportion of the population. We have no longer a small miserable fraction of destitute, or an added layer of poor, but a problem general in impact, which concerns a greater proportion of the population than ever before. The cost of medical services in our day renders a larger part of our population "medically indigent" than we have realized. Accident, sickness, and unemployment spread the incidence of need, and therefore the pertinence of "welfare" services, over large portions of the population in sporadic, rather than in continuous, occurrence. The phenomenal increase in expectancy of life, the lengthening of "childhood" status, and the practical elimination of child labor have brought larger numbers and more varied types of need into the realm of welfare. Discoveries in medical and psychological knowledge have had similar effects.

There are, however, some subtle characteristics in our culture that set obstacles in the way of erecting an effective administrative structure of welfare services. They revolve around the concept of "status." And status in our culture has been almost invariably rooted in economic power. Most of the general influence in the power structure stems from economic power. And power, in varying gradations and forms, creates status—gives the satisfying image. In "miracles" only is power wielded by the individual who is economically insignificant. Economic affluence is a first step toward power. Its visible absence is a hurdle almost insurmountable. By the same token, destitution and poverty automatically spell the reverse. Social status becomes confused with ethical probity, and it has been an easy step from that to the lumping of low economic level with questionable probity and deserts.

In the simplest family structure, status and power reside in the one who provides food, clothing, shelter, protection. He is usually the father, though there are variants in that pattern. In the more complex family, clan, or tribe, or in the feudal system as it existed in Britain and in most of Europe, the pattern of power became more complicated, but the foundation tended to be the same. Even the enormous place occupied in the history of Europe by the Church introduced no fundamental difference in the power tapestry.

It would be convenient if in the United States we could forget about status and power and about their relation to welfare. But after nearly two centuries we still find ourselves faced with a gigantic task "to promote the general welfare," both in the inclusive sense of the words of the Constitution and in the special sense of "social welfare."

Since the turn of the century a series of events has taken place in the field of social welfare that has created an unprecedented situation in Western culture. One of these events was the appearance on the scene of American social work. It would be quite erroneous, however, to credit social work with the great advance that has been made during this period. Rather it has been only one of the many conscious attempts to carry into practice a flood of theories about human relations that have slowly emerged since before the French Revolution. These came through the intellectual and ethical formulations of philosophers, political scientists, economists, and political leaders of the eighteenth and nineteenth centuries. Other conscious practices also emerged from these same sources. They include changes in penal systems, the formation and enormous expansion of trade unions, the birth and development of socialist parties in political and governmental systems of the West, the emergence of the birth control movement, the burgeoning of the concept of social insurance, and finally the massive effects following two world wars and their sequelae in theory and practice.

Social work did, indeed, introduce into the developing social structure of this century some important contributions. Some were indigenous; some were borrowed from England; a few came from other parts of Europe. One was the creation and promotion of new institutions and procedures for the service of those in need. Another was casework and an earlier technique that was best known as settlement work.

Another event of far greater importance, but closely related to the motivation that created social work in our culture, was the emergence of governmental welfare agencies on a national scale as a major component of our social engineering movement. But neither social work nor the public welfare system has eliminated or could eliminate two habits of thought about "the poor" that still dominate our culture. Both are common to all Western culture. One is that comprised in the concept of "charity" by whatever name, the other is the cult of property.

Though not always designated by that name, the tradition of charity is older than Western culture itself. It certainly antedates the New Testament and quite likely the Old Testament as well, whose authors recorded rather than created the tradition. It calls for giving material help to the poor, the sick, and the "stranger at the gates." In one form or another, the tradition is formally sanctioned and its tenets even prescribed in both the Old and New Testaments. It is further specified in many ways and over many centuries in supplementary edicts of Hebrew and Christian literature. At first an ethical precept, it later becomes a means of earning credits toward benefits of the theologically defined afterlife. The giving of charity, though not "demanded" by the theology, was clearly promoted in the teachings and recognized as a virtue of the Judeo-Christian culture. Its practice was psychologically satisfying; and when known by others it became a means of achieving prestige. The total effect was to enhance community good will. It still retains that function, and it still occupies a substantial place in the ethical outlook and intellectual commitment of our culture.

Independently, however, there grew up another tradition, no less fundamentally part of the culture. It carried a disapproval of the recipient of charity, who is judged, *ipso facto,* as of low character, low endowment, shiftless and lazy, ready to exploit the good will of the charitable, and at times indeed a menace to the economic soundness and stability of the community. This attitude of owners of wealth was strongly reinforced at times of severe dislocation of the economy. The loss of employment by agricultural labor after the "enclosures" in England created a mass of workers without roots or duties: they seemed a menace to public order. When, on the contrary, there occurred a shortage of labor, as later in the colonial economy, and after the great plague in England, the tendency was to regard the reluctant wage earners as "idle poor." In either case they would be regarded as a drain on material resources or a menace to order or both. They seemed ready to defy the class and caste structure and moral order, or to choose a parasitic existence, all at the expense of the *intelligent, hard-working, thrifty* of superior quality and status. Legislation and force were resorted to in an effort to preserve the possessions and rights of the "better classes" and to keep safe the economic and moral order.

These two apparently incompatible sentiments have coexisted. Their essential pattern was not changed by the special system of rewarding soldiers after a war with gifts of money and property. Military pension systems that in a sense were public relief of a special kind were relatively free of disapproval by the tax-minded. The phenomenally generous treatment of veterans of both world wars by the United States government, despite substantial cost to the taxpayer, have been accepted as reasonable, almost as if they were "cost of production." This may have been partly because military service had cut through all classes, so the better and the lower could achieve an equalitarian status without resentment; partly it could have been an unarticulated judgment that victory was a good return for the investment.

Neither the tradition of good will that becomes charity nor social work's new institutions and techniques can apparently overcome the resistances that stand athwart democratic acceptance of equality of all men—their right to share the resources of the abundant society. Clearly, some rational, engineerlike organization is required to prevent poverty, to insure help for those in distress, and to make smooth and effective the operation of democratic society in distributing goods and services. The new public welfare system of the United States, born out of catastrophe but shaped by philosophers, may be the most important step toward achieving that goal. Traditional charity has failed, for it was thwarted by worship of property and status. Nor has social work succeeded, for it was decoyed into technical byways and seduced by the inducements of social status and professional pride. Public welfare has yet to achieve a full-engined effectiveness in which political and social theory has overcome the compulsive drive for possession of property and power. It will be our task in this book to describe what has been done and what is being done in the field of welfare, to evaluate successes and failures as a guide to planning and improvement, and to frame it all so far as feasible within historical perspectives directed to the past for facts, but oriented to the future for purpose.

Chapter II

❧❦

The Targets of "Welfare": Destitution and Poverty

Out of compassion that has survived wars of hatred, wars for loot-
ing, wars of theological partisanship, and millennia of the exploitation
of man by man have come acts of mercy and urgings of charity. In
the long history of charity it was systematically demanded in Jewish
tradition, unremittingly pleaded for in Christian Gospels, somewhat
formally developed in Christian churches, and practiced spon-
taneously by the compassionate at all times and in all climes; all this
testifies to the persistent and almost biological presence of this quality
in Western culture. It is well, however, not to confuse this quality of
compassion and its resultant acts with the imposed regulations or

mores both in various early primitive cultures and in their present exemplars. Where family patterns, clan and tribal practices, or communal systems of production dictated the sharing of products with other members of the group, individual compassion was not very relevant. The sharing of goods was an imperative of the social structure, in the same way as was destruction or abandonment of infants or of the superannuated in those places and times where these are reported to have been accepted practice. It is, then, hardly pertinent to discuss destitution or poverty as relating to such social systems as these, for when disaster struck, it struck the group as a whole. Only when these social patterns become inoperative or incomplete do the problems of destitution or poverty become relevant.

When an individual or his family are no longer automatically recipients of the available material goods to be consumed by the group—no longer in a sense communal members for consumption and production—then the division into haves and have-nots begins. Leaving out for the moment factors of status and power in disposal of consumable goods, we have, as a minimum, those able to produce and therefore entitled to share in the consumption and those not actively participating in production and therefore not entitled automatically to share the product. Those who are accepted by definition as nonproducers, as for example young children or those temporarily incapacitated by whatever cause, are ordinarily absorbed in the social-economic structure of the family or of its extended cycle. Modern United States presents only sporadic resemblances to these early communal modes of life. Nor is there at present much resemblance to early colonial society or to its prototypes in England. From the ways of ancient Judea, early Christian organization, or medieval Europe we inherit chiefly a system of ethics and some traditional ways for dealing with what were roughly called the poor and the sick. These traditional ways are still visible in present-day practice and in some surviving attitudes that underlie them. But today it is the explicit social and political policies and the associated social engineering that rule our practice. The *appeal* for services is still ethical and moral but administration of the services becomes a matter of organization, whether under voluntary, sectarian, or public sponsorship. It is our economic affluence as a nation that chiefly determines the limits to be set to "welfare." We live in a miraculously productive, technologically superb setting, with well-nigh limitless natural resources and in the main an irreversible commitment to the democratic dogma.

The writer deliberately distinguishes destitution from poverty. Though "poverty" is the term used from the books of Moses to the poor laws of Elizabeth and appears in the "war on poverty" of President Johnson, it is *destitution,* including illness of the destitute, with which we have chiefly been dealing. There has been, and there still is, extensive destitution in the United States, but not so much, relatively, as there was at the turn of the century, either in the proportion of the population affected, or in the severity of its impact in many cases. The improvement has been greater than any of us, who witnessed it even shortly before World War I, would have dared to expect. And the improvement has been greater beyond comparison than that in the vast majority of the population elsewhere in the world.[1] It is true that in the history of the West until recent decades it has rarely been possible to distinguish between destitution and poverty. But today, in the United States, that difficulty has practically disappeared. We may now recognize measures addressed to destitution (or its specific prevention) as distinct in a variety of ways from measures concerned with poverty, though both come roughly under the heading of welfare.

Roughly, for our purposes, destitution may be defined as lack of material resources sufficient to assure survival in organized

---

[1] Some light on the great variations in income the world over—which naturally determine conditions that produce destitution and poverty—can be gained from comparative annual per capita incomes as they appear from time to time in annual economic summaries of the *New York Times.* More details are available in publications of the United Nations. The direct relations between income and the need for economic assistance of the destitute may be seen in an exceptionally informative and authoritative publication of the United Nations, entitled *Assistance of the Needy in Less-Developed Areas* (ST/SOA/28) March 1956. It covers nine countries in the Middle East, Far East, and Latin America, and is based on a series of monographs, supervised and edited with the assistance of G. W. Cole. It is an exceptionally well-organized and authentic piece of work.

society, where the various forms of familial and related structures no longer provide that assurance. Despite this rather extreme definition, with survival as the test, much, perhaps most, destitution does not become visible enough to come unavoidably to notice. One reason may be that destitution so often takes the appearance of sickness, is approached as such, and so becomes disguised in its true essence. Another reason may be that it has been confused with poverty, a far more extensive phenomenon, for which, it appears, society has been able to develop a high level of tolerance. This is true not only in the conveniently quoted biblical reference, so readily misunderstood, that the poor shall always be with us, but in the more sophisticated theoretical sense that among economic levels of society it is reasonable to expect a permanent low-income stratum, "the poor." In that way the existence of poverty is legitimized, and if one does not trouble to make fine distinctions between poverty and destitution, then destitution also attains legitimacy. There has, indeed, been a tendency to pass over the destitute as such, and to see in them merely somewhat extreme exemplars of the poor—chiefly those appealing or importuning for alms.

On one occasion the administrative head of the ministry of social welfare in one of the countries served by the Technical Assistance program of the United Nations, when the extent and severity of destitution in the realm were brought to his attention by the technical advisor, countered with the remark that "people were not dying in the streets." That, it is true, is not where people usually die, and they cannot often be seen in the throes of death. Failure to survive for lack of food is not always obvious. Malnutrition in general is not easily observable and definable. There are, of course, indirect statistical clues. For example, in a series of studies conducted by the United States Public Health Service in Hagerstown, Maryland, dealing with the virulent influenza epidemic in 1917–18, an unobtrusive but significant fact was discovered on classification of the patients by economic levels. The lowest of three economic levels as defined showed a far larger incidence of the disease even where the presence of "crowding" was factored out. And the differential death rates of patients on the three economic levels clearly reinforced the significance of the rates of incidence.[2] Another study, also under the Public Health Service, though oriented to a different type of problem, showed very similar results. Deficiency of certain food constituents was identified with the cause of pellagra[3] and inferentially with the food purchase habits of the low-income group and the demands of their budgets. Survival or food deficiency phenomena are closely related to economic sufficiency.[4]

All this is, of course, only circumstantial evidence. In any case, survival, as a sheer physiological differential between life and death, is a matter for medical science to decide when possible. For the layman, it is sufficient to determine whether destitution is something that a modern civilization should permit if it has the power to eliminate it. It is also for the layman-citizen to decide where to draw the line between destitution that *must not* be permitted, and poverty as a social-economic phenomenon to be dealt with through his command of political philosophy and his choice of government programs. Destitution can then be handled largely as an administrative problem, while poverty remains an inclusive cultural challenge.

Difficult as it is to define destitution in any scientific manner, the definition of poverty is even more difficult, especially in view of the enormous range of economic and cultural patterns in the world. Tentatively one can perhaps describe it as existence on an economic level above destitution but imposing on the individual concerned a living standard not deemed acceptable to, or characteristic of, the culture of his nation at a given time and place. There have been various other definitions of poverty. The English experience started with the identification of a "poverty line," as interpreted by Charles

---

[2] United States Public Health Service publications. Reports on influenza began to appear about Oct. 11, 1918, Vols. 33 to 41.

[3] United States Public Health Service publications, Report, Vol. 29, June 26, 1914. Also a study of endemic pellagra in some cotton mill villages. U.S.D.H. reports, Vol. 43, No. 41, Oct. 12, 1925; and *Goldberger on Pellagra,* edited by Milton Torris, Louisiana State University Press, 1944.

[4] Some extraordinarily significant and pertinent data on the subject will also be found in *Poverty and Public Health,* an outstanding contribution to the field, by G. C. M. McGonigle and J. Kirby, based on English experience (Victor Gollancz, 1936).

Booth, S. Seebohm Rountree, and their successors. In the United States an indirect way was attempted by Wilbur Olin Atwater[5] in the laboratory experiment to define the caloric requirements of an individual as a basis for calculating the minimum nutritional requirements. Also, in the United States, the federal government has attempted to define minimum standards in various ways, by statistical studies of laborers' budgets, by setting relief standards, and establishing minimum requirements of sustenance for families of various sizes. Always, it would appear, the implicit assumption has been that the concepts of poverty and destitution were interchangeable.

A completely acceptable and scientifically valid distinction between destitution and poverty would be difficult to establish. Such definition would, in fact, involve value judgments and approaches to action. Only the destitute, or some of them at any rate, have in fact been given assistance by charitable agencies whether voluntary or public. And the "survival" definition for these has been only implicit, not avowed, for avowal would have been too uncomfortable for the rest of the population. "Poverty," on the other hand, has been a coveniently indefinite concept. If elimination of poverty is the goal, in the general economic sense of assuring to the lowest income group a standard acceptable in our culture, then that subject is outside the area of welfare administration proper, that is, if we exclude the measures distinctly preventive in nature, such as old-age pensions, unemployment insurance, workmen's compensation, and various rehabilitation programs. These measures are clearly designed to prevent ascertainable destitution that may be due to specific causes. They are only partly related to a program for dealing with poverty as a basic socio-economic problem. As such, they constitute an area that should be included in the discussion of welfare but handled administratively on different patterns.

This volume is addressed primarily to the subject of virtual destitution or its prevention. The administrative tasks involved in the pertinent services require skill and constant sensitivity to the theoretical implications derived from the social sciences. At the same

[5] United States Department of Agriculture, Office of Experiment Station, Bulletin 28, published in 1896; also Bulletin 69, 1898.

time they call for a degree of humility not to assume that the services addressed to destitution can control the ideas or practices of related areas such as economic planning, political science, foreign relations, immigration. Yet if welfare services addressed to destitution are so conducted by their administrators as to refrain from participation in militant movements in the larger field, such as the "war on poverty," birth control, civil rights, or liberation from the chains that hold down minority groups, then the sharp competence of these services themselves may be dulled and they may drift into eddies removed from the mainstream of citizen interest. Examples of such limited perspectives will be found in later chapters, as well as examples of bold leadership that straddles the immediate field of administrative operations and the larger arena of social growth.

The problems of administrative management of "health and welfare" services would be relatively simple if one had only the traditions of charitable interest to consider, if the destitute were a semipermanent, self-contained group always distinguishable from the normal population. That is the way it had been presented from time to time in literature emanating, for example, from the London Charity Organization Society (COS),[6] and the peculiar measures promoted in the United States by the so-called CRA[7] and by some political and business interests apparently echoed in the now famous Newburgh episode which downgraded relief recipients and welfare officials. That is not how English scholars such as Booth and Rountree or their successors saw poverty. Nor is it the lesson of the more or less bloody history of the emancipation of the poor in Britain. For in retrospect we see that the poor were usually not a destitute minority, but the mass of the population, and what they sought was

[6] Particularly apropos the proposals for social insurance following the Beveridge Report (see Part Four, below).

[7] The Community Research Associates (CRA), technically a non-profit organization, supported by foundation funds, and service fees. It is, in the opinion of the writer, theoretically unsound in its premises as related to multiproblem families and reactionary in its social outlook; and its proposed administrative patterns are unworkable. Its operations were examined by the writer in the course of his study of the Welfare Department of Pennsylvania and comments were included in his final report to the Secretary of the Department.

a livelihood that would be distinguishable from a state of destitution.[8] The works of Eden,[9] the Webbs, the Hammonds, Hutchinson
and Harrison, and G. D. H. Cole, and others suggest that the realistic distinction between the two has often not been very great. Perhaps the chief difference may be that those explicitly destitute rather
than just poor would receive or at least be entitled to poor relief of
some sort. On the other hand, the exploited feudal vassal or, later,
the agricultural laborer still partly bound to the land, or the town
laborer militantly demanding higher wages, the indentured debtor
in England or in the colonies, or the laborer guilty of "conspiracy"
for organized demands on the employer were poor only in their own
eyes. In the eyes of those in power in the executive realm where decisions were made, they were the discontented and often the dangerous elements, and almost always the men who aspired to live
beyond their station in life.[10] They were not just the unworthy poor,
for these were already granted tentative status as applicants for
charity—acceptable or not; nor were they the worthy poor, for these
would be receiving some type of assistance and good will. These
poor were merely low-income laborers in the developing mercantile
and industrial civilization of recent centuries and residual agricultural laborers continuing their feudal and postfeudal status.

So far as information is available this low-income group
comprised a very large portion of the population of England, a relatively smaller fraction in colonial America—always omitting the

[8] It is well to recall that the experience of Britain, though technically
foreign, is culturally well-nigh indistinguishable from that of the United
States.

[9] See Part IV, below.

[10] To the scholarly mind it would be comforting to identify historical
continuity in the nature, extent, and interrelations between destitution and
poverty and society's ways of dealing with them from the ancient civilizations
of Babylon, Egypt, Judea, Greece, and Rome onward. That would be gratifying (if not particularly useful) had we adequate and trustworthy data. As
it is, we have mostly traditional concepts, the Old and the New Testaments,
the Talmud, and diverse medieval literary material. Even the more accessible material in Continental municipal history does not seem too useful.
The historian's yearning would recall it. We have closer knowledge of the
facts in English history from the fifteenth century on, but these facts do not
sufficiently match the conceptual heritage.

slaves—and later in America an increasing number of immigrants from abroad, then migrant labor, sharecroppers, Negroes, and sweatshop employees.

What complicates the problem of distinguishing the poor from the destitute is a noneconomic factor, namely the class and caste system from which Anglo-Saxon culture had only partly escaped. With negligible exceptions[11] the upper social class is the one having wealth and resources. In the typical European culture before the rise of the mercantile group—and to a considerable extent in Latin America—the land-owning group has had the power, status, and social prominence.

Social status and the corresponding station in life went hand in hand with affluence. The osmosis of the mercantile group changed the situation only to the extent that it often became difficult to determine whether, in the hierarchy of caste, wealth or inherited caste carried priority. The power structure remained on the whole untouched, and until very recent years even the French and American revolutions effected only a limited alteration. All this leaves the stigma of caste inferiority on low-income status, with or without minority-group membership.

Two facts make all this cogent for the welfare perspective of our day: the continuing massive quantity of a low-income component of the population, and the implicit status justification of this fact, redolent of the age-old aristocratic tradition. In the eyes of the wielders of power, there is still a tacit assumption that the poor are in essence a qualitatively inferior layer of society, that they are poor because of lower natural endowment than "the better classes" when they are not actually shiftless or morally inferior. With this goes a somewhat amorphous assumption, less commonly expressed today than a century ago but still extant, that sound social structure requires an upper class and status group, relatively small in numbers, and a foundation mass on a lower level. These assumptions have led to a peculiar double-edged conclusion: that the difference between the destitute and the poor is only incidental, creating problems of ad-

[11] See Warner, L., and Lunt, P. S. *Status System of a Modern Community* (Yale University Press, 1942).

ministration only; and also that too much tinkering with levels of living of both the destitute and the poor would be destructive of social stability and moral order. It is this peculiar tradition, plus occasional rebellion or danger of rebellion by the masses, that has created a militant if masked hostility on the part of those in the power structure toward the poor in general and the more visible destitute in particular. Bluntly stated—and again with exceptions exemplified by many intellectual and philanthropic leaders—the economically affluent, who in the main have also been the socially superior in status, have disliked, sometimes feared, and mostly distrusted the poor. These, in their view, have demanded more than they should rightly be entitled to in wages and sometimes in status. The "haves" generally have attributed special virtue to property and its ownership, as if that were a natural law. The right of property to create more property has been nearly axiomatic throughout history, and denial of inherited property rights has come to be regarded as immoral, unethical, and socially perilous. Property qualification for voting endured through the long colonial history, and there were strong convictions, widely held and quite vociferously expressed during the post-1929 depression, that those on relief—somewhat like those convicted of felony—should be denied the franchise.

Not until the emergence of modern economic theory, and especially the appearance of the socialist dogma in the past century, has the labor of the workingman achieved the recognition of having the same inherent moral value as that which had long been granted to the ownership of property. Previously, any claim of the legitimacy of economic returns to labor comparable to that commanded by property or capital appeared morally subversive. The marginal status of professional persons hardly alters the basic pattern. The social order as it existed was regarded as reality by rich and poor alike.

Since the motive power for service and for reform, as well as resistance to them, are emotionally rooted, it would be unrealistic to deal with the practical technical problems involved in the present inquiry without considering the pertinent historical perspectives which largely explain these emotional commitments. Philosophy and theory seem almost more important in this respect than mere events both in history and in present practice. A few of the events, however, for the United States, do stand out significantly. One of these, of particular pertinence to our subject, is the near-catastrophic depression that followed the stock market crash of 1929; another is the recognition of illness as a major component in poverty, and medical care as an indispensable requirement in relation to it. A third is the recent initiative of the federal government in dealing with the distress area referred to as Appalachia, and the still more recent action of the Congress initiating the "War on Poverty" with an appropriation of nearly two billion dollars.

In its mass aspect the unemployment that followed the collapse of the stock market in 1929 is in some ways comparable, in extent and in the far-reaching nature of its results, to the massive disaster that struck the survivors and their dependents in the great plague in England in the fifteenth century. Despite some similarities, however, the differences are enormous. In an England still under agricultural feudalism, the swiftness and the catastrophic impact of death brought a sharp and immediate shortage of available manpower and a correspondingly enormous advantage to the laborer, who was now desperately sought after; his was the seller's market. Wages, choice of place, and type of employment were in the hands of the laborer as never before. But power was still in the hands of landowner aristocracy and its political control remained practically undisturbed. The caste division became exacerbated, and both legislative and administrative weapons were wielded to keep the laborer in his place, wages responsive to the desires of the employer, and the caste distinctions intact. Records of the period emphasize repression of the laborer and the threat he presented to the established order.[12]

The situation in the United States in the 1930's was vastly different. The only similarities worth pointing out were principally in the subtle recrudescence of the repressive attitudes of the "haves"

---

[12] Some of the most pertinent if restrained citations bearing on the situation as it was in the colonies may be gathered from Henry W. Farnam's *Chapters in the History of Social Legislation in the U. S. to 1860* (Carnegie Institution of Washington, 1938).

toward the vast body of "have-nots." The actual constructive measures taken by the national government were monumental.[13] Behind these was the fact that the ultimate seat of power had, during the preceding century or more, been removed from the caste-class aristocracy to the voter, who had the politically final decision.[14] And underlying it all was the knowledge of the unemployed that they were numerically strong beyond physical control. They had, in fact, in many parts of the country created formal organizations of unemployed who exerted inexorable pressure on local authorities. To this must be added the fact that poverty and destitution had perhaps for the first time, even if only temporarily, struck a serious blow at the residual caste system. For unemployment and its attendant economic collapse of individual households had invaded a substantial layer of the middle and even upper-middle classes. It had become in many ways something like a physical disaster. It may, in fact, have established the acceptability without prejudice of the concept of the "distress area," which is now being invoked by the national government to deal with flood and other natural disasters. How far the depression itself succeeded in changing the cultural status-psychology of the country is difficult to assay. A variety of public assistance measures, including social security for the aged, have become the law of the land, and perhaps 10 per cent or more of the people automatically qualify for them. Yet the real impact and even the actual existence of many services are still spotty. Under the state-federal system not a few of the services are on a "matching" basis, and matching can be operative only when there is something in a given state to be matched. The so-called general assistance program is one of these. There are states where no general tax-supported public assistance is available, and therefore none to be matched. And these are not, in the main, states where old and venerable practice of relief for the destitute is generally available from voluntary sources. The postdepression federal measures saved the country from a possible social explosion. But they could not, despite extended and increasing

---

[13] See later chapters in this book: there is a vast bibliography available for the interested student of the period.

[14] The property test for the voter was practically gone, though literacy and color prejudice were still extant.

matching practices reflecting national ideals, persuade all local and state governments to accept and emulate national standards. The national pattern is, as we shall see, cause for pride, and it includes a social engineering miracle which by now appears safe even from reactionary assaults by the property-conservatives who seek political power for reversing the trend.[15]

Cultural acceptance of the statistically recognized incidence of economic distress and rejection of stigma attached to it are by no means complete. In the midst of the social engineering miracle achieved after the 1929 debacle attempts were made to deprive the recipients of their franchise. Standards of assistance in most parts of the country are still, and in places crudely, niggardly. There is still a stigma on the recipient. Nor has the body of voluntary social agencies generally striven to carry the torch for the new plans of public responsibility. Professional personnel and professional training schools concentrate on services largely unrelated to the condition of the destitute or the problems of the poor. There is a periodic resurgence of attempts to search out and pillory the "chiselers"; pressure to force the "legally responsible" relatives to carry the burden persists as if the social welfare pattern were unethical. Color prejudice still feeds on the status stigma. Extensive efforts were made and are still being made to draw into the picture illegitimacy, promiscuity, and marital irregularities as if these were inherently the habits of the destitute. This may not be the place to discuss all the facts and implications of the existence of illegitimate children in the world. But it is important to call attention to some of the confusions that lie behind this lightly sprinkled condemnation of illegitimacy— which under one name or another has existed as far back as we know anything about the history of the human race. Is this stern condemnation addressed mainly to the poor and destitute? Is it resentment of still another factor that creates problems of relief, along with death of the breadwinner, illness, unemployment, superannuation? It certainly appears often as a count against minority groups which already suffer job and social discrimination: Negroes, Mexi-

---

[15] The proposals of presidential candidate Goldwater and the Republican platform of 1964 were clearly frankly directed to this end.

cans, Puerto Ricans.[16] Mention should be made at this point of recent measures taken by some public assistance authorities to make available to their clients organized information about contraceptive measures well known to medicine and presumably widely utilized by the economically favored segments of the population.

In contrast to this attitude which combines or confuses a general ill will toward the recipient of economic assistance with moralistic or religious aversion to sex except as a means of procreation, there is at present an extensive and multifaceted movement toward the legitimacy of sexual intercourse and the organized promotion of contraceptive techniques. There are numerous scientific studies and a mellowing in many parts of the world of the rigid disapproval by the Catholic Church; there is financial assistance to bodies promoting planned parenthood, as for example the grant for a three-year experiment by the New York Fund for Children; specific related programs in the federal government and in numerous state legislatures, and administrative provisions in various municipal welfare departments to assist clients in family planning and birth control—these are some of the facets of a more rational modern attitude that may correct the tendency to use sex mores against economic assistance. Extensive discussions in the press have become more and more frequent, as for example, *New York Times,* March 28, 1965, November 9 1964; *Reader's Digest,* April 1964.

Whether or not the reader has accepted our tentative definitions of destitution and poverty, he may have expected some solid quantitative data. How many of the 192-odd million persons in the United States are either destitute or poor—how many are in each of these categories, if they are really distinct? No honest student could claim to have an answer. The difficulty is twofold: one of definition, the other of available statistics. Our definition of destitution is con-

---

[16] On the subject as a whole, as it relates to the assistance program, consult the factual findings in *An American Dependency Challenge* by M. Elaine Burgess and Daniel O. Price (American Public Welfare Association, 1963); also the study *Aid to Dependent Children of Cook County Illinois (Chicago),* by Greenleigh Associates, Inc., 1960. Some interesting data will also be found in *Slums and Social Insecurity* by Alvin L. Schorr of the Department of Health, Education, and Welfare (Research No. 1, Division of Research and Statistics, Social Security Administration).

ceptual, not legal or subject to laboratory tests. Strictly speaking, only those persons are destitute who have appealed for economic assistance, have been found technically eligible, and are receiving economic relief. Some figures covering most persons within this definition are available.[17] They number, roughly, between seven and eight millions. But some sixteen states have no public relief provision at all for general assistance; if they did, that number would be larger. There are also those clearly eligible in states that do provide general assistance, but who are kept out by antiquated and arbitrary rules of eligibility, such as settlement, residence, and the existence of responsible relatives even when these do not contribute. State legislatures make appropriations that may or may not cover even those eligible by their own regulations. There are therefore an unknown number of persons who are as destitute as those on relief, but not receiving any relief. To this must be added the general practice of not a few states that define destitution in one way for whites and in quite another for Negroes. The writer's own estimate, based on experience more than on official data, would add another one to two million to the persons as reported by the federal government.

These figures in any case do not include recipients of social insurance funds, for reasons and in amounts to be considered later. Nor should it be assumed that persons who do receive economic assistance are thereby lifted entirely out of the misery of their destitution. On this aspect some very depressing facts will be found in subsequent pages. But at least for them *survival,* if that is the heart of the definition, is assured.

When it comes to poverty, the dilemma both of definition and of figures becomes even more troublesome. For we have to define a floor to differentiate poverty from destitution, and also a ceiling to distinguish it from—shall we call it "solvency"?—at a low level of comfort. How many persons, then, are above the level of destitution, but "poor"? Only indirect and not strictly quantifiable statistics can be offered. In a way one has to resort to a flank attack, rather than hazard any straight answer.[18]

[17] See Chapter Three.
[18] There is more accurate information in English studies that have

A somewhat more effective approach than merely differentiating the destitute from the nondestitute, and partaking in a way of the precedent set by the English pioneers, was attempted by the White House Conference on Children in a Democracy (the decennial event inaugurated some forty years earlier), with the cooperation and participation of a number of federal departments and personnel, and reported by the Conference in 1940.[19] The conclusions reached by the staff, as reported to the Conference, stated that,

> One-half to two-thirds of the children in the cities of the United States are in families whose income is insufficient to provide the goods and services comprised in the maintenance level type of family budget.[20]

The report included the definition of "maintenance level" based on the several studies conducted previously by departments of the government. On the face of it, perhaps, these estimates would, after twenty-five years, appear to be meaningless or at least lacking in applicability. There has, after all, been a nearly tenfold increase in national income since 1940, and some 50 per cent increase in the population. There is, however, further statistical information that renders these earlier estimates more significant than they would seem to be on the surface, if we are concerned with the extent of poverty. For we are told, in the same report, that:

> At one end of the scale [of income distribution] one-half of one

---

advanced in the path opened by Charles Booth: The New London Survey, by the London School of Economics, the studies by Bowley and Hogg on Poverty in Five English Communities, the successive studies by Rountree. These have been made possible by either large statistical samples or total coverages in limited areas, and accurate data on incomes of families under consideration. These incomes were then related to a calculated "poverty line" by budget requirements per person and family. The extent of poverty was thus ascertained with reasonable accuracy. But it included the destitute and the poor in the same over-all category.

[19] *White House Conference on Children in a Democracy, Final Report* (Superintendent of Documents, Washington, D.C., 1940), Chapter VI contains considerable detail bearing on the estimates, and a series of tables and charts presenting more detailed analyses and supporting materials.

[20] Conference Report, p. 81.

per cent of all families have one-tenth of the total national income; at the other end, one-tenth of the national income is shared by 32.3 per cent of the people. Or, to put it another way, 81 per cent of the population share one-half of the national income, while 19 per cent of the population share the other half.

A comparison of these estimates with the calculations offered by Harrington[21] is suggestive but not conclusive. Harrington's figures on income distribution show an inequality of the same general type as that reported in 1940, though stated in different figures. They show, for 1958, 20 per cent in the lowest income group as having 4.7 per cent of the national income, as compared with the top 20 per cent of income recipients sharing 45.5 per cent of the national income. In absolute figures, the per capita income of the two groups, as calculated by Harrington, is a contrast of $1,460 per annum to $14,250. While neither set of estimates can be used to distinguish poverty from destitution, and the earlier calculations were centered on children, the former do, at least, include family budgets as well as family income. In both cases, however, we have figures that include both low-income levels of self-maintaining families and destitute families. They differ again, however, in that by 1958, when Harrington's figures were given, the federal-state assistance program had made considerable strides forward.

A study made in New Jersey in 1936 offers a more illuminating insight into some of the components of the difference between poverty and destitution as it is reflected in minimum needs, size of family, normal income, and economic assistance. The data, though reflecting a situation in the early thirties, have a significance that has lost nothing in thirty years.[22] Apparently on the initiative of the then governor of that state, the research arm of the Emergency Relief Administration made a study of two thousand cases to determine the adequacy of relief and some related questions. These cases had

[21] *The Other America—Poverty in the United States* by Michael Harrington (Penguin Books, 1962), Appendix I.

[22] Chart VI, p. 105, *Seven Years of Unemployment Relief in New Jersey 1930–1936* by Douglas H. Macneil, prepared for the Commitee on Social Security, Washington Committee on Social Security, Social Science Research Council, 1938.

been "receiving direct relief continuously in November 1935," had been transferred to the Works Progress Administration payrolls in December, and worked continuously during January 1936. The charts, as reproduced here, contain the essentials of the author's findings. These present the average income in dollars and also the relation of that income to "estimated minimum needs." Perhaps their chief virtue rests in the fact that the families were classified by number of persons—a most fundamental factor in the problem of livelihood. The charts eloquently demonstrate the linkage of poverty and destitution.

Some incidental implications are, however, also instructive. For example, everything is related to estimated minimum needs which, of course, vary with the size of the family. On the average prerelief or "normal" income of the families, a "point of no return" is reached at seven persons. Above this number, destitution apparently steps in, regardless. And the fact that the average size of families in the United States is a fraction under four does not help the larger families. The direct relief actually given comes nowhere within shouting distance in any size family, from one to ten or more. Even the so-called work relief income ceases to meet the needs on the minimum level of the family *over one,* even though in actual amounts paid it exceeds the relief grants of families under ten persons. And the relation between economic assistance and even minimum needs would be a travesty, were it not for the catastrophic situation in the early thirties.

But by early 1964, an event of major importance in American welfare statesmanship occurred. What had once been but an idea, and an expected proposal to be submitted by the President of the United States to the Congress, became law. The popular name of the law was "War on Poverty." On the statute books it became the "Economic Opportunity Act of 1964." As part of the President's blueprint for the Great Society it became operational forthwith, with a budget of well over a billion dollars, administered throughout the land in a complicated pattern of federal, state, and local governmental participation.[23]

[23] The law as enacted was designated Public Law 88–452, 88th Congress, S 26–42, approved August 20, 1964. A compilation of materials

A. Average Income in Dollars   B. Per cent of Estimated Subsistence Needs

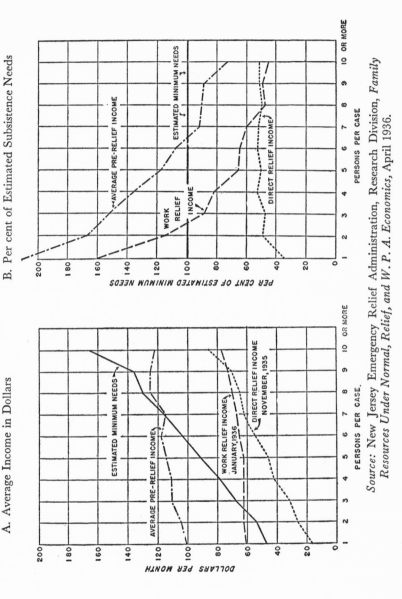

Source: New Jersey Emergency Relief Administration, Research Division, *Family Resources Under Normal, Relief, and W. P. A. Economics,* April 1936.

What is the relevance of this major sociopolitical event to the analysis of the welfare services? In what way does it rate a prominent place in the evolution of social engineering in this country? The particular purpose in this chapter has been to differentiate between destitution and poverty for a very simple reason: to emphasize the primary obligation of welfare service to work for the relief of destitution as its special assignment, and to do that job well. For administrators of welfare services in this culture to pretend to be the professional guides for dealing with poverty as a major economic-political phenomenon would seem to be both presumptuous and innocently unrealistic. Any attempt to aggrandize their status, and perhaps to expiate their failure to serve the destitute effectively by claiming an active role in the diminution of poverty, would be not only a profitless exercise but also might lead to the betrayal of their primary duty: that the destitute shall be helped; that, if possible, they should be assisted to emerge from their state of dependency.

It is becoming clear in this country, and in not a few other Western nations, that the improvement and expansion of welfare services, by steadily developing prevention as well as service, has been increasingly washing away the boundaries between the relatively limited area of destitution and the large contiguous area of low-income and large hazard called poverty. An impressive part of the population is progressively saved from the fact or the fear of destitution by a large cluster of preventive measures: workmen's compensation, unemployment insurance, pensions, a giant social security program, educational and vocational measures, wage escalation, health insurance, to mention only a few. We have thought that these preventive measures, added to the expanding welfare services, were not only eliminating destitution but very nearly wiping out the adjoining area of poverty.

But we were mistaken. The facts only partly support even a portion of this assumption. The fence that separates the realm of poverty from the realm of destitution is lower and weaker than we

relevant to the bill is also available, prepared for the Select Committee on Labor and Public Welfare of the U. S. Senate and issued by the U. S. Government Printing Office, July 23, 1964.

thought. The two are far too often overlapping. This is what became clear and has given rise to the "war on poverty." We deal here with a major social-economic diagnosis and the attempt to formulate a corresponding battery of treatments. The chief difference between welfare services and "war on poverty" is that the former is primarily an administrative mechanism for clear-cut services, while the latter is primarily an educational economic program—though naturally an administrative machinery is necessary for this also.

The major divisions of the Economic Opportunity Act would seem to emphasize that it is directed not to the destitute, but to the poor as we have attempted to define these. There are seven "Titles" in the Act, as follows:

Title I—Youth Programs

Title II—Urban and Rural Community Action Programs

Title III—Special Programs to Combat Poverty in Rural Areas

Title IV—Employment and Investment Incentives

Title V—Work Experience Programs

Title VI—Administration and Coordination

Title VII—Treatment of Income for Certain Public Assistance Purposes

This is in keeping with the declaration of purpose of the Act which says, in part:

. . . it is, therefore, the policy of the United States to eliminate the paradox of poverty in the midst of plenty in this Nation by opening to everyone the opportunity for education and training, the opportunity to work, and the opportunity to live in decency and dignity . . .

No direct reference is to be found here to welfare services proper and to the social insurance system as a whole, which are regarded in part as addressed to actual destitution and to its direct and specific prevention. That the Economic Opportunity Act is not oblivious to these latter, however, is evidenced in part in Title VII as a whole, and in part in certain provisions for the "allotment [of funds] to the States," as for example, that in work-study programs (Section 122, [b] [3]):

. . . one-third shall be allotted . . . among the States so that the allotment to each State . . . will be an amount which bears the same ratio to such one-third as the number of related children under eighteen years of age living in families with annual incomes of less than $3000 in such State bears to the number of related children under eighteen years of age living with annual income of less than $3000 in all the States.

And again, in relation to community action programs under Title II, Section 203 (b) (1):

. . . one-third shall be allotted . . . among the States so that the allotment to each State . . . will be an amount which bears the same ratio to such one-third as the number of public assistance recipients in such State bears to the total number of public assistance recipients in all the States . . .

Enormously complicated theoretical problems and immense administrative tasks face the Office of Economic Opportunity. Already the amount of published material on the administration of the Act is becoming a burdensome load for the student. The press is heavy with reports, discussions, and conflicts in federal, state, and local operational units. Only a few comments on the programs are therefore possibly useful and reasonably legitimate at this writing.

In the first place, the whole enterprise is, considering its enormous applications, in its infancy. The imagination and inventiveness that have gone into the program as a whole should command patience as well as respect by the citizenry at large and by the professional personnel of the contiguous services. In view of the variety of activities covered, the large operational personnel required, and the diverse conditions presented in various types of communities and different parts of the country, some difficulties and some criticism might well be expected. These would naturally be exacerbated and complicated by other characteristics that are still part of our culture: racial and ethnic prejudice, taxpayers' resentment, over-all social rejection of the destitute and poor, lack of understanding of the program and its purpose in general, political rivalry and competition, and the infiltration of corruption. It will take years of experimentation to emerge with a workable and reasonably efficient administration of the Act in pursuit of its purposes. Any program that is in any way addressed to the field of welfare may be expected to arouse resentment and hostility as it touches the prejudices inhering in our culture. Two types of specific criticism of the war on poverty most often heard, however, and usually distorted by a mask of superior probity should be deflated by the intelligent citizen: one is the shopworn one of "politics," the other the equally facile accusation of "corruption."

Any student of social history knows that the major operational instrument in communal and national progress has been government. Government itself has struggled to combine the pursuit of social purposes with the inescapable reality of power drives. In the more primitive periods of our civilization and again in its monarchic and feudal phases, stretching from biblical and Roman times to our day, power has been top dog. Power reasserted itself in fascist "earthquakes," and in the more deceptive masks of theological organized church and idealistic communist patterns. Increasingly, however, a dichotomy has developed that is not yet clearly understood. With the growth of democracy, government has had to become increasingly an instrument of social-economic operations. Through its power of taxation the instrument has become progressively more productive. But the essential drive for power has remained and in the Western pattern it has become focused in the political party and in local versus central conflicts. Whether the power is to be used for social good or for personal gain becomes the battleground of politics and of leaders who have become active in politics. To disdain politics is to deny democratic culture. There is room, then, for differences of opinion in party formulations as to the social good; but there is no escape from the drive for power and the assertion of leadership.

When the term "politics" is used in the derogatory sense, the accent usually is not on this philosophical aspect but on the persistent suspicion that with power goes corruption; that since government is inseparable from power, it is therefore inherently corrupt. This concept confuses government as the instrument of organized life, national and local, and government as the arena of the battle for power in organized social life. Corruption, since that is at the heart of the criticism of politics, has been at home since time immemorial in tribal affairs, business, religious organizations, royal dynasties, guilds and trade unions, and even in drives for charitable funds.

The promise of the program created by the Economic Opportunity Act of 1964 is far greater than any combination of initial missteps, and the inevitable abrasions in the power struggle among political parties, political leaders, national, state, and local government units. It has a particular significance for the field of welfare services, for its successful operation should reduce the ratio of the destitute in the population, and perhaps diminish the number of multiproblem clients who present particularly trying areas for welfare service.

PART TWO

THE FIELD OF WELFARE
SERVICES TODAY

In the immediately following chapters the emphasis will continue to be on the concern in our present American culture with the destitute and, to a lesser degree, with the poor. True, particular individuals and families may pass and repass the border between the two, if only temporarily. But the essential differences remain. What is noticeably changing is the fact that the operations being devised to serve these categories tend increasingly to overlap. The chief difference may be that responsibility for aiding the destitute rests solidly on the welfare service agencies, while the problems of the poor as such tend to coalesce in the general economic problem of the mass of the population. An example of the differences in responsibility for these two areas may be, on the one hand, the matter of dependent children (several million of them, as will be seen) receiving combined federal, state, and local assistance, and on the other hand the beneficiaries of the Old Age and Survivors Insurance administered impersonally throughout the land by the federal government.

Perhaps even a decade or two ago this dichotomy would have been both logical and in a sense final. We have now entered, however, into a phase of economic-political evolution so extensive and significant that a totally new perspective may have to be adopted in which both the destitute and the poor as well as the welfare services relating to them may have to be rethought. They may have to take their places in a social engineering enterprise based on the concept of a new distribution of the national income involving what has been designated a "guaranteed annual income" in the labor philosophy, and a "floor under family income" by the National Commission on Technology, Automation and Economic Progress.[1] More important than the phrase "floor under family income" is the paragraph in the Commission's recommendations in which that phrase is used. It reads:[2]

> Technological change and productivity are primary sources of our unprecedented wealth, but many persons have not shared in that abundance. We recommend that economic security be guaranteed by a floor under family income. That floor should include both improvements in wage-related benefits and a broader system of income maintenance for those families unable to provide for themselves.

Undoubtedly the Commission would have included one-person families in its report had it deemed emphasis important.

So far as all this has a direct bearing on existing welfare services and on other probable development in the foreseeable future, the following may be worth particular emphasis.

---

[1] Report of the Commission submitted to the President and Members of Congress, August 1964, Volume I, (U. S. Government Printing Office, February 1966).

[2] Commission Report, p. 110.

1. The "unprecedented wealth" referred to by the Commission now provides resources in our national economy beyond comparison with any past period. Within this generation the gross national product has increased more than tenfold. Various procedures affecting the national income have already been put into operation under diverse names and forms, as, for example, phenomenal increases in wages, fringe benefits, retirement provisions in labor unions, insurance to cover unemployment and work accidents; provisions for vocational training in general, for the handicapped in particular, for the aged, widows, dependent children, the mentally ill, to mention some of the more important.

2. The political structure of the nation as a whole is responsive to the needs and wishes of the people as never before, the cultural acceptance of democracy having passed beyond the stage of lip service, despite the residual burden of racial, ethnic, and cast prejudices; and it has risen above the remnants of aristocratic hegemony, of feudal patterns, of oligarchic and monarchic traditions, and even of the uncontrolled sway of wealth and capital in the earlier periods of our national life. Nor has it succumbed to any serious extent to the power-structured pretense of democracy in Communist political and social systems.

3. The philosophically recognized effectiveness of government as an instrument of public will and as an obligated servant of public interest has made it possible to assign to it extensive administrative powers in a variety of important areas such as health, welfare services, conservation of resources, recreational opportunities, transportation, highway development, and educational programs. Gradually, moreover, national standards and the utilization of national taxing resources have made possible the reduction of worship of states' rights and local autonomy, except as these are essential factors of administrative decentralization and local citizen interest. There are still archaic remnants of meaningless localism, but these are gradually retreating in favor of community participation and a variety of geographic mergers.[3]

[3] An interesting example of the persistence of this formal localism is cited by the Commission. "In 1962," says the report, "the San Diego Metropolitan community had 11 municipalities; the Phoenix area 17; the

At this point, the reader may be wondering why there is not more specific and documented information presented on this large new wave of total economic planning as illustrated by the guaranteed income, negative income tax, and similar proposals. Certainly the important events in the welfare field of the future are going to be in that direction. However, it would be impossible at this time to offer a definitive and statistically adequate picture of this seething area of bold, hopeful pioneering. It would be even more impossible to propose or to describe administrative structures for making it effective. Large-scale plans and discussions on the subject are now pouring forth in the press and in socio-economic technical literature. At the same time, present operational welfare activities are increasingly drawn into the inclusive larger plans. But the practical, daily, and still enormously important administration of welfare services cannot be neglected and swept under the carpet just because more impressive and more inclusive plans are in the making. Emphasis in this volume is on present operations, and that must remain the central topic. It is fortunate that these operations can now be seen as increasingly integrated in the great planned economy of the future. Growing public discussion and legislative experimentation is something that the interested reader will have to be prepared to keep in perspective in the next decade or two. As examples of current discussions in the press and of the caliber of those participating in them, the following items are selected as a suggestive sampling to be added to messages to the Congress by the President of the United States:

The floor under family income as recommended by the National Commission on Technology, Automation and Economic Progress has already been mentioned. The term used by the Commission is a synonym for guaranteed income (whether achieved by negative income tax or outright grants). A simple statement by an economist and former Assistant Secretary of Labor sums up the essence of the situation. Says Daniel P. Moynihan:[4] "We seem

---

Houston area 25; the Cleveland area 75; the St. Louis area 163; the Chicago area 246; and the New York Metropolitan region 1,400 local governments. Small villages, school districts, towns, counties and even states have lost much of their original relevancy as operative entities." Commission Report, p. 99.

    [4] Currently director of the Joint Center for Urban Studies of

somehow unable to recognize that what it means to be poor is not to have enough money." As simple as that. The statement is contained in an article proposing a system of family allowance (which is a more limited approach to the same end) such as is currently in effect in Canada and, according to Moynihan, in "almost sixty nations"; it covers a number of other items in the new economic planning.

A similar approach, also by way of the press, is suggested by one of the best-known economists and diplomats in the United States, John Kenneth Galbraith.[5] "The past theory," he says, "has been that the only way to cure poverty is to make everybody a productive citizen. . . . But the people who are poor in the United States are those who are *excluded* from participating in the economy. . . . I am by no means certain we can or should make everybody participants." In partial support of this statement he states that "about 30 per cent of the children who are in poor families— with incomes under $3,000—have no visible male parent. The family is headed by a woman . . ." In commenting on measures in no man's land, as it were, between traditional poor relief or "welfare" and the new method of over-all economic planning, he judges that "Sargent Shriver[6] has done an imaginative job under very trying circumstances. It is also my impression," he continues, "that the best of the programs are of enormous value." He mentions particularly the Job Corps, Head Start, and the Youth Employment program.

A more detailed and earlier analysis of the negative income tax, straddling the areas of traditional welfare and of economic planning, and also being promulgated in the press, has the titillating

---

M. I. T. and Harvard. Interrogated at a Senatorial seminar including Senators Abraham A. Ribicoff, Jacob K. Javits, and Robert F. Kennedy— *New York Times Magazine*, February 2, 1967.

[5] Paul M. Warburg Professor of Economics at Harvard, particularly well known for his book *The Affluent Society* and as U. S. Ambassador to India in 1961–63, interviewed by Anthony Lewis of the *New York Times*— *New York Times Magazine*, December 18, 1966.

[6] Head of the Organization for Economic Opportunity—popularly called "the war on poverty."

title: "Washington Should Pay Taxes to the Poor,"[7] by Michael A. Reagan, professor of political science at the University of California (Riverside). Professor Reagan cites a variety of pertinent statistics, as well as offering what might be designated as cultural comments. Of the statistics, the most illuminating may be his estimate of the approximate over-all cost of the whole package: eleven billion dollars annually. This, it should be noted, is not much over half of the disbursements in the federal Social Security system. More significant perhaps is his general agreement with the position of both Moynihan and Galbraith that the argument of the demoralizing effect on recipients, conceived as avoiding "honest labor," is, except for a vociferous minority, essentially unrealistic. He disapproves of "the degrading kind of means test to which applicants for public assistance are subjected in most localities" and seeks to estimate the nature of administrative structures and fiscal standards required.

The above citations have been emphasized because public opinion and the direction of cultural changes probably respond more to scholarly statements of economists and political scientists than of those professionally engaged in welfare administration or in the training of workers in schools committed to traditional operations. Moreover, the opinions of the former are sought after and effectively publicized by the press, which has the ear of legislators, political leaders, and the general public. But there is also a limited number of outstanding leaders within the welfare field who from their direct contact with operational agencies and with independent research can speak with authority on the subject and move in the direction of economic planning and cultural perspectives. Among these is Professor Richard A. Cloward, spiritual author of the novel social instrument known as Mobilization for Youth. In a series of articles by Cloward and his associates[8] the case is made and supporting evidence marshalled in a manner hardly distinguishable from

---

[7] *New York Times Magazine,* February 20, 1966.

[8] See Richard A. Cloward and Richard M. Elman in *The Nation,* February 28, 1966, and March 7, 1966, "Poverty, Injustice and the Welfare State." Also, Cloward and Frances Fox Piven in *The Nation,* May 2, 1966, "A Strategy to End Poverty."

the Galbraith-Moynihan-Reagan presentations.[9] Yet, though a faculty member of the oldest and largest school of social work, his voice is still a voice in the wilderness.

Also from the operational field, directly or indirectly, the new spirit reaches the press for debate addressed to the public. Undoubtedly, a large body of citations could be garnered in the country as a whole to illustrate this phenomenon. Limited space makes possible only a few examples: New York City Commissioner of Welfare Mitchell I. Ginsberg, for example, "asks state authorities for permission"[10]

to let his workers raise the subject of birth control;
for a system that will permit welfare recipients to keep a portion of their relief check when they work for pay;
for a simple spot-checked declaration of need to replace time-consuming and often degrading eligibility investigation.

The Advisory Council on Public Welfare in the Office of the Secretary of Health, Education, and Welfare recommended (June 1966) a *national minimum standard*[11] of relief payments, among other changes.[12]

Finally, in this grab bag of samples, we have a state legislator sponsoring "a bill designed to remove the stigma of accepting welfare aid" by changing the name of the "Social Welfare Law to the Social Service Law."

One should also note the proliferation on the "poverty" book shelf since Harrington's pioneer publication: various books like *The Poorhouse State* by Richard M. Elman; *Beyond Welfare* by Herbert Krosney; *The Despised Poor* by Joseph P. Ritz.

As these citations suggest in part, the stage is clearly set for what might be a wholesale restructuring of the welfare operations in

[9] By the same authors in the *New Republic,* December 17, 1966, "Desegregated Housing."

[10] *New York Times,* December 19, 1966.

[11] Italics supplied.

[12] *New York Times,* January 5, 1967, article by Robert B. Semple, Jr.

the nation. And it is likely that ten years hence the present situation will appear archaic and unreal. But it would be futile to prognosticate the exact features of that future welfare structure. The directions appear clear enough in some phases: assured basic livelihood through various instrumentalities for every man, woman, and child in the nation is truly in the works. The extent to which suitable operational personnel will be available is less clear. Institutional facilities and medical services are likely increasing to approximate needed requirements. But outlines are still dim as to the manner in which local and national governments will share administrative tasks; nor is the pattern of citizen participation clear in a future community setting where political realism, financial solvency, limited integration, and mutual acceptance of ethnic, racial, religious, and neighborhood groups is pertinent; and where the 70 to 80 per cent urban population will share and enjoy with rural producers the wealth and beauty of the land.

⤳ MAJOR SERVICES TODAY ⤲

Tentatively, the major welfare operations briefly presented in the following pages may be classified as services:
for livelihood,
for medical care,
for children, as a special group,
for personality therapy,
for neighborhood centers, and
to clients with many needs.

Obviously, this classification is arbitrary, and necessarily imperfect, since areas of overlapping are many and frequent. Their one common characteristic is that they deal chiefly with needs and with people who are primarily in economic difficulties generally constituting destitution. Nevertheless, for clarity in identifying the services, and for facilitating a historical perspective it is pragmatically useful to present them *as if* they were separate entities. This is particularly the case when we recognize varying degrees of participation in the services by voluntary as against tax-supported administrative structures. There is another difficulty attaching to any form of presentation, namely that relating to statistical support of generalizations. There are tons of statistics. But they are difficult to integrate and coordinate since they are derived from different sources and predicated on different definitions. And few of them remain the same from one year to the next. Some quantitative data despite these cautions must, however, be included in the present story, but they will be kept down to a significant minimum.

The last of the services listed above is a sort of catch-all concept and an everyman's land. It could conceivably be entitled "overlapping services" or "services missing and unrelated." A complex area, it is often composed of bits and pieces of the major services in a bewildering jigsaw puzzle—with many pieces missing. Realistically, it reflects the presence of multiple needs in a given case, each calling for a different type of service; and equally realistic is the fact that the several relevant services may be offered, if at all, by different agencies and different personnel. The agencies themselves are often eager to supply the service, if only the mechanics could be worked out. But often, also, the agencies compete for primary responsibility for the client. Rarely are the separate services for the several needs correlated in the way that diverse techniques and materials are correlated in an engineering enterprise. As yet, there appears to be no dependable pattern for matching multiple services with multiple needs.

Chapter III

⧫

Services for Livelihood

For some time before the great depression there had been considerable discussion and disagreement among professional social workers
as to the relative soundness of "categorical" relief versus general assistance for those in economic distress. There were valid arguments
on both sides. The "categorical" school has won the battle. A relatively small conceptual area has remained in "general assistance,"
and since practically all of it has come under public administration
and financing, former exponents of general assistance, who were
mostly in voluntary "family agencies," have retired from the battle-
field. The categories that are now the framework of economic assist-

47

ance within the governments on all the levels are principally the following:

Old Age Assistance (OAA)

Assistance to the Blind (AB)

Assistance to Families with Dependent Children (AFDC)

Assistance to Persons Partly or Totally Disabled (APTD)

General Assistance (GA)

More recently there has been added another category, namely:

Medical Assistance to the Aged (MAA)

All except the category of general assistance are entitled to contributions by the federal government to the states, provided the latter conform to certain federal regulations. The amounts so contributed also have a bearing on the components of state expenditures, as, for example, those for administration as distinct from actual grants to clients; and they are further adjusted in a complicated matching system to amounts per client under the state's system of maxima, its per capita income, and various additional regulations within the jurisdiction of state legislation.

The state in turn may set up regulations for sharing grants by local governments. These may represent variations as to subclasses, as, for example, the aged, children, blind, etc. As might be expected under the circumstances, there are enormous variations among states as to maximum grants and as to choice of categories preferentially served. Confusing and often indigestible as may be the statistics on this wide range of economic assistance, a limited over-all picture is, nevertheless, desirable, and will, in part at least, be submitted in this chapter. They should include at least:

Totals spent by the federal government;

Totals spent by the states;

State by state variations in actual amounts, maxima and minima, averages, and inclusion of categories served.

While a number of sources were examined in selecting these figures and in describing general situations of economic need out of which they arise, the major portion of the material, other than that from the writer's own experience, is drawn from the following sources:

1. Annual and special reports of the United States Department of Health, Education, and Welfare, particularly:
   a) The Annual Report for 1962 and 1963
   b) Report on Trends (annual) for 1963
   c) Characteristics of General Assistance in the United States (P.A. Report No. 39).
2. A relatively brief but unusually well-informed publication by Elizabeth Wickenden and Winifred Bell, *Public Welfare, Time for a Change* (New York School of Social Work, Columbia University, 1961).
3. *Public Relief 1929–1939*, by Josephine C. Brown (Holt, 1940).
4. *Facts, Fallacies and Future*, a report prepared for Cook County, Illinois (Chicago), by Greenleigh Associates, Inc., 1960.
5. An unpublished report on the Services of the Department of Public Welfare, Pennsylvania, based on data and published material provided by the department, in connection with a study financed by the Field Foundation and conducted by the present writer.

The data drawn from periodic publications of the United States Department of Health, Education, and Welfare and reflecting principally the activities of that department are particularly significant in the social welfare scene of our day. They reflect a totally new phenomenon that emerged in the early thirties with establishment of the Federal Security Administration. They begin virtually at zero, on Februay 11, 1936. There had, indeed, existed a Federal Emergency Relief Administration set up three years earlier, and several state emergency relief administrations as well, after the depression of 1929–33, but these were temporary, emergency operations. The Federal Security Agency, however, and the insurance system under it were new and permanent, and are of enormous significance. In addition to certain relatively minor operations, the program comprises two major parts: public economic assistance, under various designations, and Old Age and Survivors Insurance. The assistance services are supplementary to state operations. The insurance system is entirely federal.[1]

The number of clients aided by the federal-state assistance program[2] (not the insurance program) in 1963 was as follows:[3]

Old Age Assistance (OAA)	2,198,896
Medical Assistance for the Aged (MAA)	136,220
Total Aged	2,335,116
Aid to the Blind (AB)	98,390
Aid to Permanently and Totally Disabled (APTD)	461,537
Aid to Families with Dependent Children (AFDC)	3,934,542
	6,829,585

Characteristics of major importance for all these categories—with variation in detail—are:

1. They all apply a means test for client eligibility; no one is automatically eligible.
2. They are subject to specific budgetary provisions by the legislative body of the political unit that has administrative responsibility.
3. There are a variety of restrictions on eligibility beyond those comprised in the means test.
4. Part of the available funds, with the exception, usually, of the category "general assistance" (GA) are derived from the federal government, under a complicated system of matching, in which the determining factor is, in the main, the standard set by the individual states.

[1] A most complete review of the steps leading to the establishment of the present federal system is contained in the volume cited above, by Josephine C. Brown, *Public Relief, 1929–39.*

[2] Highly condensed statements and statistics covering this entire national program can be found in the annual reports of the Department of Health, Education, and Welfare. The data presented here are only a few of the major items. They are principally for the fiscal year ending June 30, 1963.

[3] It is estimated by the Federal authorities that about 775,000 additional persons receive general assistance grants not matched by the federal government.

Restrictions embodied in the state systems of categorical assistance vary enormously. Some of the results are visible in routine financial reports of the Department of Health, Education, and Welfare. Others are not so easily discovered, though many are available in the various publications of the department and through independent studies. A few comments on major restrictions are in place here, for they have a meaning to the citizen at large—if he is concerned with the character of the culture in which he lives—as well as to the student of the field of welfare.

First, the "means test." On the face of it, this is a logical and reasonable restriction, whether, as earlier, the funds came from voluntary agencies or from public funds. No one should receive public assistance unless he is destitute ("poverty" is too loose and general a term: it means merely a low level of income). Assistance programs are supposedly conducted to assist only persons and families who are unable to exist at all on the resources available to them. Then who shall be assisted? The elaborate means test system actually in effect supplies the answer. The test has two purposes: one, establishing eligibility for assistance; the other, determining the nature and amount of the assistance to be supplied.[4] In both these categories old repressive attitudes toward the poor and destitute have been rampant. Over and over again we find means test procedures and regulations made as difficult as possible so as to exclude, rather than include, applicants. These rules make them feel like social outcasts in return for assistance offered. The amount of evidence is overwhelming, and only some illustrative items can be included within the limited space here. In a number of states, however, there has been laudable progress in making the means test an instrument of justice and efficiency rather than a tool to punish the destitute. And in the federal government this realistic and scientific attitude, in contrast to the punitive one, has been particularly gratifying.

The means test as a component of eligibility had to establish the degree of deprivation that would justify acceptance of a client

---

[4] One of the few straightforward discussions in recent years of social work literature on the means test has recently been contributed by Walter C. Benkrup, an employee of the Department of Public Welfare of the State of Louisiana. See *Journal of Social Work*, Vol. 9, No. 2, April 1964.

for assistance. But this has always been a poser. The earliest procedure did not bother with the question at all. An arbitrary amount
was set, determined either by the generosity of the donor agency or by
its resources. Such was the dole. Within the writer's memory a $2.00
monthly allotment to a family by the overseers of the poor was not
uncommon; this had, of course, no bearing on the extent of need, or
the "means" available to the applicant. The solution in the end was
the budget: detailed requirements for various needs, cost of providing these, all in relation to size and composition of the family by age
and sex; often, extra allowance to meet the needs of a pregnant
wife or mother, or of some member of the family requiring special
food as for some medical conditions. But, while the concept of the
family budget in relation to family income is clear enough so that
eligibility can be judged by whether the family income is less than
budgetary requirements, the joker is in deciding what standard to
use as definition or requirement for livelihood. Every state can make
its own definition. It can utilize, if it chooses, scientific studies by
such federal agencies as the departments of Labor or Agriculture, or
it can set up its own. There is no legal obligation to use existing
scientific findings as to caloric requirement, vitamin requirement,
ethnic or cultural customs. An auxiliary joker then comes into play
when, eligibility by the means test having been established, the
amount of assistance fund granted may be adjusted not to these
standards, but to an arbitrarily set approved "relief budget." It is
not the universal practice to grant assistance on the same scale as
that used for establishing eligibility.

Other restrictive practices in use in some form in most states
reflect the centuries-old tendency of "charitable" agencies to hold
back; to find reasons for treating destitution as personal evil on the
part of the applicant rather than as a phenomenon of economic and
social origin. Among these restrictions are those based on residence,
pressure to utilize "legally responsible relatives" as sources of income
for clients, and, of course, inadequate appropriations for relief by
legislative bodies.

Residence restrictions hark back to the parish relief system
of Britain. They vary from state to state. In some states there are no
residence restrictions, though this may relate only to eligibility and

have no necessary bearing on the generosity of the scale of assistance; others may require one year, or as high as five, of residence;[5] and there are states that take indirect measures to modify this restriction by reciprocal arrangements. Residence restrictions as well as requirements relating to "legally responsible relatives" may be particularly harmful where members of the family live in different states, or where family cohesion and good will may be threatened by legal action to enforce regulations of the administration.

There are varieties of other impediments to effective and sympathetic administration of economic assistance. Some of these may be only psychological deterrents, but they may also threaten or destroy such attempts at thrift as the family may have practiced in their more prosperous days. It is interesting to note, in passing, that while in criminal procedures the accused must theoretically be regarded as innocent unless proven guilty, in areas of destitution it is assumed, except in emergencies, that the client must totally prove his distress and his lack of resources. The analogy is not exact, of

[5] It is disheartening to see the recrudescence of the residence phobia emerging in one of the progressive states of the country within recent weeks. It was shocking enough to call forth the following editorial in the *New York Times* (May 1, 1965):

ONE YEAR BEFORE RELIEF?

There is so much else that is sound in the report of Governor Rockefeller's Committee on Welfare Costs that it is surprising that it voted—even if only by a 3-to-2 margin—for a one-year residence requirement for recipients of state welfare aid.

It is inconceivable that in this state any person would be permitted to starve to death or to freeze in the streets simply because he had not satisfied such a residence requirement. Once this fact is realized, the illusory nature of any major savings hoped for from such a provision becomes apparent. All it would really accomplish would be to force communities in which persons who are threatened by such catastrophe are located to find other sources of funds to help them.

The argument that the existing situation encourages potential welfare clients to come to the state is undermined by the committee majority's frank admission that "not too many people" do so. If imposition of a residence rule should slow down any such flow, the resulting savings would be largely negated by added costs of the investigations required to enforce this requirement. Marginal economies in this direction are surely not worth the damage the step would inflict upon the humanitarian tradition of which the people of New York are rightly proud. "© *1965 by The New York Times Company. Reprinted by permission.*"

course, but it is not entirely unfair. Often, moreover, the client may be forced to strip himself of long-range resources to qualify for immediate assistance. Regulations may require the client to give up his insurance if he has any beyond an arbitrary low amount set up in the regulations; he must swear to a number of affidavits as to taxes paid or unpaid; he may have to sign a lien on his property even though this may be the most cherished part of his mode of life; there are places where he must fill out some ten to twelve questionnaires. A false or incorrect statement may bring refusal of assistance, legal claim against him enforceable in court, or possible criminal prosecution for perjury. The state from which a few of the particular restrictions are cited distrusts not only the client but also its own employees.[6] Local public assistance offices are systematically and quite properly checked by the central administration. But beyond that there is, in this particular state, a separate bureau that examines by large-scale random sampling the work of both local and central offices. And beyond that, still, there is the state auditor's office that, in distrust of all the others, conducts its own investigations. These last two actually investigate independently, entering for that purpose the client's home and destroying the confidential relationship between client and worker. This super-watchdog operation is designed not to protect the rights of the client but to find ways of reducing expenditures. And it is costly in itself.

So much for machinery. How adequately are the needs of the client met when established, his eligibility proved, and observance of regulations assured? The livelihood to be provided by public assistance is never in excess of low-income standards normally attained by the general run of unskilled workers' families. If, then, one could determine the reasonable needs of a family—let us say a poor but self-supporting family—that would seem to provide also a reasonable standard of public assistance. Evidently this is not a question of the income earned by the family, but of the needs to be satisfied for

[6] It should be noted that the greatest understanding, the most realistic appraisal of client problems, in this state was evident not at the central administration of the department, but in the county offices, by the directors, supervisors and field staff.

survival on a level customary in the low-income stratum of the time and place in question. So we are back again at the question of budget, as were the English scholars and the standard-of-living students in the United States. These standards, elusive though they are in view of diverse ethnic and cultural factors, competence of housewives, fluctuation of prices, and absolute factors of dwelling rentals, have been identified with a reasonable degree of accuracy by the federal departments of Agriculture and of Labor, allowing for urban, rural, and regional variations.

There is, in the United States, a cluster of fifty state sovereignties guaranteed by the Constitution, each more or less different in its mood and philosophy; there are in the main no national standards that determine welfare practice in any state. Standards are local or regional, and authority is local or state. Such standards as do become national are those imposed by conditions of financial contribution by the central government, consensus in the Congress, and intellectual perspectives of national leadership. This situation is reinforced by the fact that the present over-all system was largely the result of an economic emergency of 1929–35 from which the federal government alone was able to rescue the nation. Washington provides enormous financial assistance but actual administration resides in state governments. The caliber and generosity of economic assistance vary from state to state, to a degree surprising to the uninitiated. Some of this disparity is reflected in the annual and special reports of the Department of Health, Education, and Welfare. A striking example of the disparity is seen in the variation among States in the low and high average benefits paid for the same category of assistance, as shown by the table[7] on the next page.

In a different way (since federal matching of funds is governed by prescribed methods) the relative share of funds derived respectively from federal and state sources also shows a wide range, varying from 34 per cent to 76.9 per cent of expended funds being

[7] Wickender and Bell, *Public Welfare, Time for a Change,* p. 35. As stated by the authors, the range shown "cannot be explained by any known differences in levels of living, cost of living, wage level or personal requirements."

*Variation in Monthly Average Public Assistance Payments
to Recipients as of April 1961,
in the Several Jurisdictions*

	Low	High
OAA	$34.49	$110.91
AB	38.29	112.56
AFDC	9.35	48.21
APTD	34.82	133.56
GA	13.50	111.48

derived from federal sources.[8] In view of the wide range of practices in the several states as suggested by these figures, more detailed data drawn largely from one of the Eastern industrial states may serve to illustrate the problems still to be faced before an assistance program of truly national standards may come into being. The data presented are neither typical nor quite atypical—neither the best nor the worst. But they reflect the fact that in this country of general wealth and prosperity there are still truly destitute persons and families. They furnish little ground for complacency.

In the state referred to, the legislature clearly defined its conscience with respect to what it should do for its destitute citizens:

It is hereby declared to be the legislative intent that the purpose of this act is to promote the welfare and happiness of all the people of the Commonwealth by providing public assistance to all its needy and destitute; that assistance shall be administered promptly and humanely with due regard for the preservation of family life, and without discrimination on account of race, religion, or political affiliation; and that assistance shall be administered in such a way and manner as to encourage self-respect, self-dependency and the desire to be a good citizen and useful to society . . ."

The legislative intent thus set forth is then interpreted in a policy statement of the administrative body responsible for public assistance operations in part as follows:

[8] Annual Report, Department of Health, Education, and Welfare, 1963.

. . . a standard of health and decency for public assistance in the Commonwealth should comply with the following criteria:

1. The standard should maintain the physical and mental health of the recipient of assistance without impairment due to the inadequacy of the basic essentials of food, clothing, shelter, personal care, medical care and other requirements to meet generally recognized needs of the individual;

2. The standard should recognize the need of the individual in our society for social participation within his community on a scale comparable to that of his fellows;

3. The standard should be geared to maintaining, and if necessary, developing or restoring the ability of the recipient to exercise his normal function as a citizen and respected member of his community during whatever period assistance may be required;

4. The standard should be geared to long-term goals rather than short-term needs of all recipients;

5. At the same time the standard should be based upon a low cost budgetary provision for health and decency, as presently established by competent authorities. It should at no time be so high as to discourage employment and economic independence, where desirable, nor so low as to force employment upon the aged, the ill, the disabled, the mothers of young children, or children attending school.

At no time were these standards repudiated. In fact they were reinforced, in a sense, by federal contributions intended to make possible their implementation. Unfortunately, the legislature never did, and perhaps in the light of political pressures never could, implement its own intent or the policies of the administrative body: appropriations for assistance purposes were never high enough even to approximate intent or policy. The straightforward analysis of facts by officers of the department clearly shows failure to approximate the standards set. It is possible to cover here only a few of the deviations, all of them, unfortunately, typical for many of the states. The following items have been selected as particularly important in demonstrating the weak spots that may occur in any state (or municipal) welfare administration:

The "health and decency" standard

Residence restrictions

Variation among categories of assistance
The theory of legally responsible relatives
Auditing and bureaucratic strictures
Attitude to federal supplementation
Reluctant citizen attitudes.

≥ STANDARDS OF ASSISTANCE

"Health and decency" standards represent a combination of budgets established in scientific laboratory tests and of cultural factors of time and place.

Information on cost of living on relatively low income levels is available from calculations made periodically by the departments of Labor and of Agriculture of the federal government. They can be obtained by states and municipal authorities; they are so prepared as to be adjustable to differences in local conditions. Several such calculations were particularly useful during the hectic decade following the 1929 crash. They date back to the classic Atwater calorie requirement experiments of the eighties of the last century, and to a series of standard-of-living studies that go still farther back. Authorities differ as to their absolute accuracy and applicability to practical problems.[9] But within reasonable limits something resembling a "modest but adequate" budget for families of different sizes has been found useful for assistance agencies both voluntary and public. They are not always identified as "health and decency" standards, and sometimes they are called forthrightly "relief standards." But generally it has been assumed that they would guide assistance authorities in arriving at the appropriate level of economic assistance which should determine grants. Age and sex composition of families is usually included in the calculations, and additional amounts are often added for special needs such as illness and pregnancy. The basic standard of grants is, however, the important foundation of any administrative operations. Authorities occasionally admit that they fail to live up to their own accepted standards. The

[9] See, for example, English follow-up studies of the Booth inquiry and of the Rountree surveys, etc., in Part Four, below.

following citations are culled from annual reports of the Commonwealth of Pennsylvania in which the legislative intent was so clearly stated, and in which the administration admits its failure, year after year, to reach even its own "health and decency" standard, to say nothing of a "modest and adequate" one.

As reported by the Department of Welfare of that state: "Assistance is only one-third of a modest and adequate budget for a self-supporting family."

But since the grants claim to be only on a "health and decency" standard (never defined or supported) this same "one-third" turns out to be, in the words of the report: "Only two-thirds [of the cost of living] at a minimum standard of health and decency." A further illuminating general statement—evidently not one made with pride—adds that: "Since seven out of every eight persons receiving assistance are under age 65,[10] approximately 88 per cent of all persons on assistance have to live on one-third to one-half less than is needed for minimum health and decency."

There are also further comments presented in dollars and cents. So, for example, the Department calculates the adequacy of its grants as follows (for 1964):

		Standard
Living costs for a typical wage earner's *family of four,* for a month would be	$441	100%
Cost of assistance items for a *family of four* on minimum standard of health and decency	258	58%
Maximum actual assistance allowance for the same family	173	39%

Only the aged—sixty-five and over—are more fortunate: they receive nearly 92 per cent of the minimum allowance, though not nearly quite the same percentage of the standard described as "modest but adequate."

[10] The aged, as will be seen, are treated far more generously than children or mothers.

RESIDENCE LIMITATIONS

Residence limitations as applied in public assistance constitute a curious rejection of the biblical exhortation for kindness to "the stranger within the gates." Presumably the restriction has its origin—so far as this country is concerned—in the desperate state of some of the parishes in England as the unpredictable movement of laborers to escape starvation drove them from farm to town and from town to town. It represented the desire of communities to rid themselves of the financial burden of assisting the new poor over and above the old destitute. No comparable catastrophic phenomenon characterized the affairs of the Colonies. But the pattern had been established and had taken on a semblance of moral as well as legal right. In this country, as a practical procedure, reciprocal arrangements among certain states have been established whereby the nonresident person may stay where he is, but the cost of his assistance may be audited out. Thus the financial problem would seem to be resolved, provided there is some balance between the nonresident poor in one state and those of the reciprocal state.

There was the case of an old lady casually mentioned by a responsible official of a state welfare department in a committee meeting discussing general administrative problems. She was sixty-seven years old, living alone, was in receipt of old age assistance in accordance with current regulations. This amounted to $70 per month, of which a substantial portion came from federal matching supplementation. A daughter living in a neighboring state had been unable to contribute to her maintenance. Then this daughter became incapacitated, unable to support herself. So, not surprisingly, the mother took her in. Now, through no one's fault, there were two persons to be supported. The regulations of the department for this two-person family's support allowed $90 a month. But there was that residence catch: the daughter was not a resident of her mother's state. One of them only was entitled to assistance, at half the rate for two, which brought the $90 down to $45. So now two destitute women had to live on $45 instead of one on $70.

☙ VARIATION BETWEEN CATEGORIES

The only satisfaction one may achieve that would in any way take the sting out of the incredibly repressive standards of assistance in the different categories today would be to study relief rates before the social security system, during the reign of voluntary relief and public doles. But the present rates are depressing enough, whether seen for the country as a whole or for the various states.[11] In federally assisted categories the average monthly grant per recipient was as follows:

	1962	1963
OAA	$62.93	$77.05
AFDC	31.48	30.95
AB	77.47	81.92
APTD	72.00	74.80

This discrepancy among categories may not seem so extreme in the nation-wide averages, remembering that the amount per person in the AFDC families has the benefit of income cumulative with the size of the family. When compared, however, from state to state, the figures per month show the following averages per recipient, for 1962, for the low and high states, respectively:

	Low	*High*
OAA	$36.03 in Mississippi	$103.42 in California
ADC	9.15 in Mississippi	46.00 in Illinois
AB	38.13 in Mississippi	121.72 in California
APTD	34.44 in Mississippi	100.79 in California

The figures tell a stunning story.

☙ LEGALLY RESPONSIBLE RELATIVES

There appear to be no nation-wide statistics on the extent to which public authorities enforce contributions from technically "re-

[11] In the annual report of the department (HEW) comparative figures are given by states, as well as by other factors. See particularly Report for 1963, Tables 1 to 7, pp. 114–120.

sponsible relatives." The underlying theory is, of course, that the state may force such relatives to support their kin, because cultural mores so demand. These mores are incorporated in various forms in legal provisions of state legislation, and the extent of their enforcement is presumably part of administrative regulations.[12] In the state from which the following illustrative data are drawn, there are no central statistics covering this phase of assistance administration. County units are required to enforce them. The state does provide an elaborate schedule that may guide local enforcement authorities. They set forth the amount of income the responsible relative needs for the maintenance of his own immediate family, depending on the size of the family and some related considerations. From the excess over these requirements he is expected to contribute to the prospective assistance recipient amounts also set forth in the official schedule. The expected contribution, based on these calculations, is then deducted from the amount theoretically payable to the client in accordance with the department's "health and decency" standards. The amount is to be deducted, whether the legally responsible relative actually does or does not pay. If no contribution is received by the client, the latter is expected to institute court action to enforce the contribution, whether it be against parent or offspring or other relative covered by law. What this does to familial relations is not hard to imagine. The data which follow are drawn from two contiguous counties, where a study instituted by the state for other purposes yielded some incidental information on this phase of the work. The county director of public assistance, one of the many highly competent and dedicated civil servants in the field, reported a caseload of some 2,000 comprising approximately 5,500 persons. Ninety-two of the cases came within the regulation relating to legally responsible relatives. The grants for these 92 families would under normal circumstances have totaled approximately $8,400 per month, or a little more than $90 per family. The schedule in force called for about $2,400, or 30 per cent, of this to come from the relatives. The facts were these: in two thirds (sixty-one) of the cases contributions

[12] The Wickenden-Bell study, cited previously, reports that thirty-two of the states have laws dealing with the matter, though it seems to have no high regard for either its propriety or its social usefulness.

from relatives were actually obtained.[13] In only three of these cases was a court order resorted to. In the remaining thirty-one cases failure to obtain contributions from relatives resulted in a reduction of 18 per cent of the assistance due.[14] This brought the grants for the affected families down to 32 per cent of the "wage-earner's" rate of income.

Data on this phase of archaic "poor relief" are so difficult to obtain that some further details may be of interest:

In one case $10 was deducted from a calculated grant of	$ 80.30
In one case $5 was deducted from a calculated grant of	152.40
In still another, $26.90 was deducted from a calculated grant of	60.30
and $30.00 was deducted from a calculated grant of	65.30
and $56.00 was deducted from a calculated grant of	78.90

This was a small county. If the practice were a consistent state policy the figures would run higher in a much larger county. The contiguous county, upon request for the data, found only nine cases instead of the 1,300 that the same ratio would produce in its caseload. The explanation given was that in the second county the County Board of Assistance and the court regarded the whole regulation as unsound, unworkable, and inequitable. No information is available for the state as a whole.

With the enormous range of conditions over the country, of public opinion, of available resources, and of local traditions, it is not practicable to offer enough reliable detailed information as to the extent and manner in which bureaucratic and punitive auditing systems, unsympathetic citizens' attitudes, or mainpulation of federal contributions may militate against just and generous management of public assistance. They do exist and are known to many students of the field. But more impressive in many ways has been the dedicated attitude of a host of workers and administrators in the field. They, rather than top officials and bureaucratic regulation makers, really do the job, and they are with few exceptions both dedicated and ingenious. They stretch regulations as far as can be done within

[13] The actual figures are $1,846 out of the calculated allowance of $5,377 for the families involved.
[14] $566 deducted from $3,055 due.

the letter of the rules. Many instances were found by the writer where they went beyond "the call of duty," and where they drew from their own resources when none other could be found.

In the social security insurance system, which is entirely administered and financed under the federal government, none of these restrictive measures apply. There a totally different philosophical approach to the welfare system is seen. The fact that it is intended to prevent as well as to assist in the battle against destitution is a major fact too often overlooked. Despite the unquestioned power of the Congress to determine amounts of tax funds to be included in annual appropriations, and despite a wide range of attitudes on the part of individual federal legislators, there is never a doubt that the accepted obligations of the United States government in this field will be reflected in the appropriations voted.[15]

⤳ PREVENTION OF DESTITUTION

The approach to prevention of destitution, as distinct from service to those already in economic distress, differs from both administration of public assistance services, and from the "war against poverty." The struggle to end poverty as a major phenomenon has been chiefly an economic and political issue. It still is that. But there are also a number of factors prone to bring about destitution that can, with some reasonable actuarial accuracy be foretold as to incidence, and can therefore be handled on a scientific basis as part of economic-political engineering by government. Among these actuarially manageable causes of possible destitution are old age or superannuation, unemployment, industrial accidents or disease, and congenital handicaps. Unemployment and industrial hazards had for

---

[15] In a sense the federal government also imposes restrictions, but these are addressed to the states, not to individuals. And the auditors of the federal government are in constant touch with the documentation required to justify the allotment rates established. The government also makes available studies on budgetary standards, and the current rates of expenditures on "modest" levels of living. The government reserves the right to withhold part or all of its contributions if the basic conditions of its financial partnership are violated. Generally speaking it would seem the national government's attitude has been generous in the sense that it is oriented to the progressive creation of a national standard for the Union as a whole.

some years been the subject of public concern; both reform organizations and legislative interest grappled with these problems, and in the course of time state after state has provided some form of insurance plan with respect to these hazards to take the threat of economic distress from the shoulders of both employer and employee and avoid costly litigation and uncertain results inherent in court action. The problems of widows and orphans were similarly approached and eventually came to be parts of the over-all insurance plan under the federal government. The greatest advance toward prevention of destitution came about as the result of studies and plans by economists and political scientists, who saw it as a major task of social engineering rather than a specific method of helping those already destitute. The principal feature of this system, those that made it unlike categorical assistance plans, was the basic insurance pattern.

The principal insurance plan under the social security system is that of old age and survivors insurance, based on calculable premiums, expectancy of retirement at sixty-five, and the assumption that, while payment to beneficiaries would not necessarily suffice for livelihood, it would in a significant measure prevent destitution upon retirement from active employment. There are also a great many pension plans—in industry and in labor unions—based on similar patterns. Some pensions in this latter group are sufficient not only to prevent destitution but also to insure full livelihood. These pensions may in fact be received by those entitled to them in addition to the benefits derived from the federal system. There are, however, several characteristics of supreme importance that differentiate the social security system from other retirement and pension plans. First and foremost, the federal social insurance plan is compulsory with respect to the payment of premiums. It takes the form of taxes levied on both employer and employee; the former is obligated to pay his own share and also to deduct from employees' wages or salaries appropriate amounts constituting the workers' share. Even persons already in receipt of old age insurance, if continuing in employment or returning to employment, must pay the scheduled tax. In the second place, a basic equality is introduced into the system by taxing for this purpose only a stated amount of the annual rate of pay earned. At first it was the first $3,600, then the first $4,200, and later the first $6,600. This is important in view of the fact that there is a stated maximum benefit payable, as yet of a modest size, and it would be obviously unfair to tax a person receiving a high salary on the same percentage, when the benefit receivable is limited to an over-all maximum. Another and perhaps supremely important part of the system is the fact that the insured person is certain of his benefits as long as there is a United States. Whatever may be the state of the national budget, balanced or unbalanced, in or out of debt, payments will be made. In contrast, both assistance payments and pensions under nongovernment auspices may go by default or be diminished or altered by regulations. Within a recent period of months or years, for example, a large number of persons lost their expected retirement pensions when the employing corporation ceased operations.[16] Finally, it should be noted, and this is of supreme importance, that there is no means test attached to the system. Either you have qualified or you have not. If you have qualified, you receive your check for the preceding month on the third day of each month. The regulations do call for a reduction of the monthly payments if the insured person continues to earn, in accordance with a simple schedule. But after the seventy-second birthday even this restriction ceases to operate, and full benefit is paid regardless of earnings. Furthermore, any income from other sources than earnings does not call for reduction. A millionaire can collect his full benefit if he no longer works for a living. There are a number of other interesting and important phases of the system, but they are not central to the essentials of the plan. The principal significance lies in the fact that the livelihood of a person no longer able to earn his living, or that of his family,[17] because of his age is practically safe; nor does he sacrifice his rights, or his pride, or any possessions his

[16] The Studebaker Company was reported to be in this situation in 1964, this despite the fact that employer and union were in agreement that no blame could be attached to anyone (*New York Times,* August 16, 1964). In the same article, other cases were cited by number although not by name. According to that report, 1,932 pension plans were terminated for similar reasons, with an estimated average of 150 persons involved.

[17] He is entitled to additional benefits for his dependents or his surviving dependents.

thrift or good luck may have provided for him. He can hold up his head among his fellows.

Regarding this part of the public concern for basic livelihood, as with assistance data, certain simple statistics may bear eloquent testimony.

The following federal figures represent the situation as of December 1962:[18]

Families receiving Old Age and Survivors
    Insurance (OASI) benefits   13,318,300
    Number of persons in these families   18,053,400

This number is less than, but approaching, 10 per cent of the population of the United States. Unlike public assistance payments, however, benefits paid to these persons do not at present come from the general appropriations of the United States. They are derived from tax deductions from wages and salaries, and from employers, on a schedule established by Congress. These payments are deposited in a trust fund under government control and management. Roughly, fifteen billion dollars were paid out to beneficiaries in 1963, this amount increasing as more workers retire, the fund also increasing as the number of employees increases. At the time represented by the above figures, some seventy-five million workers were contributing to the fund, and the annual amount paid in in taxes was roughly the same as the annual benefit payments. It is of incidental interest that earnings of the seventy-five million employees from whom contributions come are roughly 227 billion dollars a year, which in turn represents nearly one third of the gross national income.

Nevertheless, it should be emphasized that these benefits are only a prevention of destitution—enormously important as that is—and not an assurance of livelihood. The worker must still save for his old age in all the ways that he may be able to do so. Retirement arrangements of employing corporations and of labor unions, when available, remain important, as are a large variety of types of provident planning. But the major fear of destitute old age has at last been removed or lightened, and the status of the older citizen in his

[18] Annual Report of Department of Health, Education, and Welfare. 1963.

family thereby greatly improved. The actual amounts of benefits as they reach the beneficiary are still modest. The average for December 1962 was $72.50 per beneficiary, with amounts varying with family composition from $62 to $191.60.[19] In many cases, the amount received was not sufficient for livelihood, and so, when no other resources were available, public assistance still had to be depended on to supplement the benefit. But the desperate days of destitution for the aged, the disabled, and their families are gone.

Does this acceptance of basic responsibility by government and taxpayer mean that voluntary agencies do not and cannot offer needed and useful services to troubled and distressed individuals or families? They do, and they can. But not as rivals and competitors with public programs, nor with disdain for the gigantic tasks performed by public bodies.

[19] HEW annual report 1966.

Chapter IV

⚜

Services for Medical Care

Medical care is almost as much part of livelihood as food, clothing, and lodging—and as unavoidable an expense at some time or another as the cost of food. And since, like food, it costs money, and sometimes far more money than food or clothing, the poor, and certainly the destitute, may not be able to secure the medical aid they need from their own resources. They may only suffer; they may gradually disintegrate; they may die before their time, because they do not have money to buy the required medical care. It is for that reason alone that the discussion of medical care is pertinent here. We are not dealing with medical care as such, but only with economic problems it presents to those without adequate funds. And there must also be a clear distinction between those already destitute regardless of need for medical care and presumably receiving medical service as part of economic assistance, and that larger body of persons who ordinarily are self-maintaining, but are faced with the more heavy burdens brought on by unexpected and often expensive illnesses.

The social planner may find it difficult to choose which of these groups it is more important to concentrate on. In some ways they are, in fact, the same group: one part faced with illness when already unable to provide the basic necessities of life, the other on the brink, likely to join up with the destitute if any serious medical expenditures have to be met. But who is likely to need medical care? After all, one might think, normally one is healthy; it is an exceptional situation to be ill. Unfortunately, this is far from true.[1] In studies quoted in *Readings in Medical Care* the Committee on Costs of Medical Care[2] reported that out of a million persons, in the course of a year,

470,000 will suffer no serious illness,

320,000 will be sick once,

[1] In the succeeding pages there will be a number of references to at least four fundamentally important publications. The interested reader may wish to pursue the subject in greater detail and therefore the following references of primary importance are included here as a whole, instead of itemized referrals in detail. They are:

Medical Care for Tomorrow by Michael M. Davis (Harper, 1955).

Medical Care in Transition, reprints from the American Journal of Public Health, 2 volumes, published by the Public Health Service, U.S. Department of Health, Education, and Welfare, 1949–57 and 1958–62.

Readings in Medical Care, edited by the Committee on Medical Care Teaching of the Association of Teachers of Preventive Medicine (University of North Carolina Press, 1958).

Community Resources in Mental Health, No. 5 in a series of ten monographs published by the Joint Commission on Mental Illness and Health, and prepared by Reginald Robinson, David F. De Marche, and Mildred K. Wagle (Basic Books, 1961).

There are many references and bibliographical suggestions in these publications.

[2] An outstanding organization that began its labors as far back as 1907.

> 140,000 will be sick twice,
>
> 50,000 will be sick three times,
>
> 20,000 will be sick four or more times.

A little adventurous arithmetic would show that the 530,000 persons—more than half of the total million—who were sick at some time piled up more than 830,000 illnesses in the course of the year. Now presumably there was a wide range in the seriousness of these illnesses and there is no telling how many of those 530,000 persons reporting illness managed to obtain medical care. All one can know is that they probably all needed it and that those who could pay were more likely to get it than those who could not. On the basis of recent figures showing 190-odd million inhabitants in the United States, each of the above data can be multiplied by 190 to arrive at a rough estimate of the extent of the problem of illness, and therefore presumably of need for medical care, in the economy of the nation.

How far does the problem of illness constitute a specific concern of the planner for welfare in general? One part of the question is what sort of illnesses need we be concerned about; another is where and to whom do they occur; the third, how can they be paid for, and by whom? All of these aspects become part of the concern of welfare planning. As to what sort of illness, there is a curious answer. It is not likely that there is more illness per thousand persons now than there was a hundred years ago. But, roughly speaking, people live twice as long now as they lived at that time. That gives them twice as many years in which to become ill, and so every person carries twice as many illness chances as he carried a hundred years ago. Nay, more! For the likeliest time for illness to strike is in childhood, or in old age; but the child grows up and the incidence of illness (as well as its costliness) diminishes. The adult, on the other hand, as he grows older, fifty, then sixty, then seventy, then still older, is subject to more illness, more often, and more expensive to care for. And we keep discovering new illnesses, not because they had not occurred before, but because they were not so clearly recognized as illness because medicine had not advanced so far in diagnosis, or nearly so far in discovering or devising treatment. Now we know, for example, that we have, among other things, infantile paralysis, muscular dystrophy, mental retardation, cerebral palsy, lead poisoning, and mental illness (rather than just insanity). We know the rates of incidence of illness by sex and by age groups; we have devised treatment processes from psychoanalysis and chemotherapy to miraculous surgical methods that look like magic.

We also know that illness may strike anywhere: not only in New York or Florida or Michigan, and not only in large cities like Boston, New York, Philadelphia, or Los Angeles, but also in remote rural communities, on farms, and in back country hamlets. Resources for diagnosis and treatment are not, however, distributed in such a way that whoever becomes ill, wherever he lives, has an even chance for treatment and survival.[3] In recent decades we have become particularly aware of the extent of mental illness and at the same time of its accessibility to treatment, provided that facilities, personnel, and financial maintenance can be procured. And that brings us back to the problem of poverty and destitution as related to its partnership with problems of disease and medical care.

In order to avoid unnecessary complexity it may be well to arrange discussion in these pages into apparently artificial categories: artificial because they rarely occur neatly and separately by themselves, but together they constitute the great "consumer problem" of securing "medical care." There is another difficulty, hardly less disturbing than the artificiality of their separation: it is uncertainty that data cited are within reasonable distance of the facts, in view of the speed with which changes take place. The figures quoted, for example, for 1941, and for 1951 in *Readings in Medical Care,* published in 1958, are substantially different from data published in 1961 in *Medical Care in Transition.*[4] The reader might justly ask, then, why material is presented that may be out of date even before

[3] A striking reminder is the proposal in Washington (December 1964) by the President's Commission on these diseases to spend some three billion dollars for establishing treatment resources for at least three of the "furies": heart disease, cancer, and stroke throughout the country.

[4] Particularly the article reprinted in Vol. II, entitled "Economic Analysis of Medical Care in the United States" by Dr. Charlotte Muller of Columbia University, published in 1961.

See also *The Economics of American Medicine,* by Seymour Harris (Macmillan, 1964).

it is written down. The answer is simple: since provision of medical care is one of the most important items in the welfare field, it is important at least to reach as nearly as possible a conceptual and factual approximation to the nature of the problems and extent of medical care as it concerns welfare services. With this point of view, then, the following basic categories are submitted:

1. Medical care as "free enterprise" and as social welfare.

2. The consumer of medical services, as fully self-maintaining, as "medical indigent," and as destitute.

3. The dawn of the new era: Medicare.

The field of public health service is not included in this list, not because it is not important, but because it deals, on the whole, not with the individual consumer's needs but with general administration, comparable to defense, to development of natural resources, to public education, diplomacy, police, government in general. The subject matter is medical; its activities are impersonally administrative.

MEDICAL CARE AS FREE ENTERPRISE AND AS SOCIAL WELFARE

Except as hospitals became one of the great contributions to society of monastic bodies, and later of church organizations, and except as medical missionaries served primitive tribes for the sake of religious interests through the medium of charitable medical service, medicine has traditionally been practiced as part of the free enterprise system. Persons might choose to practice medicine because they liked that sort of activity and that sort of status, just as engineers and artists might choose their calling; but once in practice they were in the free enterprise world. They sold their services, as did lawyers and architects, the price depending on such market factors as location, nature of the consumer body, competitive skill, time, place, and character of specialty. Since contact with the afflicted was inherent in the practice, it followed that the call for charitable service tended to filter into the consumer service pattern, and so, to varying degrees, medical practitioners gave service without usual compensation. This fact tended to be obscured and confused when the consumer was already served through the charitable function of "free bed," or through charitable commitment in hospital or clinic. But except for this modified consumer relationship medical practice has been free enterprise.

The principal spokesman for medicine as a free enterprise system of the practicing physician in this country and the most consistent opponent of the practice of medicine as a major task of organized society for assuring health and recovery from illness of all its members has been the American Medical Association. As a means for assuring the status of the physician as a "professional" person, it promotes *esprit de corps,* undertakes or promotes research, encourages "professional ethics," discourages intraprofessional competition, labors for effective hospital and clinic administration. It has helped to create, in the parlance of the social psychologist, the optimum "image" of the physician in the time-honored model built into the Hippocratic oath. As an organization, it has, however, been obtuse to social changes of our day, in which social welfare is conceived as a greater ideal than the worship of property and its symbolic icon, free enterprise. In this country the AMA has been the principal and unrelenting opponent of inclusion of medical care in the general system of social security. It has fought it, and declared its intention of fighting it, to the bitter end. From the point of view of medical care as a fundamental component of modern industrial culture, comparable to public education, the technical personnel of the medical profession in its formal association has refused to surrender its exclusive free enterprise status for one of organized service for the general welfare. The major forms of its war on social assurance of medical care has been its relentless opposition to what it chooses to call "socialized medicine" and its consistent attempts to minimize unmet needs for medical care in the general population. This position might conceivably have been equally unrelenting in the field of mental illness had that field developed in the same measure as general medicine in the free enterprise system.

The best source of information on these two prongs of opposition by the American Medical Association is probably the volume by Michael Davis already referred to, although the AMA's well-publicized declaration of war on the proposed (and by now operative) Medicare legislation by Congress almost speaks a volume in itself. In summing up his chapter on the American Medical Association, Dr. Davis says:

> As one surveys the American Medical Association one is impressed by the great service it has rendered and is rendering the public and the profession. One is depressed by the limitations upon that service which result from its structure, its use of power, its intolerance of criticism, its failure over a long period to keep its members informed of both sides of controversial issues. Our subsequent review of the course of events will furnish all too many illustrations of the effects of these policies in creating and widening cleavages between the profession and society. Certainly we must appreciate that it is common for the members of a vocational group to identify their group interest with the "public interest" . . . the public expects much more of physicians than of most men. Perhaps only the clergy and the teachers stand with physicians in this respect; to members of these groups the public looks for consecration as well as proficiency . . .[5]

Among the depressing factors that Dr. Davis recites in the chapter dealing with the AMA, a few are of particular interest in the present discussion. It is clear, for example, that research that in any way pertains to the free enterprise area of medical care receives quite different treatment from technical research in medical science. So, in answer to the general complaint that many persons in need of medical care do not receive it, Dr. Davis quotes a 140-page volume issued by the AMA in which the conclusion is arrived at that "there is no important section of the population of the United States that now [1939] fails to obtain the medical care it needs and desires." The flimsy nature of research on which these findings were based is examined by Dr. Davis, as are other similar "Studies."[6] More obvious proof of the AMA's resistance to any abrasion of its smooth free enterprise surface is its treatment of foreign experience with health insurance. "In Great Britain," reports Dr. Davis,

. . . the British Medical Association had opposed the passage of

[5] *Medical Care for Tomorrow*, p. 110.
[6] See *Medical Care for Tomorrow*, pp. 104–5.

a compulsory health insurance law in 1911, but after experience
with the operation of the act, the association endorsed it in 1925,
in a memorandum to the Royal Commission, subsequently con-
firmed this approval, and in an official report of 1930 advocated
the extension of the system. . . . In 1944 Winston Churchill's
government proposed a National Health Service. . . . The Journal of the A.M.A. did not mention the Conservative government's proposal, but has been unsparing in condemnation of the
National Health Service since it went into effect in 1948; has
never informed American physicians of the basic fact that the
British Medical Association officially approved the principles of
the service . . .

In light of the admitted fact that provision of medical care is one of
the most important components of a social welfare system, and that
the free enterprise practice of supplying that service—even including various types of private health insurance schemes—fails adequately to meet the needs for medical care, the conclusion is logically
unavoidable that a governmentally sponsored and planned program
of supplying medical care available to all must either supplant, or
substantially supplement, services now available. In Great Britain
social provision of medical service has been given the dominant
position, while free enterprise medical care continues to flourish as a
supplementary resource. As reported by Professor Eveline M.
Burns,[7]

Outside the Communist countries, Great Britain is the only major
country to expand the role of government to embrace acceptance
of full responsibility for ensuring free medical care (subject to
certain modest charges for dentures, eye-glasses and drugs) and
needed health services to all members of the community, regardless of the payment of prior contributions or the passage of a test
for need, or even citizenship. It owns and operates all facilities
and employs 95 per cent of the professionals. Although a small
number of institutions remain in private hands for the utilization

[7] Professor of Social Work, Columbia University School of Social
Work, in a paper presented to the Committee on Social Policy for Health
Care of the New York Academy of Medicine, October 23, 1964.

of those who do not wish to avail themselves of the public facilities, and although general practitioners, specialists and dentists are permitted to accept private patients, only about 5 per cent of health care is in fact received "outside the Service."

Thus medical care in Great Britain has become an integral part of social welfare without excommunicating private practice. It assures health care to all within the general economic structure of the nation.

⋈ THE CONSUMER OF MEDICAL SERVICES

The economics of medical care has been a major concern of a considerable number of governmental and voluntary agencies, medical and relief authorities, research organizations, labor unions, philanthropic individuals and foundations. The bibliographical material is overwhelming in amount and complexity.[8] The purely medical aspects of the subject are, of course, outside the proper concern of this volume. But our cultural history has been curiously deficient in recognizing and estimating the extent, nature, predictability, and significance of illness. Perhaps, before the scientific leaps of knowledge in the past century, and in the general acceptance of a limited life expectancy, the fatalistic attitude surrounding illness and early death was not unreasonable. Today prevention and cure of illness have attained a place in Western civilization hardly inferior to that of physical science as a whole and to industrial productivity. Knowledge of incidence of illness, of the extent of specific preventability, and of predictable recovery is of a character that has raised concern with health to a place where it shares with government, economics, and science the leading interests in our culture. Medical care is the major instrument for putting that knowledge to work. And medical care is, therefore, sought, offered, and paid for. The fact that it has

[8] In addition to the general bibliographical suggestions made earlier, special attention is called to two articles in *Medical Care in Transition:* one by S. Charlotte Muller on "Economic Analysis of Medical Care in the United States" and one by Dr. Margaret C. Klein on "Twenty-five Years of Research in Medical Economics," both in Vol. Two. There should shortly be available also a paper entitled "The Role of Government in Health Services," prepared by Professor Eveline Burns for the N.Y. Academy of Medicine, 1964.

to be paid for, and that the call for its purchase is well-nigh universal, makes medical care a major factor in the economic life of our civilization.

Units of medical care vary enormously in cost and availability; incidence is as complex as is the nature of illness; but statistical probabilities are sufficiently accessible for prediction. The problem becomes, therefore, one of social planning: government economic planning and administration. Our primary concern here is with those economically unprepared to cover the cost of medical care from their own resources, rather than with the over-all problem of medical care. Cost, then, comes first. This problem stands apart from other budget items. Cost of food, for example, is relatively standardized. There are wholesale and retail prices; these fluctuate but are well known to consumer and purveyor alike; they are uniformly publicized and are accessible to any one interested. The government publishes cost-of-living reports periodically, and these take account of local and regional variations. Some foods are more expensive than others, some more nutritious than others; ethnic and cultural factors affect the choice, but the consumer is free to buy the relatively standardized product his pocketbook permits. The situation is not quite so simple when it comes to clothing. Mink, like caviar, has a relatively standardized and communicable price, but the mass of consumers in this country is not seriously affected by even its major fluctuations. Shelter is more complex, less negotiable in the marketplace, and therefore more difficult to deal with in the family budget. Variations and fluctuation are more local than seasonal, and prices are more related to standards of living and to social status than to need. The contrasts between luxury and stringency are, in the main, more obvious than with respect to either food or clothing. On the whole, adjustments for variations in price level may be made within one's average level of living.

In medical care the situation is vastly different; neither cost of its units, nor incidence of need, can be so easily calculated by ordinary statistical methods. They are further complicated by factors both subtle and less manageable. Standardization of prices has been slow to arrive, except where local custom and tradition of general practice has kept physicians' fees relatively stable. As specialization advances, largely as a result of advances in knowledge and technique, the specialist invests more time and money in achieving his specialty, and this investment tends to be reflected in the fee; the specialist's services cost more than those of the general practitioner. This has been particularly true of surgery, where skill has a singular function and where the emergency nature of the patient's medical need may be more pronounced. A more subtle factor has been psychological selectivity on the part of the patient, who seeks a special personal relationship and a status symbol in the choice of his (or her) physician. Often especially gifted physicians—particularly in some specialties—attain something comparable to the uniqueness of the creative artist that sets them apart from their fellows, both in reality of performance and in "desirability" on the part of the patient.

All this accentuates the difficulty of standardizing both product and price in medicine, as compared with the market for food, clothing, and lodging. It has helped to create an unmatched place for the physician in our culture; one can hardly think of haggling and bargain-hunting, or of asking and receiving bids. The fear of death, of serious illness, of incapacitation, only enhance these characteristics of the situation.

Some parts of the medical care world are, nevertheless, gradually being standardized and thus made amenable to economic planning both by society and by the individual. Essential medical services, other than those of the physician, have already undergone a considerable degree of standardization, even before the establishment of Medicare and Medicaid. Among these services are those of nurse, laboratory technician, anaesthetist, radiologist, physical therapist. Some standardization has taken place in dentistry, and in hospital costs. Welfare services can profit from being aware of these tendencies in the field of medical care. Most of the progress in standardization of the cost of medical care may well be attributed to recent advances in health insurance, both public and private. This applies particularly to hospital per diem and associated medical service, including certain drugs. It does not seem, however, that comparable standardization has taken place in hospital cost itself, though it is often the insurer who pays rather than the patient. Such insurance contributes to the solvency of the hospital, but in the end the patient pays in increased premiums. At any rate, whatever the ultimate cost of hospitalization and physician's services may be, the progress toward standardization continues to be steady and a great boon in the assured availability of medical care.

Hospital costs as such, however, regardless of who pays for them, are by no means standardized when geographical distribution, type of community, type of financing of the particular hospital, and capital expenditures are considered. That is part of the inclusive problem of the medical profession, of government, and of philanthropic interest. It becomes part of concern of the field of welfare if and when it impedes access of the impecunious to medical care. Nor is it an integral concern of present welfare planning to discover or to determine in what way the operation of a hospital and of its medical services is affected by relations to medical schools, medical research, or postgraduate medical education. To put it more accurately, it is no more the concern of the welfare segment of social planning than it is that of government in general and the inclusive civilization of which it is part. Medical care, if it is not pure free enterprise, is of necessity an inseparable part of social planning.

The factor that makes these considerations more pressing for social welfare planning as a whole—and, as will appear, in the case of medical care for the indigent and the destitute in particular—is that, though we do know something of what medical care costs, or rather what is being spent for it, we have most imperfect information about what it would cost if all the medical care needed were actually being supplied. Dr. Muller's figures indicate an annual per capita expenditure for medical service in the United States in 1957 of $115 to $117. Even without allowing for increased costs since that time, the amount spent in the United States in 1964, for a population estimated at 192-odd million, would be over twenty-two billion dollars. It is anybody's guess whether the cost would run to 30 billion or 40 billion dollars if all the care needed were actually given.[9] It is at any rate certain that those in the upper income

---

[9] Both Dr. Muller and Professor Burns, in the articles cited as well as other articles in the volume cited, present interesting data as to the nature of the expenditures, that is, whether for physician, dentist, drugs, hospital,

brackets spend more, though they hardly need more proportionately, than those in the lower brackets. The British experience suggests that merely to improve the distribution of wealth through the wage and profit system, and through efficient patterns of taxation, will not meet the needs of the population as a whole to deal with events outside the wage-profit pattern. The incidence of destitution and of costly medical care require different types of planning.

Before the establishment of Medicare[10] two major systems of providing medical care when needed were utilized in this country (and elsewhere also); one through health insurance, the other through the application of economic assistance procedures. The first of these is, in a sense, a purely economic and actuarial affair. It must assume, as the basic component, medical judgment as to the types of aid needed, their probable frequency, and unit costs. It must then translate this knowledge into actuarial practice, to determine premiums, administrative costs, and safe handling of assets. Insofar as this is accomplished, health insurance would appear to be the perfect answer. It does, however, imply medical planning to control costs and to distribute facilities, such as medical and technical personnel, hospitals, nursing homes, home services, etc. What it cannot provide is assurance that premiums would be paid; what it cannot afford is to wreck the system by failure of premium payments, either through budgetary stringencies of the insured or through inability to pay in the first place by reason of destitution or illness. Some idea of the present extent and future possibilities of health insurance systems as a means of providing medical care—at least for those above the actual destitution level—may be gained from figures recently made public by the Health Insurance Council. They report that as of December 31, 1963, 145,329,000 persons were insured for hospital expense, 134,908,000 for surgical expense, and 102,177,000 for regular medical expense. Taking the largest of these figures, however, and assuming that it is reasonably accurate, there would still be between forty-five and fifty millions uninsured even for hospital expenses and nearly half the people unprovided for with respect to

---

etc., and the relative amounts that may come through personal income, insurance, or governmental expenditures, federal, state, and local.

[10] See below.

"regular" medical expense. The rate of growth of the insurance practice is shown by an increase in coverage—as reported by the Council—of 120 per cent in hospital care and some 250 per cent in surgical care. These figures are significant in a variety of ways. Their greatest significance may, however, be in the fact, so clearly demonstrated in Great Britain, that the total cost of medical care can be actuarially handled in the general economy of an industrially developed country within the realm of social welfare. A supplementary assurance of premiums has therefore been suggested through taxation, along the same lines as old age and survivors insurance, that is, social security. Failing this inclusive health insurance system, some alternative procedures have been introduced, as, for example, inclusion of medical care as part of the basic public assistance program or as a special form of assistance to those not actually destitute but "medically indigent."

What is wrong with these alternate procedures? Before the establishment of Medicare the following seem to have been the principal difficulties:

1. Persistence of the repressive, quasi-Elizabethan rejection of the poor and the destitute has pervaded services for livelihood in general;

2. Emphasis, throughout the discussion of progressive proposals, is on medical aid only to the aged, who are already largely favored over the non-aged;

3. Even for the aged, medical care for the medical indigent is available only in a portion of the states, since federal funds are only supplementary and depend on prior state provision;

4. Even public assistance is not available throughout the entire nation; by recent reports, some sixteen states have not made any such provision;

5. Restrictive regulations and limitations render the system as thus far practiced a reluctant and hesitant offering, reminiscent of the Royal Commission on the Poor Law of England in 1834.

There is little well-organized and comprehensive information on provision of medical aid in public assistance programs in general.

Such facts as are reported for example by Dr. Axelrod as of 1959 are not very encouraging.[11] He states that, for example:

Prior to the 1956 Amendments, which earmarked federal matching funds for medical care, there were not more than 20 states with relatively comprehensive medical care programs for recipients of public assistance. In the other states, the programs were considerably limited in scope, providing, for example, hospital care only, or there were serious limitations in financial support, ranging from monthly maximums on the amount allowed for medical care, to no public assistance at all for medical care in 16 states . . .

The situation is better, as has been stated above, with respect to the aged. In 1958, according to data cited by Dr. Axelrod from Social Security Administration sources, forty-nine of the fifty-three states and territories had some provision for medical care for the indigent elderly. For example, "39 [states] for drugs; 36 for dental care; 35 for hospitalization; 35 for physicians and other practitioners' services; and 34 for prosthetic appliances." It has been estimated, adds Dr. Axelrod, "that about 70 per cent of the payments made to suppliers of medical services in behalf of public assistance recipients in all four categories were made for Old Age Assistance recipients."

It is not that one would object to generous treatment of old age assistance recipients—if "generous" is the appropriate word. But since people under sixty-five may also be in need and also unable to purchase medical care, concentration on medical care for the aged can hardly be considered a comprehensive social plan.

Fortunately, it is no longer necessary to dwell on the unpleasant repressive pattern that controlled the medical assistance to the aged before the enactment of Medicare.[12] It is to be hoped that in time they may disappear also as to those not "aged."

[11] *Evaluation of Old Age Assistance Medical Programs,* a paper read by Dr. S. J. Axelrod before the Medical Care Section of the American Public Health Association, October 22, 1959, p. 268f.

[12] Some significant data on practice prior to Medicare were prepared by the writer for inclusion at this point. It is most satisfying that they can be

☙ MEDICARE—AND AFTER

No single event has occurred in the field of social welfare since the epoch-making enactment of the social security legislation of 1935 that can compare, both in immediate significance and as a milestone toward a great future, with the law enacted in 1965 usually referred to as Medicare. It provides an assurance of medical treatment at the taxpayer's expense for all persons sixty-five years of age or over without means tests, without "proof of eligibility," without bureaucratic regimentation, and with only little more than a modest drain on the individual's resources or those of his family. It recognizes that the incidence of illness is greatest in this age group, and that the earning capacity of the group's members progressively diminishes. More than 10 per cent of the population, those most subject to severe and prolonged illness, are freed of the fear and worry most onerous to any part of the population. The law was passed despite the most relentless opposition of the "free enterprise" medical profession, and with none of the demeaning aspects associated with so much of the welfare legislation and welfare practice of past generations. In itself it is a great tribute to the democratic enlightenment of this country and its culture.

Enormous as is the importance of the provisions of this law as enacted, its even greater significance lies in the very aspect that aroused the bitterest antagonism on the part of the organized medical profession. Medicare is, in fact, a great step toward "socialized medicine." That is its greatest virtue. It places the provision of medical services into the same category as public education, a public highway system, police protection, the responsibility for natural resources, and the national defense. It is significant of the long range intent of the Medicare act that it was accompanied by an amendment of the social security act—by way of Title XIX—which extends the general matching system of the federal government to medical services by the states for persons under the sixty-five-year

---

omitted now. For a complete history of steps leading to this law see *Medicare, Policy and Politics* by Eugene Feingold of the University of Michigan (Chandler Publishing Company, 1966). See also: *A Sacred Trust* by Richard Harris (New American Library, 1966).

age limit, a further, if cautious, step toward a true system of socialized medicine.

It is premature to judge the rate of advance of that system. A number of states have already legislated plans to carry out Title XIX. Plans are under way for bold moves to expand hospital facilities, to finance additional necessary medical schools, and to adjust the pattern of operations of the Department of Health, Education, and Welfare to its growing responsibilities. To those who hope and work for a more effective and more inclusive development of social engineering for the general welfare, as proposed by the Founding Fathers, the year of Medicare, 1965, will be a memorable turning point.[13]

[13] It is too early to judge how effective the administration of medical aid under Title XIX will be; how far the opponents of "socialized medicine," or legislatures watchful of expenditures and taxpayers' reaction, or the opponents of economic assistance to the medically indigent will try to press back the medical-care purposes into the old relief structure with all its resistances. Each state will cut or has cut its own pattern of Medicaid, and these patterns are likely to show the same variations in generosity as were seen in the standards of public assistance. The whole plan is already under attack. At this writing, it would be, in fact, impossible, even with extensive research, to ascertain the various components of legislation and operation by the fifty states, as they affect size of payments, income exemptions, relation to insurance or savings held by family members, obligations of relatives, or basic strictures of welfare departments with which the health services will be tied up. A nation-wide study of the situation under the auspices of the School of Public Health of Columbia University is now being projected, and plans are being made for personnel and financing of the study. But it will take time and it is too optimistic to suppose that anything approaching Medicare for the aged, or Social Security as now in operation, will come about within a decade or longer, to serve the medical needs of the total population or of the "medically indigent."

Chapter V

※※

Services to Children as a Special Group

The two basic categories of service briefly reviewed in preceding sections are the major channels in which progress has flowed from charity or philanthropy to a system of social welfare. The nature of needs has had a history as old as civilization. Sporadic and selective service had been given toward meeting those needs from before biblical times to our day. But the great change that has finally emerged is that of acceptance of public responsibility for these services; correspondingly, the financial obligation of government, whether local or national, has evolved and been formulated in a progressive definition of "social welfare." Both the areas discussed thus far have a com-

86

mon characteristic: the possible incidence of needs is as wide as the entire population, taken by age, sex, occupation, location, educational or cultural grouping, race, ethnic origin, or other characteristic. As incidence becomes fact, need is recognized and service is called for.

There are, however, special groups of persons who do not so clearly reflect a statistical sample of the whole population, whose needs become specialized, and who may require services not so easily codified as the provision of economic assistance, medical care, or hospitalization. The list of these special groups is rather large, and they are not mutually exclusive. The one thing they all have in common—in common also with the categories already discussed—is that they call upon expenditure of funds from within the total resources of the nation. Even a partial listing of these groups clearly shows that to review all of them would be an encyclopedic task, well beyond the possibility of this volume. There are, for example, the blind, the deaf and dumb, those who become enmeshed in the operation of penal laws, those suffering chronic or permanent disabilities like cerebral palsy or muscular dystrophy or chronic progressive diseases of a paralytic nature. One special group, however, occupies so large a place in the welfare problem as a whole that it must be considered as demanding an area of services in its own right, coordinate with the services already discussed. This area is the field of child care.

⚜ SERVICES FOR CHILDREN

For one primarily interested in describing services for children now available in the United States there is an abundance of sources and types of data: publications of the Children's Bureau of the Federal government; the *Encyclopedia of Social Sciences;*[1] current material from the Department of Health, Education, and Welfare; very extensive bibliographical material, easy to find and impossible to master. If one seeks information of world-wide scope, publications of the United Nations will be helpful. Widening the horizon to include cultural anthropology adds another task that

[1] Macmillan, 1930: numerous articles, both descriptive and historical.

would take a lifetime. One is puzzled by the variety of conditions, attitudes, mores, laws, institutions, practices, sponsoring bodies, inventive systems, abounding in the field. The discussion here is limited to the framework of the present social welfare design, as it is related in its essentials to general progress from charitable concern to deliberate governmental responsibility; it should touch only lightly upon practice, financial support, and, to some degree at any rate, the theoretical structure underlying the service.

What types of needs do children present?

What types of organized services do they receive?

How many children present each type of need?

How many children receive approximately the service they need?

How did the system of services arise and develop; what kinds of services have been discontinued?

What personnel is available to give service to children?

Most of these questions can be answered, though in different degrees of completeness; the most important figures relating to the present may be obtained from data supplied by the Welfare Administration of the federal Department of Health, Education, and Welfare. These necessarily differ from year to year, in a quantitatively ascending series. The report for 1963, for example, offers statistics considerably higher in totals than those presented in the 1962. But with the best will a complete picture requires more background than such a report could possibly offer. On the other hand, no single source or modest combination of sources can offer comparably significant statistical data.

A major item in the classification of children's needs is whether they are or are not in their own home. If that home is not self-maintaining, the principal need is economic assistance. This need, and corresponding service, is therefore covered within the general topic of "livelihood" discussed earlier. It is well worth recalling that, prior to the general social security legislation in the United States inaugurated in 1935, no economic assistance to destitute children could reasonably be counted on, whereas in 1963 close to three million children, as well as their destitute parent or parents, were receiving such aid. And this does not include children covered as dependents in the Old Age and Survivors Insurance program. At any rate, this is economic assistance in the child's own home when the threat of destitution is the chief problem.

Still in his own home the child may have different needs, not associated with economic difficulties, or independent of them. Among these would be, for example, control of: parental neglect or cruelty; illness, temporary, of the parent or parents; physical or mental handicap of the child; permanently incapacitating physical condition, or physical condition requiring permanent organized help; severe behavior problem of the child or some other member of the family. For these needs, entirely different services have come into existence. The services other than simple economic assistance, may, therefore, include court and probation service; enforced removal of the child from his home; special facilities for the blind, the deaf and dumb, the child with cerebral palsy or other disabling disease; temporary homemaker service; psychiatric treatment, clinical or other; institutionalization for delinquency. Evidently some of these services may require caring for the child outside his home. Some children, however, may require care outside their home because they never had any home or had lost it, permanently or for extended periods. This brings into play a different series of services, outside the home either permanently or for a considerable period. The services required then are: institutions for various kinds of handicaps, foster care, adoption service, psychotherapy or institutionalization for behavior problems.

No amount of classification and analysis succeeds in reducing the complexity of the inclusive pattern of services for children. On the contrary, the more painstakingly it is examined the more separate pieces seem to arise and to demand their place in the picture. Yet the past few decades have produced a phenomenal simplification of structure and service without diminishing flexibility of the program or variety of services to meet variety of needs.

The only way that the special place of child welfare in our culture can be seen in perspective is to set it in a biological framework. The preservation of any species—in this instance the so-called *Homo sapiens*—is based on insuring reproduction and on protection of the young until they join the ranks of competent adults. The first steps to this end have been taken by nature. They include an irrepressible sexual drive, as a first condition of reproduction, and progress through maternal care from breast-feeding to a general protective setting, primarily in the form of the family, first primary, then extended. This protective setting then becomes vulnerable or complex in response to a variety of conditions less clearly biological in nature and more in the scientific area of anthropology or cultural history.

Disturbing changes in the biological pattern come not necessarily in any particular sequence, nor are they universal in incidence, nor are all necessarily harmful to the preservation of the species. There is, for example, destruction of the child if deformed or if it threatens the supply of food for the family or the tribe. There is the urgency, by contrast, for a higher rate of reproduction to increase the economic or military power of family or tribe (also for manpower on the farm), in which case parental love may have to work out a compromise with the function of economic or military entrepreneur; in some variations of this theme, the female child may prove to be an unprofitable investment and therefore vulnerable. The arrival of "private property" in the pattern of a culture may alter the social outlook toward the preservation of the species, and those in power may purchase women as property, for pleasure or for profit, and the offspring also may become assets. Some of the Eastern potentates of this day enjoy multiple ownership of women, as wives and concubines, and ownership of many children, as objects of love as well as symbols of wealth and power.

Mores or laws take cognizance of these facts and, in some legal codes that have been transmitted through centuries, relations, rights, duties, property aspects, have been formalized and their observance administered. A considerable body of these laws has found its way into Roman jurisprudence, canon law, Talmudic and post-Talmudic regulations. Our own much-talked-of "legally responsible relatives" in the relief system is a vestigial example. The persistent feature in all this is the variety of adjustments of conflicts between the original, biological provision for preservation of the species through parents and family, and the varied and elaborate forms of social organization that extend this protection. In our Western system the biological function of the family in reproduction and in care of the child is taken for granted until its functioning becomes imperfect or inoperative. At this point, the State, that is, the politically organized social structure, takes over *in loco parentis.*

There is one step, however, that may intervene either formally or as an instrument of the State, before full functioning *in loco parentis* occurs, that is, voluntary group activity for child protection. It is a function either of compassionate charitable interest or of the vested interest of a sectarian, ethnic, or other special group. To serve in that capacity, it depends, however, on the residual power of the State, functioning *in loco parentis.* We shall see how that relationship among parent, State, and intermediate voluntary charitable organization enters into the present-day simplified understructure of child care. But first it may be useful to illustrate the conditions that may determine this functioning of substitute parenthood by State or intermediate voluntary organization.

What conditions may call for this service *in loco parentis?*

1. *Non-existence or absence of parents.* This type of situation occurs in social systems where there is no "extended family" to take over the tasks of the natural parents when these are absent: for example, it may be due to war, epidemic, plague, vendetta, fire, flood, earthquake, automobile accident. Then substitute parenthood patterns arise, such as orphanages, almshouses, indenture foster care, adoption.

2. *Parental neglect, cruelty, incapacitation.* Descriptively, this category of conditions is sufficiently clear to provide justification for the assumption of parental responsibility on the part of the authorities. The description is deficient, however, in explaining the occurrence and the logic of most of these conditions. The explanation—except in cases of incapacitation—lies in the cultural perspective of the relation of parent to child. The parent is, to be sure, provider and protector; but he is also disciplinary head of the family and has been so regarded from time immemorial. In many Oriental cultures today, in the ancient systems of Judea and Rome, in many sectors of Western culture extending to feudal powers and rights— by divine authorization to absolute monarch—the right, power, and propriety of the disciplinary function of the family head is integral. Not infrequently it includes power over life and death. Psychologically, authoritarian discipline implies use of force in the judg-

ment of the head of the family. How measure the limits of force? How separate it from anger or disapproval? How integrate it with love and guidance? If lack of self-assurance, and even a dose of sadism enters into disciplinary management, the legitimate boundaries of parental authority become vague. If difference of opinion between parents enters, if partial disciplinary rights are informally bestowed on older offspring as against the younger, how draw the line? Yet another factor may enter, for, curiously and to the modern generation not always understandably, all adults in the cultural pattern are assumed to have superior rights over children, and older children over younger ones. It is within this framework of cultural perspectives that both cruelty and neglect may occur.

3. *Children's physical or mental conditions beyond the power of parents to cope with.* This type is suggestively defined by the kinds of special services created within medical, charitable, educational, and recreational functions intended to serve children with handicaps. Some are obvious; physical handicaps have been mentioned; institutions for retarded and mentally deficient children are of a somewhat different order, but clear-cut in essence. The relevance of juvenile courts, family courts, institutions for delinquent children and youth is clear; even the history of their emergence and operation is reasonably clear. The more recent addition of child guidance clinics has progressively defined the conditions inherent either in the child's personality or in the quality of the family life in which he lives. The major factor often defining the condition of the child, namely economic insufficiency of parents or guardians, is part of the larger problem of economic destitution which affects not the child per se, but economic maintenance of his family as a whole.

Discussion of services for children as developed in the United States within recent decades may be considered as falling into two categories: that of the nature of public responsibility, and of the nature of personnel for exercising it. These require some detailed exposition.[2] It should be added that probably no special area of

---

[2] In addition to the sources of statistical data and other informational sources mentioned earlier, the *Social Work Yearbooks* may be usefully consulted. They are published by the National Association of Social Workers.

social welfare has received so much attention and has produced so much literature as that of child welfare. The difficulty for the student of the subject is not so much the absence of published material as the labor of wading through incidental details and nonessentials toward a unified picture of the whole. The situation is further complicated by overlapping areas of study within the fields of child psychology, casework technique, psychoanalytic material on child development and intrafamily relations, public school systems, and institutional specialization and management.

Public responsibilities. The prime factor in the field of child care has been the progressive and now nearly complete responsibility assumed by public authorities where the natural functioning of the family structure has proved to be ineffective. The standard of care is not yet uniform, and legal and administrative patterns also show differences as public authority is vested in state, federal, or local governments. But ultimate responsibility is clearly accepted and administered by the public. Equally important is the fact that this public responsibility is accompanied by assumption of financial responsibility. The fact that administration is not always perfect, that standards of financing are not uniformly generous, and that personnel is not always of the same standard of competence merely reflects our spotty development of cultural standards in general, and emphasizes the need for positive propaganda and education on all levels of service.

On the surface, this ultimate public responsibility is not always visible; there are many child welfare agencies under denominational or nonsectarian voluntary sponsorship operating under legal, approved patterns. Occasionally, such agencies are even entirely self-supporting, though these are rare specimens. The vast majority of child welfare services, under whatever sponsorship, are able to operate only on the basis of the per capita contribution, or total budgetary base of maintenance, by the tax-supported public bodies. Again it is important to recognize that, although much technical leadership still resides in the interested labors of nongovernmental agencies, the raising of standards is increasingly part of the function of public authorities.

By way of specification, the major child care services fall under the following categories:

1. Public assistance, principally in federally subsidized operation for aid to families with dependent children (formerly known as ADC). This is quantitatively the largest child welfare service in the country and is included under services for livelihood in an earlier section.

2. Foster-care service in families, group homes, or institutions. This service is generally on a per capita subsidy basis when conducted by voluntary agencies, either denominational or nonsectarian. There is an increasing amount of supervision by public authorities of the work of these voluntary agencies. There is, also, a sort of competition for the "public image" of this phase of child care as between public and voluntary agencies, which is sometimes beneficial and sometimes more clearly competitive. Foster care applies also to the support and regulation of adoption services, since these are mostly interlocked with temporary foster care.[3]

3. Legal operations, distributed over a variety of court structures, among which are, depending on locality and state, county courts, children's courts, family courts, probate courts. Financing is not on a per capita basis with respect to children served, but is part of the taxpayer's general burden, for the maintenance of the judiciary and of its personnel which by now covers, in varying degrees of adequacy, probation service, clinic examinations, detention homes, and related functions. Legal services addressed to care of children fall into the following chief categories:
   a) adoption, and accompanying services, which may involve foster care on the usual basis.
   b) in some localities, approval of referral to foster care, which is also subject to legal decision, usually in a children's court.
   c) protection of property rights of children where these are

[3] For many of the relevant details consult the *Social Work Yearbook,* and publications of the Federal Children's Bureau and the Child Welfare League of America.

involved in matters of inheritance or guardianship, usually under the probate functions of the court.

d) court action in complaints—from whatever source—of neglect, abuse, cruelty, or abandonment by parent or guardian; while the formal decision by the court rests on purely legal provisions, the disposition usually involves supervisory assignments to court personnel or to some agency, either public or voluntary. The important aspect of this phase of legal operation is the fact that the power and responsibility for care and welfare of the child is formally transferred from natural parent or guardian to the State through its judicial department, which may also assume administrative responsibility in determination of persons assigned for care of the child, and funds to be used for that purpose.

e) administration of criminal laws in relation to children found to have committed illegal acts. This by definition is totally a service administered by public authorities, more specifically by courts, and under court jurisdiction by probation and parole officers, and by institutions for the care, training, education, and rehabilitation of youthful offenders. These institutions may be sponsored by state or local governments, or they may be normally sponsored by voluntary agencies either denominational or nonsectarian. In the latter case, however, major support is derived from tax-supported public authorities. These institutions constitute a very large segment of care, and have in the course of nearly 150 years since the establishment of the first "House of Refuge in New York City" experienced a range of quality in their work that still has not settled down to generally dependable level of excellence or a sufficiently integrated cooperative service with other components of service to children and youth.

Much as still remains to be done to build a comprehensive and uniformly satisfactory system of service for children, at least the basic and total responsibility has been accepted by community and taxpayer, and the residual repressive attitudes so prominent still in the general field of economic assistance have largely disappeared. To a considerable extent general improvement has come from a high degree of intelligent and increasingly informed competence of personnel in the service. This is seen in several sectors. A larger proportion of trained caseworkers chooses to enter the child-care field than that of general economic assistance, at least as the latter is now constituted. A substantial proportion of scholarships for social work training tends to go in this direction. Statistics on this point are still crude, largely due to the confused classification of manpower with reference to public assistance, family casework, and child welfare work.[4] Judges in relevant courts are often though not uniformly chosen in the several judicial state groupings with an eye to their interest in, and knowledge of service to, children. Probation officers in courts dealing with children, though still appointed in many places as political patronage, are increasingly drawn from trained personnel, and in many places are given organized training and opportunities for improvement of their knowledge after appointment to their posts.

In institutions, more and more of which are becoming of the cottage rather than congregate type, there are specialist consultants, including psychologists, psychiatrists, and psychiatric caseworkers. More attention is being given to the qualifications and competence and to the importance of the service of cottage parents, group leaders, and group instructors. Medical care is taking an important place, and child guidance clinics in one form or another are brought into regular service. Basic education in regular public schools is widely offered to children in institutions or in foster care, and their isolation from general community life is being diminished by a variety of inventive administrative procedures. In all areas of services for children, even of those who may have to face prolonged or permanent institutionalization, there is increased effort to maintain or to reestablish natural relations with parents and with the community life of parents.

[4] The *Manpower Study,* conducted by federal departments and national voluntary agencies, published in 1960, fails to give entirely intelligible answers.

There are at least two factors that would seem to account for this positive and hopeful outlook for services to children and for their nearly unobstructed flowering into a full-fledged social welfare program in the not too distant future. One is that, like the care of the aged, the welfare of children occupies a large place in what might be described as the sentimental sanctions of our culture. Even more, perhaps, than the aged, they draw to themselves the love, concern, and imaginative interest of people in all walks of life, in all economic and social classes. Even though in origin this may be part of our biological heritage, it has become a prominent phase of our culture. Support has come to this interest from a second factor, namely the contiguous areas of interest of other parts of our culture. One is that of education. By definition, the interest of education is centered on the child, and in the course of time that interest has extended up and down in the age spread, from two-year-old nursery school toddlers toward full adult life. The elementary school system has perforce become one of the most extensive administrative operations. Within its intellectual leadership, the system of recreation, of research in pedagogical techniques, of special concern with various kinds of disability and handicaps, has created administrative provisions that at many points become the common area of education and of social services. There are, of course, still weak spots, as for example the slow development and frequently unimaginative integration of treatment for problem children (and problem parents) with the general administration of classroom work. But progress has been steady in both urban and rural centers, despite the disruptive influence of race prejudice and rejection of minority groups.

Another contiguous area has been that of research in child psychology, both "normal" and "abnormal." This has arisen first perhaps directly within the educational field—for example, from Froebel, Pestalozzi, Montessori—then in the realms of technical psychology, later supplemented by psychoanalytic interests. The last has been chiefly responsible for the recent trend toward setting up child guidance clinics within the school administration, in the general community, and in the field of medical service. An incidental but important development, due to the overlapping interests mentioned, has been the convergence in the services to children, from several disciplines, of educator, psychologist, physician, caseworker, recreation leader. This convergence of personnel has been helpful in better coordination of agencies that serve the child in their respective fields. This has been true in health and welfare departments, school systems, recreational areas—muncipical, denominational and nonsectarian services, settlement and neighborhood houses.

One very important area of services to children has, however, been unable to advance at the rate of speed that has occurred in the field as a whole. It is that of foster care and adoption. In both these (partly interrelated) child welfare activities the quantitative problem as well as that of technical operation has become increasingly difficult and burdensome. While there are inherent difficulties of many kinds in providing substitute parents for children when their own are not available—difficulties greater in our industrial-urban civilization than they were in the systems of extended family and tribal responsibility—the principal cause of the trouble lies in the cultural and economic dislocations, and in the ethnic, religious, and racial blocking of an integrated solution. It is common knowledge that the uprooting of the accustomed life of Negroes and Puerto Ricans in the United States, as they leave their economically or socially unpromising homes for urban American centers, disrupts family life, normal channels of support, and marital responsibilities. The "promised land" of Northern urban United States brings unemployment, social rejection, inadequate school opportunities; and the results are often a harvest of children without adequate families, homes, or food and shelter. So the need for foster homes is multiplied.

Cultural change in sexual mores, liberation from disciplines and restrictions no longer found valid, an enormous increase of individualistic outlook on life without accompanying information for contraceptive practices, have resulted in a very great increase in illegitimate births, among "native whites" as well as among the less affluent nonwhites. As a result, large numbers of babies in hospitals, and children in families without normal support, enter the difficult arena of search for foster care. Many studies of the problem have been made, but few effective solutions found. The color line remains an "absolute" not yet resolved, and the number of children in need of foster care is expectedly higher in any minority group that is still economically disadvantaged. Any disability of the child, physical or mental, increases the difficulty of placement. With the choice of institutional care generally out of favor with the leading technicians of foster care, and despite sectarian facilities in line with institutional history, innovations have been sought with some success. Group foster homes for limited numbers of children, conducted by persons selected as suitable for the purpose, have apparently been one of the promising forward steps. Location for foster care within the normal community areas appears to have been a promising direction of development. But the plight of the Negro child seeking placement is still with us. Adoption has been a perennial hope though it cannot meet the quantitative demand; and again disparity due to color and presumptive religious affiliation between available children and prospective, willing adoptive parents remains unresolved. In certain areas, sectarian groups have insisted that children be placed in adoptive or foster homes of the same religious faith as their natural parents; or when the parents are unknown that they be placed in alternating sequence in families of the three major faiths. This is just another complication in the difficult task of matching child to foster parents.

One very interesting experiment in the foster care field has recently given promise to open up new avenues of successful placement and deserves special mention. The plan is based on the fact that the number of families receiving public assistance is greater than the number of children requiring foster care placement. Among these families also, as among the prospective foster children, there is a disproportionate number of nonwhite families. Since the major problem in these families is economic, and the quality of family life not necessarily more disturbed than in the general population, it seemed reasonable to expect that many of these families might be suitable as foster homes, if the income from payment for foster children could be added to the assistance grants, thus further easing family budgets. Traditional regulations for choice of foster homes would have made these families automatically ineligible. The experiment was directed therefore to the possibility of using public assistance families as a source for foster homes. The idea seemed promising, and a foundation provided necessary funds for the experiment and requisite research to test its soundness. As yet, unfortunately, the results of the experiment have not become known and information on the usefulness of a bold new idea not been made accessible to the general child welfare field.

Whatever may be the technical and special developments in the near future in the field of services for children, and however much these developments may be advanced or retarded by what seems at the moment to be a disproportionate interest in abtruse psychological studies, at least this field does not have to struggle against the parsimonious and repressive tradition of the field of economic assistance as a whole.

Chapter VI

❧

Services for Psychotherapy

Strictly speaking, all therapy is, by definition and by historical fact, a medical function, even though in recent decades the term "therapy" has been more loosely applied in the social sciences in general.[1] Services for medical care were discussed in a previous sec-

[1] The major reference for the field as a whole, as of this writing, is the series of monographs published by the Joint Commission on Mental Illness and Health, published by Basic Books, Inc., in 1959. The particular monographs chiefly examined for the present purpose were: No. 2—*Economics of Mental Illness* by Rashi Fein, Ph. D.; No. 3—*Mental Health Manpower Trends* by George W. Albee, Ph. D.; No. 8—*Community Resources in Mental Health* by Reginald Robinson, Ph. D., David F. DeMarche, Ph. D.,

tion chiefly because of the economic problems they present to lower income groups and to that segment of the population in this income group which has a relatively high incidence of illness. In part, this discussion of psychotherapy will also show how it is conditioned by economic factors. At present the burden of general medical care is probably more of a problem still for individual and family budgets than for government. Mental illness, on the other hand, would seem to be a larger drain on public resources than on those of the individual. Whatever may be the relative burden on public or individual budgets, it is large enough for inclusion in the social welfare structure of the nation. There are two other important reasons for discussing this service here. One is the extent to which nonmedical personnel are inextricably involved in this field; the other is the rate of growth of the field, both as one of service and as one of contemporary culture. From this latter point of view, it is more fruitful to speak of therapy as applying both to personality problems of adjustment and to definite mental illness.[2]

Physical illness is recognized by its bodily symptoms, and in our civilization its occurrence is addressed, for treatment, to the physician. That there is also illness of the mind has not been so generally recognized or its symptoms so easily identified until relatively recent times. The term "mind" is used in this connection as denoting not so much intelligence as emotional experience and capacity to relate to cultural commitments as they affect personal relations within and outside the family. There may be a greater range and greater fluidity in symptoms of mental illness than in those of a physical nature. However, ability to carry on relatively

and Mildred K. Wagle, M. S. S. A. The study as a whole was authorized by a unanimous resolution of Congress and was financed by grants from some twenty-one organizations in the field, including three major foundations.

[2] Mental illness and psychotherapy are discussed here in the pragmatic sense as they are generally spoken of in medical and in psychological literature. Despite the many years that have elapsed since Freud and his successors established definitions, there are still many aspects of the subject on which no agreement by experts exists. Says Dr. Thomas Szasz, Professor of Psychiatry in the New York State University at Syracuse, for example, "I submit that mental illness is a myth . . . mental illnesses cannot exist in the sense in which bodily diseases exist."—New York Times Magazine, June 12, 1966.

normal activity in self-maintenance and in social relations is interrupted in mental illness only at the outer, more intensive edges of the range of symptoms. Imperfect "mental health" can be "lived with," therefore, as long as it does not present too striking symptoms of disorder or discomfort. At the extreme end of the range, mental illness has been designated "insanity" and, generally speaking, it has been so handled. The handling, over the centuries, has been, unfortunately, chiefly custodial, and the quality not always humane or understanding. Treatment or therapy in the medical sense has not had much more than a century of consecutive history. It is fair to say that symptoms of mental illness in the less dramatic range—excluding feeblemindedness in its various forms and organic diseases of the nervous system—have come into focus largely as a result of psychological research of hardly more than a hundred years, highlighted more recently by theories introduced by Sigmund Freud. There is a recognized range of gradations from what is loosely called normality (or mental health) through stages and varieties of deviations of neurosis or "abnormal personality" patterns to psychotic medical entities; stated another way, from personality problems to psychoses.

With respect to setting and conditions of therapy, a pragmatic classification would be into two categories: institutional (both inpatient and outpatient), and noninstitutional (comparable to private practice in general medicine, where therapeutic practice is conducted within the framework of normal social and community setting). There is, perhaps, a less clear-cut definition of "clinic" in this field, for it may be, and often is, not clearly an outpatient medical service, but rather an organized psychotherapeutic activity in a school, a settlement house, a welfare office, or a child welfare agency. In hospitals or clinics therapeutic service is almost universally under the control of a psychiatrist. But the whole professional staff is not necessarily medical. It may also include, in varying proportions, psychologists, psychiatric social workers, and psychiatric nurses. In fact, considered as a whole, mental therapy personnel often includes these four distinct disciplines. The proportion varies largely from hospital to clinic to private practice. In view of the importance of this fact, some pertinent data selected from the report of the Joint Commission on Mental Health and Illness will be cited below.

First, it is important to recall certain characteristics of the field as related to service in general and as bearing on the economics of its financing. There are some fundamental differences between incidence of mental illness, its duration, and the relative place it occupies in the therapeutic services of public or community management and of free enterprise practice. In contrast to most kinds of physical illness, for example, one may go all through life with more or less "mental[3] discomfort" constituting a personality problem, and either never be aware of it or not regard it as requiring therapy, though he may be troubled by it 365 days of the year. In physical illness, this is rarely the case: the discomfort and confinement at home or in the hospital are temporary; recovery is expected and, in the overwhelming percentage of cases, takes place with limited loss of time or income. So we have either extended periods of illness with no incapacitation on the one hand, or brief periods with temporary incapacitation on the other. But in serious cases of mental illness the situation is quite different. Here long-term incapacitation and hospitalization is the rule. Some statistical data obtained by the Joint Commission are exceedingly significant in this respect. For example, more than half of all hospital beds in the country are occupied by the mentally ill; yet only 6 per cent of the total population is estimated[4] to suffer some serious mental disorder. Equally significant are other findings of the Commission bearing on this general point:

. . . of the 500,000 resident patients in State hospitals [for the mentally ill] one-quarter have been hospitalized for more than 16 years, one-half for more than 8 years, and three-fourths for more than 2.5 years.

The contrast between hospitalization for the mentally ill and that

[3] Throughout this discussion, for convenience, the term "mental" is being used, even though "emotional," "neurotic," "psychic," or even "psychotic" often may be more accurate terms.

[4] Joint Commission on Mental Illness and Health, Monograph No. 2: *Economics of Mental Illness* by Rashi Fein. Also other monographs in the series referred to, as, for example, *Mental Health Manpower Trends*.

for other medical reasons is even more striking when one compares the daily census of all hospitals and admissions with corresponding figures for psychiatric hospitals.[5]

In 1955:

	(1) Total U.S. Hospitals	(2) Psychiatric Hospitals	Per cent (2) of (1)
Average daily census	1,363,024	740,295	54.3
Admissions	21,072,521	356,377	1.7

All this has a bearing both on the manpower problem and on that of costs. But the ways that the two problems are related are not too simple. On some points, statistics and explanations are available; on others, they are scarce or unclear. Cost of maintenance in hospitals for the mentally ill as compared with general hospital costs is, for example, relatively low. It covers little more than physical care, including food, shelter, clothing, drugs, etc. Professional personnel, on the other hand, as compared with general maintenance staff, is more expensive but relatively low in numbers. As a result, and because mental hospitals are relatively large, the per capita per diem cost as reported for 1956[6] varies from $1.84 in Tennessee to $4.74 in Connecticut, and $5.51 in the District of Columbia. Compared to general hospital costs, which are rarely less than $20 per diem and often over $40, this is not excessive. But the length of stay per patient in the general hospital rarely exceeds a week or two as compared with figures cited earlier for mental patients, which run into years. Even so, in view of the large proportion of hospital beds used for the mentally ill, the cost for the average daily census cited, of more than 500,000 in state hospitals for the mentally ill, ran, in 1956, to some $662,000,000, and by 1965 it may well have been closer to one billion dollars. To this must be added the figures, not now clearly available, for a large number of patients on "parole" in the community, still requiring drugs and a degree of professional

[5] Monograph No. 3, by George W. Albee, Appendix, Table 5.
[6] Monograph No. 2, by Rashi Fein, pp. 28–29.

supervision. These figures do not include expenditures from federal funds for veterans and for the armed services; nor do they include any of the expenditures by way of grants-in-aid for the general field of mental hygiene and for research.

In the area of mental health the manpower problem and part of its economic consequences are somewhat unique. Practitioners in the field, at the apex, are psychiatrists. They exercise control in hospital care. Their competence would have to include all aspects of mental illness that have an organic base and where chemotherapy, physical therapy, institutional environment, and personnel are involved. Outside hospitals, and to a lesser extent in hospitals and in a variety of clinics, the therapeutic personnel includes, besides psychiatrists, also psychologists—particularly clinical psychologists—psychoanalysts, both medical and lay, social caseworkers in a variety of administrative relationships, and sometimes members of the clergy, either with or without some additional training. Apart from psychiatrists and psychologists who specialized in psychometric testing, persons engaged in mental therapy are practically all practitioners within one or another of the psychoanalytic schools of thought and practice. This implies existence of a number of agencies devoted to the training of therapists, either after medical training or independently.

There are several complicating factors in the field of psychotherapeutic practice that makes its inclusion in the social welfare structure difficult and also obstruct a systematic analysis of the manpower problem. In the first place, tax-supported services—including hospitals and clinics—carry, as indicated, the major burden for care of the mentally ill. In that way they constitute the public, institutionalized services. Outside these agencies lies a combination of voluntary agencies, mostly nonprofit,[7] and a large body of practitioners who operate clearly in the free enterprise system. The voluntary agencies are, in the main, either family agencies, no longer concerned with economic assistance, or child welfare agencies, or, in some instances, child guidance clinics. Personnel in the several

[7] There are also, as in the medical field as a whole, proprietary institutions, clearly intended as business enterprises.

operating agencies is composed of the same types of practitioners, and their training is obtained in medical schools, in universities having curricula in psychology, or in training schools for social workers, or in training schools for nurses. The demand for their services is highly competitive: they are wanted and bid for in hospitals and clinics for the mentally ill, in social casework and child welfare agencies, in a variety of public agencies, and in the large area of culturally conditioned prospective patients for psychotherapy, or prospective patients of psychoanalytic therapy.

The free enterprise phase becomes, however, a bit more complicated than it is in the general medical field. There is a much larger effective demand for "psychotherapy" in the middle and upper economic classes, where the cost is no serious problem, than in the lower income classes. Therapeutic interviews, lasting usually fifty minutes, may be held once a week or as many as five times a week, and the treatment rarely is of less than several months' duration. In fact, a substantial body of patients in this group may be more or less continuously under treatment for as long as five or ten years or even longer. Since cost is related to interview sessions, this may represent a large outlay of money on the part of the patient. When, as is often the case, several members of the family may more or less simultaneously by receiving this form of therapy, the cost may be beyond reach of all but a small fraction of the affluent group. It is only natural, therefore, that demand for services of the most prominent of the therapists presents a competitive economic picture and tends to draw the already limited supply of specialists into the economically more rewarding areas of service. This, in turn, makes them relatively less available for training of additional manpower, and for service to lower economic levels and to destitute clients of public assistance and of clinics for low income groups. It similarly affects their availability for school systems and for outpatient clinics in general.

While fees in this free enterprise or subsidized clinic and training service do not compare with usual fees paid to surgeons, they are more cumulative in effect, both with respect to the paying client and with respect to the receiving therapist. It is one, though probably a lesser, inducement for attracting therapists to this field,

as compared with the intrinsic and stimulating nature of the theoretical aspects of psychotherapy.

By and large, the economically limited income group cannot
afford, and in quantitative comparison does not receive, psychotherapy in proportion to the incidence of need for it, except when it
comes to hospitalization. The sliding scale fee system is in effect in
many clinics and voluntary family agencies, ranging from almost
free to a maximum of some $15 or more per session. The really free
service available in relation to need in public assistance and similar
groups is, however, negligible; and whatever the discrepancy may
be between need for general medical care and the cost of care
actually obtained, that discrepancy would seem to be far greater in
the field of psychotherapy—with the possible exception of those
hospitalized for extended periods of time.

There are estimates available on costs of service in mental
illness as there are for the medical field as a whole. As yet, data for
the two kinds of services and their relative cost are not offered in a
unified form. It is difficult to obtain an integrated picture from any
combination that can be drawn from the sources referred to earlier.
To the lay person, interested in the general field of social welfare,
some of the variants may be suggestive, though they hardly add up
to a scientific whole. Fees paid by the economically comfortable
class rarely come to less than $15 per session, whether for one or for
five sessions a week. Occasionally, one hears of $7.50 per session
charged to persons of moderate means when treatment extends over
a series of years. In the economically higher class, $20 per session
is not above the customary standard, $25 not rare, but $50 per ses-
sion would occur only among wealthy patients. From the viewpoint
of the individual's budget, extended therapy running to $5,000 a
year (on the five sessions per week basis) is not unusual; but since
it necessarily takes much of the therapist's time, his income may still
be modest in comparison with the fees of a surgeon for the same
economic class.

We do not know how much of the "disposable income" of
the population of the United States now goes into direct fee payment for psychoanalyst, psychiatrist, psychologist, or social case-

worker in private practice.[8] In this connection, some of the Joint Commission's estimates on manpower may be suggestive. These estimates do not differentiate, except in some of the more detailed specifications, between manpower available in the free enterprise sector, alone or chiefly, and in the manpower utilized in hospitals or clinics supported by public funds, by professional organizations, by training provisions in universities, or by federal subsidies. A few of the general findings may be of interest.

In commenting first on the long-standing shortage—in some instances, nearly complete absence—of competent and specially trained professional personnel in mental hospitals Fein judges that the situation "has been aggravated rather than relieved by a tremendously increased demand for mental health services in other agencies—for example, schools, courts, and prisons—as well as in private practice."[9] His summarized findings are presented somewhat as follows:

> Surveys of State and county hospitals have revealed budgeted positions for physicians and psychologists standing nearly 25 per cent unfilled. We are approximately 20 per cent short in filling budgeted jobs for psychiatric nurses and social workers. . . . Even if available jobs were filled the staffing of public mental hospitals would fall short of the minimum standards for adequate care set by the American Psychiatric Association. . . . By this criterion our hospitals are *20 per cent* adequate in nursing staff and *36 per cent* adequate in social workers. The adequacy is 45 per cent for physicians (with heavy reliance on foreign interns and residents) and 67 per cent for psychologists.

This is important from our point of view, for it repeats in somewhat different form the same tendency that exists in social work[10] to de-

[8] Some speculative estimates are made by Dr. Fein, but he makes no claims for their accuracy.

[9] This and the immediately following material are drawn from the "staff review" of the monograph on *Manpower,* prepared by Jack R. Ewalt, M.D., director of the enterprise. The more detailed figures cited afterward (and on an earlier page) are derived from a series of more than 75 tables in Appendix I of the volume.

[10] See later chapters in Part Three.

vote our resources for training, not for the services that most need personnel, but to serve the impressive images of professional and social status. The monograph continues its analysis of available manpower for the several types of personnel required. As for the principal and most essential professional personnel, namely psychiatrists, the "staff review" continues:

. . . about 600 [medical graduates] complete resident training as psychiatrists each year. The net increase in psychiatrists is somewhat less, due to deaths, retirements, and foreign physicians returning home . . . *only one-third of psychiatrists become fulltime employees in hospitals or clinics. Another third enter fulltime private practice,* and the remaining third divide their time between private practice and salaried positions. . . . Because of the superior attractions of private practice, the greatest shortage—it is self-evident—occurs in the area where patients with major mental illness are concentrated—in public mental hospitals.[11]

Some of the reasons for the shortage of medical personnel in this as well as in the general medical field may not be entirely accidental. An article dealing with the subject points to some deliberate efforts to restrict trainees. It cites the economist Seymour Harris to the effect that "It is unfortunate . . . that there are definite signs of restrictionism in some professions. Medicine is a notable example. . . . The raising of medical standards has to some extent been used as a mask to conceal the feather-bedding practices generally associated with trade unionism. . . . A frontal attack on restrictionism . . . in medicine will increase the number of desired openings."[12]

[11] Compare the discussion in a later chapter of the concentration in social work training on "casework" in voluntary family and child welfare agencies as against the massive demand for services in the public assistance field.

[12] Quotation from an article in the British publication, *Medical Care,* October-December 1964: "The American Medical Association and the Supply of Physicians; a study of the internal contradictions in the concept of professionalism," by Elton Rayack, Associate Professor of Economics, University of Rhode Island, prepared with the assistance of grants from the National

Certainly, in the field of mental illness and health, there is no evidence of such restrictionism. Yet the sad statistics on the availability of psychiatrists quoted above continue with respect to other professions required. Psychologists, for example, are badly needed. Though their number has increased relatively faster than that of other auxiliary professions, they are still not up to "adequacy." An indirect example emerges from the report of an experimental program for mental health consultants for institutions for the aged, conducted under the Community Mental Health Board of New York City (1964). Reference is made in the introduction of the report to the fact that "From the beginning of the program members of four professional disciplines were utilized." A glance at the list of consultants shows: one Doctor of Medicine, two Masters of Social Science, and nine Doctors of Philosophy. The majority on the list, to judge from their academic degrees, are psychologists—certainly not physicians and almost certainly not social workers. To return to the matter of shortages as discussed by the Joint Commission:

> At the end of World War II, we had about an equal number of psychiatrists and psychologists; overall . . . the number of psychiatrists doubled in the post-war decade. But, meanwhile, the number of psychologists quadrupled, with the result that there are now about 16,000 psychologists. At first glance, this increase appears encouraging; in a way it is. But only about one-third of all psychologists engage in clinical services. . . . The larger number are employed as college teachers. The second larger number of psychologists are employed by the Federal government, mainly for research, some of it related to mental health. Private industry employs a sizable number for aptitude testing and for personnel, management, and market research.

The estimate by the Commission of a need for "an additional 50,000 social workers by 1960" and the reference to the fact that "schools of social work train not more than 2,000 a year" raise some interesting questions for the social work profession and its schools.

Science Foundation and the Research Grants-in-Aid Fund of the University of Rhode Island. Consult also *The Economics of American Medicine* by Seymour Harris (Macmillan, 1964).

As will be shown in a later chapter, "casework" is the major interest in schools of social work; and students enter that field by preference, so far as numbers can show. The content of their training certainly emphasizes psychological and therapeutic subjects both in classroom and in field practice. Psychiatric casework as a specialty has more than a shade of glamour above general casework. One would think that the graduates would flock into the field that would seem to need them most. But, in fact, not only is there no great rush into the service of institutions for the mentally ill, but when actually in that service they are expected to deal with administrative matters rather than with direct therapy, and so, in Dr. Ewalt's words,[13] though the social worker is "a key figure in any clinic or hospital proposing to provide competent care of mental patients, including attention to his social and economic circumstances, [the social worker] presents a rather vague image in the minds of people . . ." Actually, the social worker, despite her interest in dynamic psychology, finds herself, in hospital and clinic, less in the active therapeutic role than psychiatrist and psychologist, and more in the manipulative, administrative, and environmental area, as further comments in the report clearly indicate. It would seem, therefore, that both the training interests distinctly in the mental health field and those in the schools of social work have to face a task that they have hardly touched.

As to the subject of psychotherapy and its place in the social welfare structure of the country as a whole, some questions would seem to be of a crucial nature:

What proportion of the general public is in need of psychotherapy at some level short of hospitalization? We do not know, except in isolated spots.

Are there more persons in the community at large who need some limited psychotherapy than persons who sooner or later will require hospitalization? We do not know.

What proportion of persons, high or low in the economic scale, can manage such problems of personal maladjustment as they may have, and perforce must manage, with respect to food, lodging, recreation, social life, and community situations by their own efforts

[13] Monograph No. 3, p. xvi.

through their basic biological resiliency and adaptability, without therapy, and yet without catastrophe? We do not know, and as of now would not know, except by counting those who ought to, but do not, get to hospitals, and those who commit suicide or possibly crime. It may always be anybody's guess.

The field of mental illness and mental health enjoys one advantage of tremendous value as compared with some other parts of the social welfare structure. *It has fewer enemies.* Sophisticated layers of people in our culture are intrigued, and have been intrigued ever since the emergence of psychoanalysis and its vast social and status implications, with mental health, especially as—more or less—the other fellow needs it. Moreover, the mentally ill person is not, by definition, an economic threat as is the person on relief, the "chiseler." Our culture has not yet accepted the "destitute," and as yet the War on Poverty would seem to be on probation. At any rate, for the moment, psychotherapy has a better "image" than public assistance. Social Security has made the cultural grade, except as free enterprise medicine and the individual grumpy taxpayer are irritated. But mental illness and mental health are accepted concepts; federal funds, state mental health bodies, community mental health programs, research on all levels, are approved. A well-articulated and generous place for mental hygiene in our country's social welfare structure seems reasonably assured, even though as yet far from adequate in schools, courts, and institutions.

Chapter VII

Services to Neighborhoods: The Settlement Movement

The unique characteristic of settlement and neighborhood centers that have become so prominent a factor in welfare history in this country (and of some other Western nations) is the fact that needs were defined and services offered on outside initiative rather than as a result of help requested. The imaginative and socially sensitized members of the comfortable and secure segment of the community recognized that forces outside the lives and experiences of the disadvantaged were responsible for these needs; that these had to be seen and studied at firsthand; that help needed was not always simple, nor always to be given by gifts. This social sensitivity of originators of the settlement movement[1] was conceptualized by observation of the effects of social change in industry, political life, and community behavior.

The first significant step that started the movement was a purely individual, impulsive act by Edward Denison, in London a full hundred years ago. In 1860, he took up lodgings in Stepney with the idea of persuading some young men to throw in their lot with dwellers of that underprivileged neighborhood. No substantial progress was made, however, until the Rev. Samuel A. Barnett founded Toynbee Hall in London in 1884 as a direct sequel to Denison's original move. The group of workers inspired by Barnett's urgency came from among Oxford and Cambridge graduates to initiate what then became the Settlement Movement.

The universal characteristic of the settlement house, or of the neighborhood center as many of them have more recently been called, is the fact that it is an operating agency, established in and for the inhabitants of a limited geographical area, and is concentrated on discovering the needs of that area and seeking to find services to meet those needs. But that is only the external common fact. The living pulsating component is less simple to describe and to evaluate. In the first place, every such early settlement house owes its existence to some inspired person whose leadership gave direction, urgency, and propulsive power.[2] Consequently, differences from one settlement to another may be expected and have, in fact, occurred. But organizationally and functionally that fact does not seriously affect the basic pattern of the settlement house or neighborhood center as an operating agency.

---

[1] For a brief but authoritative history and interpretation of the Settlement Movement consult the article by Paul U. Kellogg (the late editor of *Survey* magazine and spiritual leader of the "Pittsburgh Survey") in Volume XIV of the *Encyclopedia of Social Sciences* (Macmillan, 1934). Even though the article is dated 1934, nothing of major importance can be added for the subsequent years, unless it be the indirect influence of that movement upon the more recent public housing development for low-income groups.

[2] Some of the most outstanding of these are mentioned by Kellogg, and some are responsible for far-reaching innovations in service and social propaganda, as, for example, Jane Addams of Hull House, Chicago, and Lillian Wald of the Henry Street Settlement, New York.

The common characteristic of neighborhood centers and settlements (some call them community centers) is that they provide a locus and a stimulant for much needed services for inhabitants of the neighborhood. These services were at first predominantly recreational and therefore particularly important, for they supplemented the educational content of public schools and emphasized the inherently educational value of recreation for children.[3] They then extended to recreation for teenagers and adults, and soon introduced into the physical plants of these centers gymnasiums, swimming pools, large halls for dramatic staging and musical performances. It was natural for groups of all kinds to find places in these centers, for example, trade unions, mothers' groups, civic organizations.

The next important service offerings that came by way of the centers were those promoted by health agencies. And so there came clinics of all varieties, including such specialties as the promotion of birth control. More or less related to this phase was the propaganda activity for better housing and associated purposes. It was not long before educational and group activities led to the establishment of arts and crafts, and the movement for promoting musical education, especially for the talented offspring of the low-income groups of the neighborhood, who otherwise might never have had opportunity to enter and to advance into musical prominence.

One of the most important of the contributions to national welfare arose in fact from the health service activities of the "center," in this case the Henry Street Settlement in New York City, and the introduction of visiting nursing service by Lillian Wald, the head of that settlement. The extent of the influence of this innovation in the field of health, hygiene, and medical care in this country is difficult to overestimate; its contribution to the well-being of the low-income group has been, and still is, one of the great achievements of the settlement house movement.

So much for the common characteristics of neighborhood centers and settlements. Certain differences have arisen between these two types of service centers that are obscured in part by the

[3] There was at the earlier stages a far greater recognition of this fact, especially as set forth by its most effective exponent, Joseph Lee, now rarely mentioned in current bibliographies.

fact that the personnel employed in the two types has much in common, and that the programs of particular exemplars are not always distinguishable. The real difference lies in the character and purposes of the sponsoring group. These purposes affect location and the neighborhood versus larger geographical services; but, more importantly, they affect the original intent and aspirations of the settlement movement. The sponsoring group of the original Toynbee Hall was only apparently sectarian. It was centered around Rev. Samuel A. Barnett, a member of the clergy. But the group was not sectarian in outlook. "Barnett and his associates," writes Kellogg,[4] "set the type in consistently rejecting sectarian bias and evangelical intent." The simplest way, though necessarily not entirely accurate, is to say that neighborhood centers (including some calling themselves settlements) had become instruments for maintaining, promoting, and extending the interests of ethnic, sectarian, and occasionally political groups of the low-income population in the area. The services rendered to the neighborhood were not necessarily diminished, but they tended to be channeled to the favored representatives of the sponsoring group.

Particularly in the case of the young and young adult group was this tendency of selective specialization an increasing phenomenon. In many instances the orientation tended away from the neighborhood and the disadvantaged group. The accent became increasingly the cultural and religious interest of the sponsoring group, rather than that of the original sponsors, from Barnett to Jane Addams. So the YMCA, YWCA, YMHA, and YWHA drew more and more of membership from areas that could hardly be called neighborhoods, and from layers of the population that could hardly be distinguished from the middle and upper middle classes.[5] A tendency developed in many places, in fact, to set up neighborhood centers in and for neighborhoods whose inhabitants were of the cultural or sectarian segment of the sponsoring group. Occasionally

---

[4] *Encyclopedia of Social Sciences,* Vol. XIV.

[5] It is of some significance to note here that even the Boy Scout movement, with its extraordinary potential for educational recreation, eventually became channeled—though without explicit formulation—into the principal sectarian fields of sponsorship.

it also happened that a center could grow into a community enterprise only nominally related to the original purposes of the sponsors, and devoted to general dramatic, cultural, and musical interests of the community as a whole.

But there have also been instances where the purposes of the settlement movement itself were distorted and subverted to the group preferences of the sponsors. A few examples known directly to the writer may serve to illustrate the tendency. In one case—a settlement house established in the spirit of the leaders of the movement—a substantial influx into the neighborhood of Negro and Catholic families progressively brought the young members of these groups into the settlement house. Unobtrusive arrangements were made by its management to find supplementary locations for program activities for these newcomers rather than have them dilute the major cultural clientele of the settlement. Eventually plans were made, in fact, to find an entirely new location for the agency, one that would be safely within the environment of the sponsoring culture.

In another instance, a decision had been made by a sponsoring group in a large industrial city to move the agency bodily to another location; they would start anew there without complicating racial and cultural factors to deal with. There have been other variants of this type of adjustment. But actually they may represent, on the whole, not a violation of the settlement idea but a new series of service offerings, adapted to conditions typical of urban development, where ghettos develop in neglected and poverty-stricken areas whether the local population is hetrogeneous or uniform. Such ghettos have been Jewish, Chinese, Negro, Puerto Rican, Mexican, and other. Centers have been established increasingly by sponsors of ethnic, religious, or cultural groups similar to those in the ghettos except for economic class and social status. Often the centers would be indistinguishable from parish or church annexes, except for the actual group activities and the expansion of recreational and cultural pursuits. The number and adequacy of such centers have depended in part on the extent to which such minority groups had developed an upper economic-social contingent in the community, in combination with explicit group identity and awakened social responsibility. The Protestant YMCA and the Jewish Welfare Center have therefore been more numerous and more prosperous than centers devoted to Mexican or Puerto Rican ghetto service.[6]

As of this day, when urban inhabitants far outnumber the rural and semirural population, and when awakening of social conscience is not so esoteric and epoch-making an event as was the establishment of Toynbee Hall and Hull House, it is possible that operation of neighborhood centers under whatever auspices and however restrictive in clientele may be more extensive than the expansion of the settlement movement as such. Surely neighborhood centers under such separate sponsorship cannot match the general divisive influence in our society of the sectarian, cultural, racial, and economic forces for fragmentation. If, then, settlement houses continue to be a smaller and smaller numerical segment of the total neighborhood centers (and housing development centers) that fact may not represent regression in service or in political egalitarianism. But they do represent a unique type of social experiment, still vital, and still potentially important in the welfare scene and in the problem of "operational personnel." It is, therefore, useful to spell out some of their characteristics.

The range of services in settlement houses has already been indicated, and it is probably still greater than that of other types of neighborhood centers. It is also clear that in the light of its conceptual purposes the settlement still is a consistently potent factor for general civic advancement and education for social outlook of its clientele. And there continues to be, in the typical settlement house, a very interesting three-part component of the personnel involved. The respective roles of these three are clear enough, but their activities often combine in a total tapestry in which they are not always functionally distinguishable. Roughly, the three components may be designated as: lay sponsors, operational staff of the administrative and service activities, and residents of the neighborhood in various groupings.

[6] It should be noted that the YWCA group as a whole, though in some ways a neighborhood center, has made a far more significant contribution to general social welfare progress than other special groupings.

The lay sponsors established the original foundation of settlement work. They were not only the channels for financing the work, but as volunteers they performed the task of organizing groups, lectures, classes, discussions. They were primarily university graduates who were stimulated by leaders to observe and to develop a sympathetic and philosophically meaningful understanding of what industrial and political innovations meant to the working classes. In a sense, therefore, though giving volunteer service, they were themselves the educational beneficiaries of their labors; for it helped them, despite their middle-class security and aristocratic social life, to learn the realities of the standard of living, the preoccupations, the troubled discomfort, and the rebellious reactions of the low-income laboring classes and their families. It also gave them a glimpse of the housing and living conditions of the London laborer. In the United States, though the caste system of Britain was absent, there was enough of a chasm between the lives of the sponsoring group and the neighborhood residents to offer the same kind of educational chance to the middle-class volunteers. Jane Addams, with Hull House as her "parish house," constantly emphasized this value to residents and volunteers of her settlement. This contribution of settlement houses to the education and larger social perspective of its sponsoring group continued to characterize the movement, even as the financial prosperity and solvency of settlements, with their increasing service programs and payrolls, began to bring serious problems to management of the organization. Funds had to be sought increasingly from personnel beyond the active volunteer group, and settlements joined the ranks of voluntary agencies struggling for existence. The original sponsorship type had to be supplemented by and diluted by members of the community who could help to assure financial stability and substantial programs. This financial difficulty is not merely an additional fact; it is a major one, as will be seen in the story of the much publicized Mobilization for Youth.[7]

The second component, the employed staff, is responsible for administration and service programs. Administration itself demands

[7] See below.

considerable personnel, especially as program expands and prospers. A full-time executive has to be supplemented by departmental assistants, secretaries, and staff for physical maintenance of plant. Then there is personnel for recreation activities, club leadership, instructors in arts and crafts from sewing to pottery; leaders in dramatics, music, painting, and sculpture; adult education personnel, from teaching English to foreigners to general cultural subjects. All these, while presumably having some interest in the settlement movement itself, must be recruited primarily for their competence. Here and there a volunteer not in need of compensation may become available and occasionally a member of the lay management may be interested and available. Volunteers to supplement staff and keep the payroll within bounds may be utilized. But a paid, professionally competent staff is an absolute condition of successful operation. A part of that staff, on the administrative and supervisory level, can presumably be useful only if they are imbued with ideals promulgated by the leadership—lay and executive—and within the ideological tradition of the agency. This is true also, though perhaps to a lesser extent, of other neighborhood centers not strictly classed as settlements. To these staff members must be added students in training, especially in group leadership and recreational activities. Yet another staff group is usually organized for the management of summer camps, usually part of the total program structure of American settlements.

There are various degrees of coordinate status between representatives of the sponsoring group and professionally oriented members of the staff structure, degrees and patterns varying from place to place and from agency to agency. There are also varying patterns of relationship between both the above groups and members of the third contingent, namely, residents of the neighborhood—or of the total community of sponsorship as is the case in the "Y's." This relationship is less relevant to service aspects, which tend to become matters of professional or artisan arrangement, always conditioned by budgetary considerations.

The extent to which the third component—neighborhood residents—is involved in the operation or leadership of these agencies is difficult to determine. Nor is the pattern uniform. The original pattern of Toynbee Hall became less and less a working model for successive emulators, as distinctive and elaborate service programs took increasing priority of attention, and as administrators became too numerous and too heavily burdened with responsibility to match the stature of Barnett, Addams, Woods, and their disciples. Moreover, ethnic and religious sponsorship, which numerically has become far more extensive than the local type, has tended to remove essential leadership to those in charge of these larger sponsoring groups.

A curious and unexpected test of this relationship between sponsors and residents and one that has yet to be evaluated may be taking place at this time in the operation of the Mobilization for Youth in New York City. This is theoretically an experiment and demonstration in intent but, like many demonstrations in the welfare field, it has tended to become a new type of agency program rather than to remain an experiment. Its relevance to the settlement and neighborhood center movement arises from several features of its origin and structure. It has, like the settlements, a geographically limited area of operation, in which it accepts certain responsibilities for the well-being of residents. This area is occupied primarily by families of low-income and limited opportunities, and in ethnic and racial composition among the less advantaged members of the community. In recent years the area has experienced somewhat disturbing outbreaks of juvenile lawlessness and gang feuds. For these and related reasons the area as a whole has seen the opening over the years of a number of settlement houses as well as other welfare centers.

But, as in other parts of the voluntary welfare field, financial resources had not kept pace with the needs to be met and with the new expanding types of services deemed to be important for the area, particularly for the younger members of the resident families. Relations between sponsoring management and local residents had been good, but how far that fact represented real integration between the interested benevolent management and residential families is not clear. The technical employee group could not command the time and resources requested for adequate services. A conviction had grown up among leading personnel of the several settlement houses that increasing resources were imperative; and that it was high time to experiment with what had come to be termed "saturation services" to see whether a full complement of adequately supplied services would solve the various problems of health, recreation, employment opportunities, clinical help, and educational needs.

A carefully planned series of moves resulted in the commitment of federal, municipal, and private foundation funds for providing these saturation services. One aspect of this new undertaking that is pertinent to the present discussion is the relation among the three above mentioned personnel components of the settlements and the new corporation created to supply the resources. To a degree not yet clear, the several settlements accepting new funds from the new agency had to surrender some of their "sovereignty" in management, programming, public relations, and administrative structure. The new agency had become in some ways similar to a holding company in the business world, but without the assured permanence and historical continuity of the component settlement and neighborhood center membership. New lines of authority, new images of purpose, new patterns of relationship to municipal departments, research bodies, and the shapers of public relations, new rivalries among agencies and among personnel, were in the making. And surely a new test was in process, of the theoretical and human aspects of the relationship among middle-class sponsors, government authorities, an army of employed personnel, and the yet undefined character of the residential family matrix. Something quite new may be learned and come into existence. Something old and proven may wither.

If Mobilization for Youth had been only a local experiment, even though it soon involved the city government, party politics, and political debates, it would have been a limited if exciting episode. Funds for the program were obtained from foundations, city budget, and federal sources, in amounts that were, in their way, record-breaking. MFY is, in fact, now (1967) a local voluntary agency, with a series of branches in public schools and neighborhood centers within the area of its origin in New York City. But the long-range influence that this new welfare implementation offered far exceeds either saturation services or neighborhood center civic patterns. At least three major national movements roughly simultaneous in origin and presenting similar aspects soon appeared as movements tending in the same direction. They represent both theoretical innovations and also almost explosive events. One is the focused interrelation between delinquency and poverty as portrayed by Cloward and Ohlin in their book, *Delinquency and Opportunity*,[8] and the establishment of the President's Committee on Juvenile Delinquency;[9] another is the civil rights movement with all its side effects; the third, and perhaps most important, is the national legislation creating the Organization for Economic Opportunity which developed the community organization bundle of programs.[10] The local community component has remained vital, if varied. Mobilization for Youth, though limited in operation and cost compared with these three movements, is inseparably associated in origin and spirit with them, and remains a significant episode in the progress of social welfare, even beyond its neighborhood implication. But the striking and important fact of our welfare structure is that responsibility for the well-being and livelihood of the depressed portion of the people is being accepted both as national policy and as subject for local community organization, be it Mobilization for Youth, Headstart, or guaranteed income of national scope.

---

[8] Richard A. Cloward and Lloyd E. Ohlin, *Delinquency and Opportunity: A Theory of Delinquent Gangs* (The Free Press, 1960).

[9] See also *Beyond Welfare* by Herbert Krosney (Holt, 1966).

[10] The program developed under OEO for prekindergarten education of culturally deprived children to compensate for their cultural lag and upgrade them to normal achievement levels is one of the most popularly accepted of the OEO programs.

Chapter VIII

⤞⤝

Services for Clients with Many Needs

The preceding chapters have dealt with roughly distinguishable types of service, corresponding to the distinct ascertainable needs of the client.[1] Admittedly the classification as presented is both rough and not quite comprehensive; it is made with an eye to the organization of servicing bodies as much as to the specific need of the client.

[1] The term "client" has become a generally accepted, convenient designation for the person or family in need, and implies that a contact for possible service has been established between the client and a welfare service agency. By way of a convenient extension, the term relates also to any person or family presenting a need, even though no contact has actually been established but logically should be.

It is functional or operational rather than analytic in relation to the condition of the client. It does not negate, however, the infinite variety of personal patterns of the client, or the different meaning that the same discomfort-producing and unsatisfied need may represent for one client as compared with some other. It is akin in a way to the propriety of classifying the species as *Homo sapiens* without attributing a standard quantum of wisdom to all its members. Nor, in the operational sense, is the designation of a given service as applicable to a stated need of any client any less legitimate than the acceptance of a standard monetary system, even though the value of the dollar for the purchase of one kind of commodity has no relation to its value in procuring a totally different commodity or service. It is taken for granted that a person's specific need is part of that person's total being rather than some inanimate interchangeable molecule; and though the particular means of satisfying that need may be the same when offered to two different individuals, their use of that means may serve differently their several complex individual purposes. No one would claim that a slice of the same loaf of bread may not in general serve to appease the pangs of hunger in two totally different individuals. Within limits, the situation is similar with respect to services, whether they relate to economic need, medical care, psychological support, or leisure-time activities. If one insisted on the unique nature of each type of need for each person in the light of his unique personality, and if it were necessary for that reason to individualize each unit of service correspondingly; if, moreover, there were possibly several needs at the same time, and in varying degrees of intensity, one would have to deal with all the permutations and combinations presented, multiplied by the number of individual systems of soma and psyche—and one would have to give up before one started.

Admittedly the foregoing paragraph presents an exaggerated picture. It is in focus, however, of this much reality: that in every client's case a considerable degree of individualization must be sought in assaying his needs; that a degree of ingenuity may often be required to combine the requisite services with the nature and number of needs presented, the individual character of the client, and the specific established and recognized service categories available at a given time and place.

It is regarding the utilization of the diverse services required (and available) that a major problem faces the welfare service system, a problem calling for services to clients with many needs. The simple reality as it emerges is that the same client may and often does have several needs at the same time, calling for different kinds of services, and these in different combinations. How shall these services be given? How can they be given—by the same agency, same personnel, or some elaborate design, flexible and adequate? How, in fact, are they given if given at all? The simple answer is that there is no effective and dependable system now in existence to assure requisite services for the multiproblem client in this country at this time.

A variety of procedures have, however, been evolved with different degrees of effectiveness, or have been experimented with from time to time, though none of them would claim a perfect philosophical foundation or comprehensiveness of plan and resources. The principal methods utilized for clients with many needs have been referral, diversification, and coordination.

Referral has a long and hoary history, and has often been utilized, depending on the ingenuity and devotion of the worker, on the esteem enjoyed by the referring agency, and, of course, on other resources being available. Referral, as a system, implies several things. The agency may offer only a limited type of service, and the applicant-client is not aware of that fact; or it may be limited in funds, personnel, or other quantitative imperatives. It may have policies of service not related to the nature of the need; these may be sectarian, social, geographic, ethnic, or theoretical. In these days of private fee-payment agencies the policy aspect may include the client's income status. In public agencies, the additional factors of residence, "settlement," or, in some instances, citizenship status have been pertinent. At any rate, when for any reason the agency first contacted by the applicant is not or considers itself as not being in position to render the service required, it refers the client to some other presumably suitable agency. It may do so and has consistently done so even when it actually does provide the service within its resources, upon discovering additional needs in the situation of the client that it is not in position, for whatever reason, to serve. It then seeks to guide (and to refer) the client to some other agency for the additional service required. Such referral requires that the worker know of other services available and be familiar with their policies and their limitations. The worker has to exercise perspicacity in selecting the most suitable referral. Otherwise, the process might turn into a "run-around." It is in part to meet the demands of the referral process and in part, perhaps, as a defense against the "professional beggar" that the social service exchange system was devised more than a half century ago.[2] In many communities, of course, there is sparse provision of agencies (other than the local churches) so that the referral system is automatically inoperative, and much needed service may not be available. But that is part of our basic welfare service problem, rather than a difficulty of referral.

The distribution of service agencies even in the largest and richest metropolitan areas has not reflected a planned pattern for providing whatever help might be required by those in need in the form or quantity appropriate to those needs. In the main, before emergence of the national social security system and the plans in effect in a few individual states, the cluster of agencies in any locality had come into being as a result of philanthropic imagination and devotion of leading citizens, or vested theoretical or institutional interests, such as churches, religious groupings, ethnic or racial groups, trade unions, etc., or foundations or foundation-nurtured activities, or residual and continuing philanthropic agencies established generations ago.

Finally, referral as a system may often turn out to be a one-way street. It does not follow that an agency to which referral has been made is able or willing to accept the client referred for service. Aside from policy questions, judgments in the individual case may differ, staff or resources may not be available. And then there is

---

[2] It is not generally known by the lay public that the information so expertly organized in the social service exchange gave no hint of the problems of the client but merely listed the agencies that had had some contact with him.

that time-honored waiting list. There is no defense against the waiting list. Many a client has passed beyond suitability of service when his turn came for the active instead of the waiting list.

Diversification. The simplest and most logical way to deal with the multiproblem phenomenon would seem to be to diversify the services of the agency or of the sponsoring body. A suggestive pattern for this solution may be seen, for example, in the outpatient clinic systems. There, the variety of illnesses is matched to the varied specialists in the medical service. In some ways—though admittedly different because of the free enterprise system involved—the group medical practice organizations also offer a clue for diversified service. Inherent diversification, though not under that label, is represented by the cluster of services under the federal-state-local authorities described in an earlier chapter dealing with services for livelihood. More specific examples may be seen in municipal welfare agencies in cities like Philadelphia, Pittsburgh, and New York, for example. Entirely different in form but similiar in essential purposes are the Salvation Army Services, the programs of the Society of Friends (Quakers), and, in some places and some ways, Catholic agencies. There are also single private agencies where a degree of diversification has taken place. A family agency may have related services for the aged, for children, for homeless men or unmarried mothers. An organization primarily concerned with disturbed or delinquent children may conduct several institutions, psychoclinical and casework services, experimental and research projects in school systems or clinics. But these are exceptional rather than common patterns, and usually limited in diversification.

Coordination has been the favorite concept, or hope, or catchword in the history of welfare services, especially in the early decades of this century. It is based, aside from its inherent logic, on the assumption that the services to be coordinated actually do exist, and also on the untested and innocent belief that coordination of agencies is the same as coordination for the explicit needs of the client. Actually, coordination as distinct from referral has been addressed to administration, sponsorship, and financing rather than to client-oriented service. It has served, to a limited extent, to reduce competition, rivalry, and power drives. The long history of welfare councils, community funds, functional committees, and conferences is realistically pertinent more to diplomatic and financial problems of agency-entities than to the weaving together of diverse services to meet the complex needs of clients. Perhaps the greatest coordinator in reality has been the resilient and biologically persistent client.

What then is the answer, if there is any, to the search for providing services to the client if resources are actually at hand? The answer is not one but several. Little can be done unless these is consistent, continuing study of the distribution of needs and of patterns of complex needs, both qualitatively and quantitatively, with particular attention to the structure of public services. Such studies might then be converted into agency structure, personnel differentiation, and budget distribution. In a modified form they could be the basis for manuals, one for the worker, another for the client. And with continuing routine studies the requirements of budget, service, and staff could be altered as conditions in the country as a whole, or in a given community, are altered.

One reminder may well be in place here. Many of the problem complexes, especially those of a psychological, vocational, educational, and medical nature, occur in the economically comfortable classes as well as in the low-income group. At present, the classes in which economic stringency is not present can and do find much of the help they need in the free enterprise system. In that system, however, they can be easily exploited, for there is no control over the operation of technicians in the free enterprise arena. When welfare services are tackled in the same way that we have tackled the school system, elementary, high school, college, and university—or as we have tackled public health, sanitation, police, and recreation services—multiproblem as well as single problem situations will be handled with less anxiety and better results.

PART THREE

WELFARE METHODS AND OPERATIONAL PERSONNEL

Chapter IX

⧨

Components of the Field

If we think of persons rather than activities, there are two major components of the field of welfare: first, and most important, the beneficiaries, either those receiving services or those legitimately belonging to the group but not actually receiving benefits; second, the agents of society through whom services are administered. In a way the definition of the first group constitutes the proper arena for social scientist and philosopher, for it is the nature of "life and labor" that defines who needs to be served. It is, in fact, leaders of men and interpreters of life who have shaped instrumentalities for service also. In our own day we recognize these interpreters as hav-

133

ing been the real architects of the subsequent agencies of service. Among them would be, to mention a few, Adam Smith, John Howard, Francis Place, Robert Owen, Karl Marx, Dorothea Dix, Jacob Riis, Edward Denison, and in more recent years Clifford Beers, Jane Addams, Sir William Beveridge, Abraham Epstein. Also among them would be numerous members of Royal Commissions, Congressional committees, and political leaders like Senator Robert F. Wagner and President Franklin D. Roosevelt; and always journalists among whom, offhand, the name of Lincoln Steffens occurs as a good example.

The visible instrumentalities for carrying on services from the impersonal machinery of social organization to the beneficiaries or clients are the operating agencies and their personnel to whom the task is assigned. They are, perforce, the wheel horses who labor, while the inventor-leaders produce the ideas and inspiration. These visible instruments are, in turn, two-sided affairs, consisting of agencies or corporate bodies of administration and human personnel who, as officers or employees, carry on actual operations and give form, color, and perceptible purpose to activities. Occasionally, in rare instances, the administering personnel may also supply the inventive leadership that defines and identifies needs and mobilizes motivations.

Agencies have included a varied assortment: local community organizations formed for charitable purposes, churches, cultural and ethnic groups, fraternal orders, philanthropic foundations, overseers of the poor, parish officials, monasteries, hospitals, almshouses, orphanages, guild organizations, newspapers raising fresh air funds, neighborhood centers such as settlement houses, public school systems conducting playgrounds and special classes, and so on without number. A basic dichotomy of a different order of both historical and administrative interest is the division in this country between two classes: tax-supported agencies, federal, state, and local, and Voluntary agencies, supported in a variety of ways, many of them depending to a considerable extent on subventions from tax-supported sources. Both types of sponsorship have existed in the field of welfare activities since early colonial days. Both have exhibited considerable variety, and both have been influenced by emergency situations as well as by gradual unfolding of cultural responses to changes in the economic and political setting. Our immediate interest centers in the rationale of their theoretical structure and in part in the quantitative distribution of services. Neither has escaped the influence of philosophical and political pressures or the impact of technological development and population growth. Each has responded, however, in different ways except where technical services have imposed their own standards, as, for example, in medical care, psychiatric treatment, and educational services for children.[1] Public or tax-supported agencies of necessity operate under the legal control of whatever political area has jurisdiction over them. Their principal problems are in the civil service systems affecting personnel and in the political control of their financial appropriations. They cannot escape bureaucratic requirements or the complicated controls and functions inherent in the division of authority among local, state, and federal governments. This is especially true because of the great diversity of political patterns, the stages or varieties of culture in the different regions of the nation, the changing distribution of rural and city life, and the varying tax systems in effect.

The voluntary agency in the field of welfare, while subject to laws governing corporate operation, licensing and other restrictions imposed on medical, eleemosynary, or philanthropic agencies, is not directly subject to legislative and executive control of government bodies. It is, technically, outside the realm of civil service regulations. The voluntary agency is entirely free to select its own functions and area of activity. It can decide what services it chooses to perform, what clients to serve or to exclude, what funds to raise and how to do so; and it can choose its operating personnel as it likes. Ultimate control rests in the lay management group which determines programs and policies and in various ways shares responsibility with the technical personnel employed.

Whether tax-supported or maintained by voluntary financ-

---

[1] The historical sequence of development without which much of present-day practice would be difficult to assay will be sketched in later chapters.

ing, and under whatever sponsoring bodies they may be conducted, the principal areas of "welfare" commonly include:

Support, in general, individuals of families unable, for whatever reason, to function as economically independent units. This field used to be to a large extent, although always inadequately, in the hands of voluntary agencies. Now it is, still inadequately but to an incomparably greater extent, served by public bodies. Their clients, as we have seen, number many millions of families and individuals.

Support of those who by reason of age or disability are incapable of self-support and who are not adequately supported by family or relatives. To some extent this group includes veterans of recent years, for whom public responsibility has achieved a new and dignified standard.

Support, specifically, of widows and mothers and children who do not have a breadwinner to provide for them.

Provision of medical and hospital care for those unable to provide this care from their own resources. Simple as this sounds it has been one of the most difficult and controversial areas of service. It necessarily includes physicians' services in the home, in hospital, clinic, and sanitarium. It involves the highly debated issue of socialized medicine, public and private hospitals, a variety of group and individual insurance plans, and enormous amounts of capital investment. As yet it is difficult to estimate how much of this service, when not covered by the patient's resources, rests on voluntary and how much on tax-supported agencies.

Provision of institutionalized care from temporary stay to permanent custody—some for care and therapy for themselves, some as protection of the general public. Few, except as they come from the affluent economic classes, can be cared for at their own, or at their families', expense. Such people tend to be overwhelmingly a responsibility for tax resources.

Assistance to persons not overtly in economic need, but suffering from psychological disturbance or disability sufficiently intense to render them at least unhappy, and in some cases unable to carry on normal social functions. It is not clear yet how large a portion of this group is, or should be, the taxpayers' responsibility.

Fringe-benefit recipients as we have begun to identify them in pension schemes, veterans' programs, educational bodies, and trade unions.

Tax-supported systems addressed to economic security in general, including old age, unemployment, industrial accident and disease, and sickness in general.

Miscellaneous services given under sponsorships of borderline nature, and in overlapping areas, yet partaking often of a welfare character due to the economic factor involved. They would include leisure-time activities for young and aged, under religious, municipal, educational, and health organizations of bewildering variety and complexity. They would include special education and care for retarded, physically or emotionally handicapped, and deteriorating children and adults. This is a disconcerting area of service, for neither sponsorship nor the characteristics of the clients lend themselves as yet to clear-cut definition.

Correctional programs—another borderline area, only some parts of which have been recognized as being indisputably in the field of welfare services.

This is by no means a complete list, but it should serve to define the general terrain. The outstanding common characteristic of all these is an emphasis on material welfare. Less obvious in the list is the psychological component of welfare. We may take it for granted that difficulties in obtaining a livelihood are practically always accompanied or followed by psychological malaise, while the more severe psychological traumata, whether based on economic difficulties or other causes, soon tend to become economic problems as well. And when the irritant factor of status rejection is added, psychic health may suffer as much as economic welfare.

This procession of services, while enormously influenced by shift of the center of operational gravity from voluntary to public agencies, has also been influenced to no small degree by the shift, in a confused pattern, from concern with material welfare to interest in the psychological welfare of the prospective client. This latter shift was further complicated by two distinct but related factors: the type of interest that tended to preoccupy personnel in voluntary agencies, and the emergence of interest among both agency and personnel in what became known as the "techniques" of social work.

⚲ TECHNIQUES OF SOCIAL WELFARE

Unlike some other fields in science and practice, the field of social welfare has experienced a peculiar and disconcerting trend of orientation in recent decades, characterized by emphasis on techniques more than on purpose. This excessive orientation would seem to be unique in the cultural and sociopolitical field. Yet it has been so obvious and inescapable that it must be evaluated in relation to purposes as well as to instrumentalities.

The subject as a whole has been under intensive discussion during the last three or four decades and is not yet resolved. It is becoming perhaps more clearly a controversy rather than merely discussion. It relates to the entire field of the so-called techniques of social work. These will be presented in the ensuing chapters as specialties in the operation of services. But the fundamental differences relating to general orientation apply to all the techniques and are particularly important to the field of training and to the schools for training the operational personnel. The best way, perhaps, despite the apparent personal coloring of the statement, may be to reproduce part of a correspondence between the writer and one of the outstanding representatives and exponents of social casework during the past century in this country. A portion of that correspondence follows:[2]

If there were no substantial differences among the seasoned members of the profession, these pages would not have to be written. One would merely set down within the hierarchy of authoritative status, or within the categories of expertness in fields of specialization, those things that the occasion demands and in such language as one's literary idiosyncrasies prompted. There are, however, far-reaching differences among us who have labored within the past four decades of this maturing profession: differ-

[2] Letter addressed by the writer to Gordon Hamilton, Professor of Social Work in the Columbia University School of Social Work, in the summer of 1953.

ences in the interpretation of the meaning of our history, differences in social values and ethical concepts, differences in the meaning attributed to concepts of general currency in the profession, differences in those interests and groups that we regard as closest to ourselves, and, perhaps most important, differences in what we hope for, look forward to, and are willing to labor and fight for. With respect to some of these matters, you and I are in agreement, with respect to some we differ sharply, and there are subjects within our scope of professional interests where a deceptive use of common terms makes clarity and understanding difficult.

A good place to begin is a remark you made to me as we reviewed our little spat at the Council meeting apropos the proposal for a "day to discuss publicly sponsored social services." You said approximately this: "It is true that I have been more interested in process . . ." I wondered whether at that moment you appreciated the import of this simple animadversion. For you are, as we need not argue, one of the very few leaders of the profession. I would find it hard to line up a dozen that are fit to share the dais with you. If I could line them up, I think you would be speaking for most (though not all) of them. But if one followed down the line to the next stratum of dignitaries, the executives and supervisors, and further to the rank and file and to graduating students, your point of view would prove to be increasingly held. Process has it. She is queen, and her realms have been widening—but widening within a circumscribed area where casework and group work have dug into a relationship terrain, and where, I think, the need for service has become an evanescent concept. Here I want to interpose a remark that all that I am saying represents not an attempt to define *the truth,* but accents of truth. Everyone is right. The question is how widely significant is each one's right, and to what degree of exclusion of the others' *right* concepts.

Why should I be objecting to this devotion to, or emphasis on, process? After all, the most distinctive and important contributions of social work in the past half century *have* been in developing process, and in developing a conviction of the importance of process, and in the imperative demand that there be dependable vehicles of this process, namely a professionally self-conscious and competent body of practitioners. In my reading of the history of the past four decades this is what has happened:

1. Process has obscured purpose.
2. Leaders have chosen process as their chosen material for perfection and have caused a loss of interest in purpose on the part of the profession.
3. Process has gradually slid into specialties, of which psychoanalytic treatment (even more than concepts?) is the chief, and progressive education, civic activity, and a diluted form of sociological and anthropological "ideas in action" have been camp followers.
4. The social causes of disturbed behavior, the nature of social responsibility for either dealing with the causes or for supplying treatment, and the social engineering tasks for dealing with them have been lost sight of, and interest in them has evaporated.

These statements sound like old hash to you. But consider the history both of the purposes and of the processes, and look at them in the light of the history of Western civilization as a whole. Or else, if you prefer, chuck history and antecedents out and start without the chains of sequence or evolution. In the second alternative you can look at social work as if it were a matter of recent creation—3–4 decades. From the point of view of process as the over-all perspective, what would you have? Do this as if one were not arguing. Process-wise what would you include? Surely not the need for economic security, or for economic assistance, or for raising standards of living. Therefore, on the whole, one would have no truck with social insurance, little more concern with assistance, very little to do with group work agency activities, for these are either in the field of education or of recreation (a forgotten interest in social work), or the provision of social activities for the economically underprivileged, when they are not props for churches and ethnic groups.

Process-wise still, would you include rectifying or reducing personal maladjustment (casework, group therapy, psychotherapy)? Certainly *not*, unless the client came to you as an individual practitioner of the process, or as an agency employing such practitioners, for process as now envisioned does not include seeking out clients. They must be self-motivated. And from the point of view of the process, there would then be that of (*a*) the social caseworker who includes family and social aspects in diagnosis and therapy, (*b*) the clinical psychologist and psychiatrist, and (*c*) the group therapist.—And from the point of view of the existence of the agency it would have to be (*a*) profit-making, (*b*) non-profit or limited return, (*c*) research and educational, and in a way, all of it "functional" so far as the clients' initiative is con-cerned.—I need not develop this further, especially because you say that process is only part of the story, it does not exclude pur-pose. There is merely a preference for one or the other. But do the leaders of the profession have a right to choose one as against the other, or the lesser instead of the greater demand upon them?

Here my "prejudice" comes in: I think purpose is the greater of the obligations, process is the lesser: the lesser to be distinctive, yes, but only as it serves and enhances the greater of the purposes. *My* perspective in other words would give a high place to process as it advances and perfects the central purposes of social work. And here I would find the key concept to be that of *social re-sponsibility*, and the scope of service that of *need* and among the *needs* I would include *economic* self-advancement, normal rela-tion to one's fellows, physical and mental health, and self-expres-sion. What sort of scheme of social work would emerge from this way of thinking about it? Let me repeat what I regard as the key concepts, in the order of their logical sequence: need, social responsibility, then process. But these three concepts only make sense in determining the present scope or future ambition for social work, if seen in historical sequence; not because history in itself matters (it may be only antiquarianism) but because it actually has determined the present pattern and its various emphases, and because the present scope is *by definition* only the moving threshold of an incompletely grasped and unpredictable future pattern—one that we seek to promote or try to alter in the making.

Historically (and very roughly, of course), the forces that operated to formulate social work, at least in Western civilization, seem to have been three-fold, and all three very different:

1. the cohesive or cooperative one: here mutual aid, charity, kindness, sympathy, love of one's fellows, humanism and kindred motives belong. They get mixed up with ethics, religion, tribal consciousness, family unity etc.

2. the forces of control or regimentation: that is the ex-
ploitive and dominating one. Practically throughout the
history of Western civilization there has been the ruling
class, under various patterns and descriptions, and the
mass of people (up to 95 per cent or more of the population). The interests of the two classes despite cultural
unison were different—concentration and increase of
wealth and power on the one hand, and mere livelihood
on the other, although the latter again and again turned
into a struggle for sharing its goods or actually reversing
possession and exercise of wealth and power. The long
history of mores, laws, and administration in public, civil,
and criminal laws (including variations of poor laws)
reflects, if in a confused way, the attempts of the ruling
classes to keep the masses in their places, and to maintain
a large differential of power and resources. Most of the
motivations behind the feudal system (including the
church) and the English poor law belong in this category.

3. the forces of social planning for social efficiency. Here we
have institutions, philosophies, "constitutions," science
and, in this rough hurly-burly of review, "technique" and
therefore process. Within this category come the very
powerful forces represented by important writings—
Plato, Aquinas, Marx, Ward, Beveridge, then Octavia
Hill, Denison, the Fabians, Mary Richmond, and the
New Deal sequence.

By this time, as I knew would happen, you and I are both
getting tired of this. Moreover, a clear and logical exposition of
the more specific corollaries of the foregoing would certainly take
innumerable pages and endless patience. I, therefore, shift now to
a few dogmatic statements on some of the subjects mentioned in
your letter, and one or two additional items, to wit:

Democracy   Education
Research   Psychoanalysis
Social Action   Professionalism
Public Welfare

1. *Democracy.*   Again and again I have heard this term used by
group workers and caseworkers as if it were something
special contained within the framework of social work technique. Aside from the fact that a *quality of democratic feel-*

ing is absent from most of the personnel involved in social
work (I'll come back to this briefly, the democratic ideology
and the forces for the activation of that ideology have had
their origin and development almost wholly outside social
work, and in fact they have had a difficult task to enter into
social work at all. There is one exception to this, and that
exception comes to honor *process:* In the operation of casework (more than of group work) there is an assumption
and a practice of democracy comparable to that of medicine, where once a patient is a patient, his treatment is
predicated on a quasi-Christian democratic pattern as if
every human being were as worthy as any other, as if (in
the eyes of God) every soul is as good as another, especially
perhaps "the least of these," etc. Except for this fact of
democracy as a foundation of the *process* itself, there is little
of it in the function and status of Boards, in the regimen of
agencies, in the outlook of executives; it is difficult to maintain it in the worker-client relationship because it fundamentally contradicts that relationship. Teacher, supervisor
find it functionally difficult, and some individuals, by early
tradition, education, and temperament find the democratic
validity inaccessible. You, for example, have it in the head
but not in the bones; Katherine Tucker, though a socialist,
could not manage it; Antoinette Cannon, despite external
characteristics, was born with it as with a halo—and many
like me, essentially unworthy in composition, struggle madly
to attain it, and with sweat and blood constitute useful
components.

Now to come back to the main theme: *Democracy*—
Democratic concept is a *social phenomenon* (a fact of history) that provides the explicit or articulated rationale of a
struggle of the masses against domination by the ruling
classes, by expressing not the reversal of power concentration (revolution) but an equalization of power in society
comparable to the pattern represented by the distribution
of separate biological organisms in a structured or functioning social order. This phenomenon, and its verbalization,
begins roughly with the Protestant reform, achieves a high
peak with the writers leading up to the French revolution,
and through parliamentary reform, American revolution,

Chartism, Owenism, and Socialism constitute the basic social aspiration of our day. And because modern social work is "of our day," it falls into that pattern, a modest conformity, not a technical innovation.—In a logical sequence which would be too boring to develop, it leads *in my mind* inexorably to public service in social work, both in strict theory, and because pragmatically the resources are only accessible in that way. Inasmuch, moreover, as private philanthropy is structually inconsistent with this democratic concept, it, and the Board structure behind it, is doomed if democracy is to stay and grow.—And the quality of technique in private agencies has nothing to do with it.

2. *Research.* As your perspicacity has already discovered, I do not have, and never have had, much interest in research as such. It has always, to me, been subordinate to purpose. I suppose that, by analogy, to me research is "process" and *therefore* subordinate. What *has* interested me is the importance of logical, rigorous thinking (that itself being a process, subordinate to effective living, and living being the irrational and undebatable purpose of our existence; and living in this sense is not only nonrational, instinctual, but also philosophically beyond our capacity to understand or justify). Why the importance of rigorous, logical thinking within this framework of pragmatic philosophy? Because it is a corrective against undisciplined intuition, because it tests the conformity of our actions and their results to the purposes intended, it tests consistency between social values (which may be non-rational but of supreme importance) and the means employed for their achievement. It helps build more suitable processes, may lead to inventions, improvements, effectiveness in social engineering and in the processes of technical application. It is a precaution against complacency, self-delusion, ideological arteriosclerosis.

For these reasons I have never pressed for research as an area of importance in itself (cf. "culture" by Hurlbutt, public welfare by Dunn, casework and group work by the majority of the faculty, etc.). For greater detail, I suggest you look at my paper on "The Contribution of Research to Social Work," published by the AASW (Otto can get you a copy), possibly my paper before SWRG published in the NCSW procedures about 2 years ago, and the prospectus for a research center prepared for the School under my chairmanship (the original).

3. *Social Action.* Here again I have not been carrying banners in front of the White House. The reason why this subject is important may be that we have never looked at it *dispassionately*, never *seriously* weighed it for curriculum. With faint praise, and pious nods, we allowed its atrophied and desiccated concepts to rest in our curricular museum of antiquities. From the point of view of our concern as social workers, I see two divisions of social action having different priority values in our kit of professional obligations. One is social action concerned with such things as minimum wages, the Wagner Act, Housing Programs, McCarran Act, etc. The other is social action for ADC, for health insurance, for high standards of relief and other assistance benefits, for adequate foster home care, for institutions for disturbed children, etc. For the first group of purposes our functions seem to me to be those of an auxiliary, partnership, contributive, or cooperative kind. They are *"reform"* movements, the business of citizen, statesman, politician and of self-interest groups, like tenants, Negroes, ethnic groups with close immigrant ties, etc. Initiative does not come, or need to come, from within social work and actually has not come from our field (except in the early days when we were reformers as well as operatives). But for the second group of items the situation is very different. Here the activities or services are specifically "welfare" or social work practice; here we know better than anyone else the nature of the need, and *could* know if we cared to, the extent of it or of them. Here the initiative and the recognition of social responsibility belong to us. How can we achieve these purposes? By slow accretion? By a little larger budget to this or that agency? By persuasion and "cooperation"? By the educational method of casework, by curricular changes, by "leadership" of Boards, etc., *ad nauseam?* (You see I do feel strongly here.)

Within these fields of ascertainable purposes our prior obligations are very clear to me. And here we have signally failed and are consistently failing—indeed, in leadership, in

education, in curriculum. I see no extenuating circumstances. The techniques or processes for social action are different from those of "casework, group work, and community
organization" or for that matter of research. All right, so
we might have to add a partially developed minor process
to our process teaching. But to my mind the purposes would
justify it. And remember I am not talking of *social action*
in general; I am talking of social action for social work
purposes, where our obligations are primary and where we
have—historically—once acted, then talked, and now just
nod.

Now I think I'll quit. Unfinished and loose ends blowing in the
wind. Actually I am pessimistic about the future of the profession
as such. I see it fragmented, disoriented, its outlook pigmied, its
introspective capacities disturbed. Why should I specify! Life is
speeding by—whithersoever it is headed—and we are not the
only flotsam and jetsam on the future waves. Compared, anyway,
with the incompetence of the human race in running its affairs—
cf. Korea, Mau Mau, McCarthy—social work may be doing no
worse than others. Meanwhile, the standard of living is going up,
poverty is being pushed back even though not by us, colonialism
is on its way out. If we survive at all, we will be a better lot.
Among other things of lesser pessimism, behold I have ended
this——

Chapter X

Casework, the Major Technique:
Origin, Growth,
Loss of Direction

The explanation of the impulse to help one's fellow humans is something for biology and psychology to offer. By the time it becomes part of the culture and mores of the group we are pretty well outside the realms of biology and animal psychology. We are dealing with pressures of social organization and the patterns imposed by requirements of communal life. It is not important to debate whether the quality of mercy is inborn as an instinct or the flowering product of social life. We may take it for granted that somehow it existed and received social approbation. That approbation stamped it as a virtue and increased the probability of its practice. It did not find its way

147

into the Ten Commandments but received urgency both in the Five Books of Moses and in the New Testament. It reached a glorious flowering after Rabbi Hillel in the life of Saint Francis and drew, century after century, an army of lesser lights into the service of the Church. It became codified in the rules and regulations of the Jewish community throughout the Diaspora. All this, however, did not succeed in making the history of the poor law a pageant of brotherly love. True, there occurred abuses and exploitation of the community by the beneficiaries, to the point where the financial burden on parishes often became unsupportable; and the subjects of benevolence often vented their ire on the economically secure and socially comfortable. In any case, the history of relief of the destitute and of hostility to the poor is one of the darker phases of development of Western culture. There were, moreover, cross purposes between the indiscriminate alms of religious bodies and the interests of disgruntled property owners and local authorities. It is against this background that we must see the attempts at orderly management of charitable activities over several centuries of experimentation in England and on the Continent. For an exhaustive treatment of the problem as a whole, the reader is referred to the works of Sidney and Beatrice Webb[1] and to the numerous sources they examined. It is important to recall at this point only that there were many problems arising in the administration of poor laws, and in the uncoordinated charitable activities of church, community, and individual benevolent persons.

The first effort at efficient management of poor relief by individualization of the problem and systematic coordination of effort and resources was in Great Britain in the experiment conducted by Sir Thomas Chalmers, economist and clergyman in Scotland in the early years of the nineteenth century. The experiment was short-lived and is important in the development of casework chiefly because of its individualization of treatment, imaginative pursuit of resources, and automatic recruitment into service of the parish clergy. The accent was on efficiency and economy of administration,

----

[1] Especially their *History of the Poor Law and of Local Government in England.*

though combined with the belief that the character of the beneficiary also would be improved. Indirectly it led later to the charity organization movement and creation of the London Charity Organization Society where, once again, system and efficiency were the watchwords, for the field of charitable activity had become chaotic.

More of the sympathetic approach came in fact from quite a different source: the efforts of Edward Denison, Arnold Toynbee, and the settlement movement as a whole. They realized that they did not know enough about the lives, motives, troubles, and struggles of the poor; that they had to savor the nature of the environment and of the forces that depressed, and the sources of the vitality that inspired the poor. For two generations the settlement movement that emerged from this beginning has had a tremendous influence on many phases of social work, particularly on civic interest, leisure-time activities, and health services, and on attitudes of some social and philanthropic leaders. It appears to have had little effect on the emergence of casework[2] as the predominant social work activity in the United States. Perhaps the most direct line of succession for casework was from the charity organization movement in England, its emulation in this country, and the independently exercised influence of economists like Amos Warner and Simon Patten in the United States.

Whatever the demonstrable genealogy of its emergence, casework made its first formal appearance with the activities of Mary Richmond. The first major statement of its principles and underlying philosophy was the publication of her *Social Diagnosis*. This, with some later added material, became the bible of caseworkers. It retained that status for at least three decades, until it was gradually crowded aside, though not totally displaced, by literature inspired by appearance of the psychoanalytic school of thought. *Social Diagnosis* was a major intellectual creation of a profound and lucid mind, compounding wide reading with experience unremittingly testing and being tested. It was further reinforced by the discipline of teaching. Mary Richmond taught casework in the early years of what was

---

[2] The term itself probably came into use about the turn of the century and may have had its origin in the case method of teaching as practiced in law.

then the New York School of Philanthropy and later the New York School of Social Work.[3] Later, she became director of the Charity Organization Department of the Russell Sage Foundation and, in that capacity, the spiritual guide and hard-fisted promoter of casework in "family agencies" on the continent of North America. Up to the creation of the federal social security system, it should be recalled, voluntary agencies held sway over relief of the destitute, even to the point of active attack on public relief operations. The influence and pressure of this movement actually succeeded in having public relief systems discontinued in several communities. The principal overt reason for this pressure was alleged to be the presence of "corruption and politics" in public agencies.[4]

Over the years casework and agencies conducting it became the leading exponents and chief visible exemplars of social work and more particularly of economic relief services for destitute families. Casework personnel in voluntary agencies still regard themselves as being at the heart of the service, and until recently family agencies, privately supported, still have carried a venerable cloak of leadership, even though these agencies are now a negligible component in the field of service to destitute families. Whatever may have been the origin of the use of the term "casework," it is certain that the underlying principle was that of individualization of the situation of the client in somewhat the same way as the physician in his approach addresses himself to symptoms, causation, and then the pertinence of appropriate treatment of the individual patient. Always he regards the patient as an individual, and only remotely as a member of a group; and the reason for his concern with the patient is illness. The reason for the clients' appearance in the family service agency, in the vast majority of cases, was economic distress, a specific thing requir-

[3] Now the Columbia University School of Social Work. The author was a member of one of the early student groups taught by Miss Richmond.

[4] This may have been quite a disingenuous reason. The writer was engaged at one time by Miss Richmond's department to make a study of community measures in the unemployment situation in 1921–22. Among some fifteen communities to be included in the writer's list were Denver and Detroit, where the family relief operation was under public agencies and conducted by outstanding professional executives. Miss Richmond deleted these two cities from the list because of their "public" sponsorship.

ing, at the heart of treatment, economic assistance in some form or another.[5] The forms were many, centering, however, around material relief. The physician does not regard the patient (except in occasional types of situations) as culpable for his illness. The destitute person or family has, however, always been stigmatized as personally culpable, and as a member of a culpable or "unworthy" group.

The diagnostic approach as defined by Miss Richmond and her disciples did not explicitly subscribe to this moral rejection of the destitute. But neither did it militantly counteract it. It continued to emphasize, in effect, the fear that relief might pauperize, make dependent, or weaken the character of the client. The casework approach and the social outlook of its exponents, both individual and corporate, were as a result not significant factors in battling causes of poverty or the more immediately pertinent parsimonious and degrading standards of assistance. Public policy for economic assistance and social security, as promulgated in the thirties, failed to receive the enthusiastic support that might have been expected from persons and agencies whose place in the scene came because destitution was widespread and poverty rampant. The movement and public promotion of widows' pensions, for example, as a measure of social engineering was practically disregarded by the casework group. Family casework agencies were not among the promoters, and Mary Richmond and her followers actively opposed it. In the writer's recollection a chief reason given was that any widow and her children in need were being effectively cared for by voluntary agencies and none, to speak of, would qualify or require public widows' pensions. In the State of New York where Miss Richmond's activities centered, the law was passed and offices were set up to give service. There proved to be a host of clients qualifying and needing support. Casework—as persons and as agencies—had failed the needy.

In the late twenties and early thirties there was widespread discussion of proposals for unemployment insurance systems as a means of reducing both recurrent destitution and general poverty

[5] See publication of study conducted in the New York School of Social Work, *Basic Statistics in Social Work* by Philip Klein and Ruth Voris (Columbia University Press, 1933).

resulting from the periodic occurrence of extensive unemployment. Family casework agencies were, again, with a few exceptions, conspicuously missing among those actively favoring legislation to this end. Through the personal interest of the then chairman of the Charity Organization Society of New York[6] a grant was obtained from the Carnegie Foundation to finance a study of the effects that such legislation might have on the work of family casework agencies and on their clients. The task was assigned to one of the schools, and the work was conducted under the general supervision of the Director of the School,[7] who was recognized as both the leading authority on casework in the country and as a man of extraordinarily wide interests. He maintained constant touch with the project, carefully read the final report, and transmitted it to the publishers for immediate publication.

The study itself was based on about half the caseload of the family agency affiliated with the School. It analyzed in detail provisions of the bill pending in the state legislature, and ways in which the provisions would meet economic problems not necessarily related to unemployment, so that a considerable residuum would still remain requiring the agency's financial assistance. The ultimate disapproval of publication by the agency was based not on the data presented but on the then current casework philosophy. The objection was that the subtle, complicated, individual image of any case could not be broken down into its components in such a way that the unique and indivisible image of a case could be grouped with any component parts of the image of other cases in any quantified presentation. The material had been analyzed by the staff member into (1) problems presented, and (2) treatment suggested in relation to the problems. Whatever might conceivably have been the technical legitimacy of this reason for refusing the imprimatur, the far more important fact is that a serious and costly study bearing on causes and possible remedies in cases in the sample with respect to their economic problems as destitute families was denied publica-

---

[6] Walter S. Gifford.
[7] Porter R. Lee.

tion; and that the even greater significance that the study might have had for the over-all problem of poverty was denied to public knowledge.

And this brings us to the next important development in the story of casework technique in the United States, from the place it occupied as a national and carefully designed method for improving service to the destitute to its present almost total preoccupation with the psychology of the client. This preoccupation derives from the discipleship in the theoretical structure of psychoanalysis and in the resultant pattern of treatment applied to the client and his diverse difficulties. There is a general tendency to apply the term "psychiatric casework" to this present casework procedure. This seems, however, a misnomer and distorts slightly the actual story of the entry of psychiatry, as distinct from psychoanalytic procedure, into the welfare field.[8]

In 1908 a book was published by Clifford W. Beers[9] presenting the far-reaching conclusions that emerged from his life and subsequent release from an institution for the mentally ill. This book was the foundation of the mental hygiene movement in the United States, principally through the founding of the National Committee for Mental Hygiene. One of its most persuasive expositors was the quondam director of the committee, Dr. Thomas W. Salmon. He had a direct influence on introduction of psychiatric units in prisons and reformatories, and indirectly affected the thinking and attitude of many executives and workers in the general field of social work. There were others who had similar influence, including, for example, William Healy, author of *The Individual Delinquent*. It is anybody's guess how far the entry of these imaginative psychiatrists would have influenced the treatment of welfare clients had not psychoanalysis swept all before it: public opinion, clinical psychology, education, and casework. Whatever may have been the effect of this "new look" on the orientation of Western intellectual culture, it cer-

[8] On this point, see the next chapter, dealing with casework technique.

[9] *The Mind That Found Itself*, Longmans, Green and Company, New York, 1908.

tainly swept the practice and teaching of casework, and the policies of operational agencies, away from any previous concern they had had with destitution and poverty.

A detailed history of this "conversion" of casework is probably not important for our present purposes. What happened may roughly be summarized by saying that the trend was first toward "casework equals social work" while still largely within the field of economic assistance. Then casework became "psychiatric casework," though it was not quite so bluntly stated. This latter change became in a sense more legitimate as operations massively swerved away from relief to hospital social work, case treatment in institutions, the extensive Veterans' Administration activities, child guidance clinics, and so on. Curiously enough, however, less of it went to mental hospitals and similar services.[10] By the middle twenties the casework teaching staff in schools of social work comprised almost exclusively persons drawn from agencies committed to psychiatric orientation. Most of them had themselves undergone psychoanalytic therapy, and soon an increasing portion of the student body who were "majoring" in casework also underwent personal psychoanalysis in various degrees.

Parallel with this new orientation in classroom teaching came corresponding orientation in field practice assignments. Agencies in which field work practice was arranged for students were administered by devotees of the new trend, supported by psychiatrist consultants committed to the new trend, and by similarly oriented casework consultants and subexecutives in casework operation (supervisors). The accent became overwhelmingly psychological and psychology came to mean psychoanalytic theory. In supervisory practice and in reports by field work supervisors to school faculties there appeared increasingly factors of psychological judgment and decreasingly problems of economic maintenance, although family budgets continued to hold an important place for years in operations of casework in family agencies.

Recognizing that casework had become a self-contained concept and activity, and that it had to be practiced in specific agencies,

[10] See Chapter Four.

it is not surprising that some special groupings of caseworkers came into existence, which set up organizations of their own, at first separate from the general professional organization. The most impressive of these was that of the "psychiatric social workers," who by designation and by concentration in certain types of agencies emphasized their severance from the general economic field. Emergence of this particular organization was further accentuated by the heavy demand for caseworkers in veterans' hospitals, a large field after World War II, and in child guidance clinics, another very important field of operations and one that also tended to emphasize separation of casework from the function of economic assistance. Two other groups also emerged, less distinctive and less tendentious: school social workers attached to public school administrative units to help deal with children presenting problems in classroom or school activities; and hospital or medical social workers, whose free exercise of casework service was generally impeded by the fact that, like nurses, they were limited to a secondary status in relation to doctors. All this specialization and group consciousness served to emphasize the drifting away of casework from serving the impoverished, even before the critical period ushered in by the major relief and economic system that followed the 1929 crash.

Two other developments occurring within this phase of welfare are also of interest to the philosophic observer of the field, as well as to the culture of our day in general. One is the schism in psychoanalytic theory which had its repercussions in casework and influenced training school development to a perceptible degree. The other is the emergence of "private practice" of social work on a fee basis in a "free enterprise" pattern. So far as the schism in psychoanalytic schools of thought concerns us here, it relates only to the secession of the followers of Rankian analysis from that of Sigmund Freud. No comparable divisive influences for casework have come from the Jung, Adler, or other rebellions against the Freudian system of psychoanalytic thought, nor has modification of the system by Karen Horney or by the more scientific researches of Harry S. Sullivan or Franz Alexander influenced casework appreciably. So far as the schism has affected casework practice it was confined mostly to the influence of a small minority of training schools, their facilities and students. One thing only seems to be clear, namely that the factional division in schools of psychoanalytic thought still further removed casework concern from problems of the destitute or poor.

The rise of private practice is, in a sense, the last word in the abandonment by casework of the call for material assistance of the needy, whether conceived of as traditional charity, redistribution of wealth, prevention of destitution, or service to the destitute. In a sense private practice has grown out of the psychological orientation of casework. But other influences have also been at work. As casework took on more and more a professional outlook, the attention of the worker turned also to himself as much as to the client. This tendency was reinforced by the extensive practice of caseworkers themselves entering into analytic treatment. The constant contact with psychiatric consultants not only reinforced this habit or outlook, but developed an ever-growing sense of partnership with the psychiatrist or psychoanalyst. He was aware, moreover, that the psychiatrist was in the main a "free enterprise" practitioner, while the worker was only an employee, with limited salary, under administrative control and supervision—the supervisory function proving often very irksome to the worker.

To all this were added at least two new factors in the casework world. One was development of the fee system in casework agencies, this reemphasizing the technical specialty of the work, and at the same time pushing forward the urge for status recognition by drawing into the clientele more and more middle-class clients instead of those economically dependent. Another was the growing pattern of clinic structure for personality problems, in which psychiatrist, psychologist, and caseworker were a team, thus tending to elevate the caseworker to a status of sensed equality with the professionally recognized status of psychiatrist and psychologist. In fact, it became increasingly common practice for the self-employed psychiatrist, psychologist, or clinical psychologist to have an associated caseworker for more effective practice of total therapy. The general operational system of the therapist concentrated on the psychic (including, of course, the emotional and familial) components of the patient; the procedure was always to deal with the patient in the office privacy of the therapist. Therapy would be generally confined to interview with the patient alone and only rarely would it include members of his family or others enmeshed in the social experience of the patient. It was natural, then, especially after developmnt of the team operation pattern, to call in services of the caseworker, who was in possession of the essential psychological understanding but could also deal outside the therapist's office with other members of the social setting of the patient. It was not a long step from this to the independent operation of the therapeutic program by the caseworker either in cooperation with the therapist or on his own. And so they would enter the free enterprise system as individual practitioners, to earn their livelihood from fees set by themselves from clients who were in position to pay those fees, and who thus, by definition, were members of the middle class instead of applicants for material assistance for themselves or their families. How effective this casework or therapy is in cases where there is not a distinct, medically definable neurosis or psychosis is something not strictly pertinent to the present discussion.

We can now consider briefly some ways in which casework personnel and agencies carrying on casework service responded to events after the 1929 crash. It must be borne in mind that the rank and file of caseworkers in voluntary relief agencies were employees and did not make the policies of social work organizations that had been carrying the responsibility for dispensing relief. The policies of these agencies were determined by their boards of directors, largely influenced by the executives employed by them. The outlook of these, and their pattern for employing workers, had already been substantially deployed in the direction of psychological therapy rather than of economic assistance. When the massive loss of employment began to make demands on their resources beyond their normal rate, they were faced with the impossible task of raising funds incomparably beyond their past efforts or successes. They failed to admit that a major national call for economic assistance and for the prevention of destitution was a matter for the government to handle and for the taxpayers to finance. The particular events that took place then, and the way in which they affected development of the national welfare physiognomy, belong to another part of the story. Here we are concerned with what bearing they had on what had been the increasingly leading role played by casework in the evolution of a social welfare program in the United States.

One of the principal confusions for which neither caseworkers nor agencies in which they work may be blamed is the inherent semantic trap in the term itself. Casework was originally employed as a means of individualizing service to the client. The case was the particular individual or family. Individualization in service to the destitute or to the poor or to children in trouble would naturally have to take into account economic, familial, medical, vocational, and psychological factors. This would necessarily be the diagnostic phase. Treatment would correspondingly also be multilateral. But since casework had become overwhelmingly a psychological relationship therapy, by the time the massive call for personnel in the great depression came, neither training nor inclination nor available numbers required for the emergency task were suitable or adequate.[11] The day of the investigator had arrived, and caseworkers did not relish the title or the task. As a whole, then, they remained alien to public assistance.

There have been, indeed, a few remarkable instances of leading personalities within the casework field who sought to call attention to the neglected but important areas not touched by the psychoanalytic trend of the votaries of casework technique. One, Alice Overton, introduced the operative concept of aggressive casework when on the staff of the New York City Youth Board, a concept quite at variance with the relationship domain of thought. Two others, curiously enough, were earlier among the leading exponents of the psychoanalytic movement in the field: Charlotte Towle[12] of

[11] The more restrained and realistic development in Britain, where the "cult" aspect of casework and professionalization (described in later chapters here) had not taken command of the field, can be noted in at least the two following publicatios: *Some Impressions of Social Services in Great Britain* by an American Social Work Team, published by the United States Educational Commission in the United Kingdom, 1956, especially in Chapter I, by Arlien Johnson; also, *Social Case Work—Principles and Practice* by Noel Timms, published by Routledge and Kegan Paul, London, various portions. A more uncritical acceptance of casework *in toto* can be seen in the French-language text entitled *Social Case Work* by L. B. DeBray and J. Tuerlincky, both of Brussels, Belgium, published some time after 1953.

[12] Now deceased.

the Chicago University School of Social Work, and Bertha Reynolds, perhaps the most profound of the personnel in that field. The efforts of those three are worthy of places of honor in their area of service. And there may be others, also, not known to the writer. But in the field as a whole there appears to have been little response; they were eddies in the professional stream but did not succeed in changing the current in their time.

Chapter XI

✠

The Hierarchy of Techniques in Social Work

With schools of social work definitely established as the chief instrument for training practitioners in the field, it was inevitable that subject matter to be covered in the training program would be systematized in such a way as to give maximum preparation for employment and at the same time offer a recognizable academic curriculum with suitable specialization. Personnel needs in agencies in which prospective employees would be hired and academic or theoretical concepts underlying agency services had to find an integrated expression in the curriculum. By the second decade of this century a basic curriculum had been established with casework as the most clearly defined activity, and group work as a somewhat less clear-cut second; some time later, but still within the early formative period, community organization was added. These remained the categories within which the professional training cluster developed, while a variety of supporting and supplementary courses were introduced, both for conceptual enrichment and for sharpening the skills of students seeking agency employment. Techniques applicable to other fields in the social sciences and to activities contiguous with social work were also included but they were not regarded as peculiarly social work techniques. For example, research is a generic technique, applicable to all physical and social sciences and differing principally with respect to material handled and goals selected. It cannot be designated as peculiarly a social work technique.[1] The same is true of administration and social action. To what extent the three major technical categories claimed by social work education are equally valid and self-contained is something on which probably no general agreement would be reached either within the profession and schools or by persons outside the field.[2] None of these latter "techniques" any longer occupy quite the prominent place in social work school curricula that they did before social security and public assistance were ushered into the basic structure of national welfare services, and before psychoanalytic material was given its present dominant place in the social work schools. All three are practiced along with many other procedures and functions. All three are, moreover, practiced outside the field strictly designated as social welfare or social work. They are found in school systems, in psychiatric and mental health services, in outpatient clinics, in trade union activities, and in churches. Nevertheless, since they are so widely associated with the specific field of training for social welfare, it may be useful to indicate their identifying characteristics.

[1] For reasons that will be given later, research is, nevertheless, discussed in this chapter *as if it were* a technique in the sense presented here.

[2] Although the term "social work" is used in this and some other chapters of the book, there is, by now, no really defensible designation of the field by that term. It is habitually used alternately with "social welfare," but what was for some four decades carried on to a limited extent by voluntary agencies under that name is now incomparably more extensive as social welfare, or public welfare, or social security.

Casework is referred to, though with considerable misgivings, as the fundamental process of all public assistance, and wishfully sought after in clinics, hospital social services, child welfare services, probation and parole work, and theoretically imperative for marriage counseling, service to unmarried mothers, school pupil problems, and a host of other services. Elsewhere we have discussed the question of how far caseworkers and their technical commitment have served to alleviate destitution and poverty. Here the attempt is to identify the principal components of casework as a technique now taught and practiced.

The central concept is, implicitly, that of individualization, though one rarely finds it stated so directly. That, of course, is not in itself peculiar to casework. But it was the significant beginning, as contrasted with its predecessor almsgiving, charity, dole, a coin to the beggar, a meal at Christmas, some cast-off clothing, or later the almshouse. The concept of individualization was treated as a bridge between identifying causes of distress in a particular case, and help or treatment appropriate to alleviating it. The term "diagnosis"— borrowed from medicine—is useful in describing the nature of distress in relation to ascertainable or probable causes. Lack of adequate food, clothing, heat, shelter, are the crude and principal components of distress. Others occur in various combinations, and in ways that make the distinction between the nature of the distress and its causes less and less sharp. Illness, loss of employment, physical handicap, neglected children, drunkenness, quarreling in the family, abandonment by father or mother, incompatibility, and a host of other conditions are ascertainable, with cause and symptom often indistinguishable. "Diagnosis" as used in medicine fails here in that neither symptom nor cause lies within the confines of one person, but are spread over family, community conditions, varying mores and cultures, changes in the economy, in politics, in public opinion, and in resources. These are expressions of social life, and diagnosis becomes changed to social diagnosis, the first step in individualized social service. So far so good. But as to help or treatment, the analogy begins to be less clear. In medicine, roughly speaking, treatment is applied directly to the patient, and the means of treatment are practically within the control of the physician, omitting for the moment the question of financial resources. In treatment of the social welfare client, control over the apparatus of treatment becomes diffused. A variety of instrumentalities may have to be drawn upon. These may be distributed among a number of agencies or types of agencies, which would have to be involved without the kind of control or authority enjoyed by the physician. A complex pattern of cooperation, manipulation, persuasion, and a complex coordination of resources may be called for. Successful coordination requires a plan and personal ingenuity on the part of the caseworker. This ingenuity and the knowledge requisite for using it are usually referred to as casework skill.

At this point, a major distinction must be made between public assistance and social security operations on the one hand, and the older system of voluntary service agencies on the other. In public economic services social diagnosis becomes primarily establishment of eligibility; resources are within the agency itself, and therefore treatment becomes use of the agency's resources. The area in which ingenuity and specialized knowledge can be used is reduced, and the regulations of the agency assume major control.

In the determination of eligibility one must recognize the complicated interplay between state-controlled systems, subject to legislative decisions in each state, but supplemented in various degrees by the federal government and the federal insurance system independent of state legislation. The former deals mainly with categorical assistance systems.[3] The latter is principally Old Age and Survivors Insurance. Inasmuch, however, as the matter of providing economic assistance is paramount, rather than what is thought of as casework, and inasmuch as funds granted are not generally adequate for even a low standard of livelihood, funds for personnel are usually limited to what is requisite for determining eligibility and for checking on continuance of eligibility by periodic reviews and recalculations.

[3] OAA, AFDC, AG, APTD, GA. See Chapter Four, above.

There are differences of opinion in the field as to how far, in programs for economc assistance, governments should go beyond determination of eligibility and required budgets, and the obligation—moral if not legal—to provide economic assistance that does not degrade the client or hold him to a level of livelihood out of keeping with the general cultural standards of the land. Beyond that obligation are two choices of practice: to regiment the lives of the client on the old moralistic theory of worthiness or unworthiness, or to help the client overcome whatever difficulties may stand in the way of his taking an honorable and useful place in community life. On this second choice, in keeping with democratic and cultural standards of our land, casework in its best sense of individualized service is necessary and justified. How much, then, of casework technique is pertinent to this totally rehabilitative point of view for economic assistance or for other types of help or both? The literature on the subject is enormous: books, articles in professional journals, proceedings in conferences, minutes of "workshop" sessions, students' theses for master's or doctor's degrees. During the past two or three decades of professional development, however, less and less is said about external conditions and more and more about influencing the client; and influencing the client is progressively conceived of as a process within the psychoanalytic structure of ideas, processes, causations, and motivational elements. Curiously enough the advent of public assistance services, both categorical and general, has been a sort of happy liberation to family casework agencies, for it has relieved them of the burden of economic concern with the client and provided further justification for centering their attention on the intrapsychic components of the client's distress. Casework has, in fact, flourished in this sense in voluntary family agencies, child welfare, marriage counseling, specialized psychiatric agencies, and latterly in private practice.

Perhaps it may clarify this generalization to list, if somewhat roughly, certain components of casework theory and practice as usually present in professional discussions. The client's situation is regarded as involving:

1. unfavorable general conditions, social and economic, which are beyond his powers to control or change;

2. specific external situations that cause distress: lack of material goods, adequate housing, health care and so on;
3. inadequate personal competence to meet the stresses suffered, to take command for reshaping these external limitations, or to effect personal changes in attitude so as to "do battle" with conditions as they are.

Of these, the first is obviously not within the individual caseworker's power to achieve or to affect. It is for the agency, insofar as its policies include that type of interest, for civic bodies, for government, and for individual citizens among whom the caseworker can be a citizen among citizens. Certainly there is no professional technique involved here. The second type of situation affecting the client has become the technique of environmental manipulation, at which caseworkers had become quite expert, utilizing all sorts of resources and procedures, with ingenuity growing out of practice, and effectiveness increasing with experience. Today the third item is overwhelmingly the major technical hallmark of the caseworker. To this end he (or, far more frequently, she) has developed the technique of relationship therapy. This is a set of procedures of infinite variety, comprising almost entirely psychological concepts built upon psychoanalytic foundations. It is par excellence the casework technique as professed and taught today.

In view of the frequent reference in these pages to relationship therapy, since the meaning of this term may not be familiar to the general reader, it may be well to indicate what is intended to be conveyed by that phrase and how it came about. In the course of the transition from the Mary Richmond concept of casework to its present form, an interesting intermediate stage emerged from the University of Pennsylvania School of Social Work, locus of the Rankian School of casework teaching,[4] designated at the time as nondirective approach. In essence, it represented an assumption that any change in the client's situation would not result from service or guidance by the caseworker; rather it would result from producing in the client a psychological understanding and consequent motivation that would

---

[4] Usually referred to as the "functional school," as interpreted in *A Functional Approach to Family Case Work* by Virginia Robinson and Jessi Taft (University of Pennsylvania Press. 1944).

lead to appropriate steps by the client toward resolution or adjustment of her problem. The attainment of this motivation would arise from the affect relationship achieved between client and worker, and it was the task of the caseworker to foster such a relationship. The premises on which this conception is based include in the first place the definition of the client's problem as having both external and intrapsychic components.[5] Of the external problems that of economic distress had been, as we have seen, progressively excluded as a concern of casework; there remained external problems such as vocation, employment, physical or mental handicaps, relations with spouse, children, and others. These would then eventually be dealt with by the client himself. The psychological apparatus for bringing about the ability of the client to achieve solution of these problem components is the establishment of such reciprocal empathy and acceptance between worker and client that the joint feeling tone with respect to problems would result in appropriate steps on the part of the client to achieve adjustment, improvement, or rehabilitation: motivation gradually emerging from the relationship. The process of achieving such a reciprocal relationship was derived chiefly from psychoanalytic theory, with the interview as the specific instrument. A fundamental understanding of psychoanalytic theory by the worker is implicit, and a *sine qua non* of the procedure. On that basis, talking it out with friend, pastor, or other professional personnel would not fill the bill.

There are, indeed, subsidiary administrative requirements. Since the instrument of relationship therapy is the interview, there are questions of the content, sequence, duration, frequency, management, recording, summarization, supervision, and, almost universally, consultation and guidance by the psychoanalytical participating staff. Defining the borderline between psychological insight of caseworker and of psychoanalyst has, on the whole, been avoided. There are further technical problems arising out of the specific type of agency in which the caseworker functions. For example, there are modifications imposed by an institution for delinquent children, a

5 Compare the title of a recent book by Dr. Florence Hollis, *Casework, A Psychosocial Therapy.*

psychiatric clinic, a court, a probation service, a public school system, a foster home service, adoption and other services. But these are not problems of casework techniques as such; they are the problems of the setting and functions of the agency.

The safest way to discuss the technique of casework in a general descriptive enterprise like this is to say that it exists, and that the reader will find ample material in the literature to satisfy his interests. No part of the field of social work has produced a comparable plethora of published material in books, periodicals, and conference reports. No part of the training program of social work schools has comparable number of courses or as many course units, syllabi, or credit points. In addition, a very large number of case records used by many teachers of casework might be regarded as part—though unpublished—of the technique materials of the field.

About 1930, in the early days of the new casework approach, a new and remarkable effort was made to sort out by both inductive and deductive methods the nature and procedures of casework under the leadership and guidance of Porter R. Lee, Director of the New York School of Social Work, and with participation of practically the entire faculty of the school. This effort resulted in the publication in 1933 of *Social Case Work: An Outline for Teaching,* containing a series of some five detailed, annotated case histories, and syllabi. It was intended as a major interpretation and guide.[6] Shortly after its publication, however, it ceased to be regarded by those in the casework field as being either an interpretation or a guide. Miss Richmond's original contribution, previously the bible of casework, continued to serve as a courtesy item, but with little actual use being made of it. Casework had become relationship therapy within the psychoanalytic field of conceptual structure. There had to be retained, naturally, some recognition of nonpsychic factors, and there was also an attempt to establish rapport with sociological thinking. The underlying commitment, as a whole, often stated in casework teaching may be identified in condensed form as stated by two of the recognized representatives in the field,

[6] Published for the School by the Columbia University Press, edited by M. Antoinette Cannon and Philip Klein of the faculty.

published in the *Social Work Year Book* of 1960.[7] Mrs. Perlman writes:

> Stimulated by the so-called shell-shock cases of World War I, prepared by earlier clinical studies in delinquency and mental retardation, and impatient to find answers to the many problems of human behavior which perplexed them, social caseworkers in the 1920's grasped eagerly at the new knowledge which psychiatry was offering. There ensued a period of immersion in Freudian psychology, chiefly in the search for understanding of the motivating and irrational forces in man, which had thus far eluded the caseworker's understanding and hampered his effectiveness in dealing with troubled people. While this swing from study of the outer to the inner forces produced some distortions in professional perception and activity, the gradual incorporation of dynamic psychology added a new dimension to casework's body of knowledge about human development and behavior. . . . From this period on most of casework's psychological understanding was psychoanalytically oriented, chiefly Freudian, with a small sector shaping its theory and practice by the contributions of Rank. Secondary changes and mutations of behavioral theory and its implications for practice have continued to occur reflecting changes and developments in psychoanalytic theory. . . .

Since that article was limited in space, the term "practice" is used as if its meaning were self-evident, which, of course, is far from reality. Nor is it very helpful to add to it Mrs. Perlman's basic definition of casework, namely that

> The particular purpose of casework is to help people who are suffering some impairment or breakdown in their adequate social functioning and to restore, reinforce, or enhance the performance of their daily life . . .

[7] One excerpt from the article on "Social Casework" by Helen Harris Perlman of the Chicago University School of Social Work; the sequence of the items in the quotations is somewhat altered to the needs of this exposition. The other excerpt is by Lucille N. Austin, of the Columbia University School of Social Work, from the same publication.

For reasons attributable in part to the difficult, and at times abstruse, quality of psychoanalytic concepts, and in part to a bureaucratic structure that had grown up in casework agencies within which field practice of students is conducted, supervision had come to assume a somewhat self-important status in casework technique. Moreover, the practice was increasingly adopted of embracing the case supervisors so operating as quasi-faculty members in schools of social work. It is in this light that a separate article in the *Social Work Year Book* appears, dealing with supervision, rather than including it in the general casework article. It reads, in part, as follows:

> Social work teaching has . . . been predominantly interested in making adaptation from psychoanalytic personality theory. Psychoanalytic theory furnished no clear statement of a learning theory. It did supply a theory of the nature of learning problems having to do with anxiety and its role in inhibiting learning. Unresolved libidinal and aggressive conflicts were demonstrated to be the cause of blocking and damaged ego capacity. These problems were seen to interfere with the mastery of learning tasks and the use of learning opportunities. Transference problems also were identified in the problematical relationships between teacher and pupil. Quite naturally this theory was put into use in the delineation of learning problems, and in the development of individualized teaching method with students and staff in social work.

Unavoidably, certain administrative concepts have gained entry into the casework service. A case became a case only when "opened," and ceased to be one when "closed." Statistical reports have therefore covered the number of cases opened or closed during the month or year. The workload of the individual caseworker depended automatically on the number opened and closed, and left an "average." Since the tool of service was the interview, the number of interviews per client took on an administrative as well as a qualitative aspect, as did consultation with supervisor or psychiatrist. The opening of a case became a formal step, involving one, or at times more than one, interview. It had to determine whether the case was suitable to the particular agency's policy and program, and not necessarily whether an agency more suitable existed in the community or was available. The interviewer would determine whether the client was able, or would become able, to benefit from the agency's services, whether he or she would cooperate or resist. By definition, therefore, these aspects of casework are not applicable to public assistance programs, where eligibility is prescribed and where economic assistance in accordance with regulations is the paramount objective. At most, therefore, in the vast majority of public assistance cases environmental manipulation, in addition to economic assistance, is all that can be offered rather than relationship therapy. While this distinction is not absolute, it applies in the mass, so that casework is limited to other types of service than economic assistance, public or voluntary.[8] Additional administrative procedures involving little by way of conceptual material are, of course, unavoidable in all individualized service, whether economic assistance or casework. Cases may be "reopened," "referred" to other agencies, transferred to other departments or workers, accepted on emergency levels, or—except in the public assistance categories—placed on the waiting list. The waiting lists are as yet the great unresolved problem of many services: welfare, health, custodial, hospital, and a variety of special institutions.

The other great unresolved question in casework is that of ascertaining results. Merely closing a case is no test and is not claimed in casework technique as a test in itself. Presumably, when a problem is presented and a solution is achieved, that fact may be subject to numerical reporting. Relatively few cases respond to such a simple test. Economic self-maintenance, permanent or temporary, might be accounted for in numbers, but the achievement of that result has become irrelevant to casework practice as such, and even in public assistance the concept is rarely applied: one merely discontinues payment when periodic recheck shows a closing of the gap between means-test amount and income from all sources, the means test be-

[8] There are, of course, supervisory and other administrative measures in public assistance programs that may be no less ponderous than those of casework.

ing not a test of adequate self-maintenance but of conformity with regulations. Occasionaly, as in adoption or similar objectively identifiable instances, specific results can be stated and counted without being distorted by subjective opinion. One might suggest, of course, routine research-like procedures that would take account of presenting symptoms, improvements measured both qualitatively and in terms of time elapsed, and number of interviews consumed. Some analysis of research of this type carried on in the field thus far will be attempted in later pages;[9] but even if such analysis were technically feasible, the required manpower and lack of intellectual commitment by the casework world would cancel it.

It all comes down, therefore, to competence on the part of the caseworker to produce relationship results, to judge them without the inescapable bias of the producer with respect to his product, and to prove the interchangeability of practitioners of presumed equal competence to produce the same or similar results in a given case. This latter way again may, by definition, be impossible, for a relationship between a client and one worker cannot easily be duplicated with another worker in a scientific weight-lifting sort of enterprise. How, then, is the caseworker to assure competence within the limits so defined and without elaborate and costly research?

As yet, an adequate test, by results, of the caseworker's practice has not been found or introduced in the technical armory of this operation.

In two other social work techniques, the painful problem of testing or proving results has not quite had to be faced. On the other hand, neither group work nor community organization have aspired to the achievement of so definite a technical status as casework, nor have they hitched their wagons to quite so shining a star as psychoanalytic psychology. The history of both these techniques is shorter than that of casework. Moreover, despite the fact that both have retained a foothold in the curricular structure of schools of social work, their quantitative importance in the job market is so much smaller than that of casework (even without counting public assistance) that pressure for development of techniques and the search

[9] Under Research as a Social Work Technique, later in this chapter.

for teaching personnel and for experimental tasks has been of a lesser order. In fact, there has been some tendency to merge the two techniques and to use personnel interchangeably, at least in administrative and teaching area.

✑ GROUP WORK AS A SOCIAL WORK TECHNIQUE

Perhaps the best way to describe this technique—despite the earnest efforts of its practitioners to give it a coordinate status with casework—is to say that actually it does not exist. Its activities do indeed exist and have probably existed as part of the social welfare field longer than casework itself. They were part and parcel of the movement initiated in England by Toynbee Hall and continued in a flourishing sequence in settlement houses in the United States.[10] True, settlement houses have offered other services also, and functioned in civic reform, but they have consistently carried on the central group activities. These have been chiefly of a recreational nature, of the utmost importance in slum areas, and for all ages and in all forms. They have had their full justification in providing play opportunities as part of education and in promoting play as an educational component. They have provided much-needed leisure-time activities for young and old; they have opened to disadvantaged persons avenues for music, drama, arts, and almost all of it in groups. But group work technique has had small part, if any, in the promotion of these activities. There has been some formulation of concepts but not enough to be dignified by being called technique rather than activity.

The activities have almost invariably been programs of agencies, their goals and content serving agency purposes. The YMCA type of program, the Boy Scout type, the settlement type, variegated activities developed as adjuncts to churches, synagogues—all these served their clientele in groups. The ultimate purposes of sponsors may have revolved around religion, minority interests, labor union activity, health, or education, but the principal activity has been recreation. Inevitably the conduct of such activities required considerable organization, management, and administration. Age

[10] See Chapter Seven, above, on Services to Neighborhoods.

grouping, for example, is very important in all recreational programs. Where nationality, race, religion, or other determinant of cohesion is emphasized, administrative procedures of the agency have to be formalized accordingly. There have been, also, some intensive and elaborate efforts to develop competent group leadership and group activity record-keeping. For some reason, perhaps by way of competition with the technical self-assurance of the casework field, personnel in group work has worked hard to establish a "professional" content for social group work as a process. It would seem that they would have fared better and would not have lost any prestige had they frankly addressed themselves to activity programs. There has been enough diversity in programs and in sponsorship to satisfy those really interested in the work, especially in view of the high proportion of administrative as compared with rank-and-file positions, and corresponding opportunities for financial advancement. There are enough points of contiguity with political, educational, sociological, and artistic disciplines to satisfy multilateral interests, and a wide field of supplementary work in summer camps, day camps, and other leisure-time operations. The training facilities and status offered by social work training schools remained accessible. But the appeal of professionalism has apparently outweighed satisfactions of self-expression, and the semantic seduction of the social sciences has added to the problem.

From its conceptual exponents, it is exceedingly difficult to gain an understanding of social group work as a technical pursuit. In the same *Social Work Year Book* cited earlier concerning social casework, the following exposition of group work appears:

Social group work is one of the basic methods employed in the professional practice of social work. It shares the philosophy, values and goals, bodies of knowledge and professional skills which are germane to the profession of social work. As is true for all social workers, the group worker is committed to practice which meets human needs, recognizes the worth of the individual, and accepts responsibility for helping to advance the well-being of the individual and his society. . . . It is in and through the group that members or clients are helped by the social group

worker toward increased, improved, or changed social functioning . . .

There is more of the same, before the writer comes to the names of
some of the agencies[11] in which the group work is carried on, speci-
fying

> the Scouts, the Y's, Boys Clubs, Campfire Girls, Catholic, Protes-
> tant and Jewish organizations, or the Salvation Army; in 4-H
> Clubs, public housing projects, correctional institutions, and resi-
> dent and day centers for children, adolescents, or the aging . . .

It is, in fact, not the fault of the group work personnel—at
best a small minority of social work manpower[12]—that one can gain
little guidance as to the technique; nor is there literature on this part
of the field comparable in a specialized sense to that of casework.
Here, it would seem, is a valuable service in the field of social welfare marked by the compulsive drive for professional recognition.
And schools of social work do not appear to have been willing to
give up the traditional trinity of its techniques by helping teachers
and practitioners to face the real values they serve, and the reasonable limitations that they must accept.

COMMUNITY ORGANIZATION AS A SOCIAL WORK TECHNIQUE

It may be inaccurate to say that the training schools or the
field as a whole refer to "community organization" as a technique
quite in the sense that casework uses the term. Rather, the exponents
of community organization have always presented their procedures
and purposes as programs. Calling for citizen participation and
leadership, for communal planning of social services, for financing
and budgeting them, and for maximizing the coordination and cooperation of the service agencies, these have been a larger part of
their programs. As might be expected, both coordination and cooperation would constantly run into rocks and shoals of various

---

[11] See also Chapter Seven on neighborhood centers and settlements,
above.

[12] See the Manpower Study quoted in later pages.

vested interests of both individuals and agencies. Consider it techniques or programs, or community life, some facts about the history of this part of social work and its relation to purposes of social engineering are imperative for its understanding and evaluation. And it should be borne in mind that throughout the history of what has usually been called community organization, the area of operations has been principally in the voluntary field, and in a preponderant measure it was so handled in the curricula of schools of social work.

Much has been said and written about the planning phase of community organization in social work, and much has actually been done by the agencies carrying that responsibility by way of fact-finding and research. But this has been, in the main, secondary to their financial and coordinating functions, and has, on the whole, been a lateral development rather than part of direct purpose. It should be recognized, at the same time, that, as compared with service agencies and possibly compared with training schools themselves, community organization agencies may have produced, with respect to fact-finding, more and better material.[13] The major contributions of this group of agencies were, in any case, made during the period when, in the United States, public welfare was practically unborn and hardly seriously conceived. Their importance has been primarily in the fields of coordination and financing of voluntary agency programs. It therefore followed naturally that they have been called, as a group, either Welfare Councils or Community Chests, though neither designation accurately describes them.[14]

The first such attempt for cooperative financing appears to have been made in Liverpool, England. Next came the one in Denver, Colorado, in 1887. There followed others, some twenty years after Denver. By the time World War I had gotten under way there may have been as many as twenty Community Chests. The largest ones came into existence, as a matter of fact, as War Chests to meet the pressure for funds resulting from needs associated with war efforts. It had become increasingly clear that, for a variety of reasons, fund-raising by individual voluntary agencies was expensive and pre-

[13] See material on research and surveys, below.

[14] In a sociological sense, undoubtedly "community organization" would cover a very different group of concepts.

carious. The pooling of efforts, and the chances of drawing all the major social and financial leaders of the community into the Chest or United Fund, offered a higher probability of supporting member agencies. Inevitably this also increased the imperative need to set up cooperative, coordinative, and consultative machinery, and so Welfare Councils by that or similar names came into existence. This phase of social work development has a place in the historical perspective of social welfare, as does its evaluation in the modern task of social engineering. If, as is reported in the *Social Work Year Book* in 1960, there were over 1,200 United Funds in the United States about that time, and perhaps 700 "welfare" or "health and welfare councils," they must be included in the panorama of social welfare programs. It is, however, as programs and welfare philosophy that they must be seen, rather than as techniques, which is the place given them in school curricula and personnel analysis.

If techniques are at all appropriate to this area of social work they would seem to fall into three categories: financing and budgeting, coordination, and communal planning. Whatever technical procedures could be subsumed under these categories were, had been, and still are being employed by individual voluntary agencies as well—in fact, sometimes in competition with "community organization" agencies. They are practiced outside the technical field of social welfare also, by chambers of commerce, political party units, fraternal organizations, churches, the March of Dimes and kindred nation-wide health movements, Olympic sports activities, and countless other movements.

Financing by the community chests, contrary to normal business practice, is completely distinct from budgeting. It is a sales technique, with all the appropriate psychological gadgets included. Quoting again the *Social Work Year Book* of 1960, we see a straightforward statement:[15]

The planning and conduct of federated fund-raising campaigns has been developed into an art, practice of which is being con-

[15] It may be noted that the passage which follows would apply equally to nonlocal agency fund-raising, as, for example, the various national drives for health movements such as cancer, heart, muscular dystrophy, etc.

stantly refined and improved. Increasing use is being made of scientific methods of evaluation, study and analysis. Attention is given to human motivations, economic and social structure and process, personal satisfactions and relationships, nature and theories of leadership and the like. Numerous campaign devices have been introduced and improved or adapted. . . . Basic to campaign organizations and procedures are the ideas that: (a) every individual and corporation with income or resources is a potential contributor to the community united campaign; (b) amount of each contribution should be in proportion to resources and relative magnitude of economic or social activity of the con-tributor; (c) a vigorous and individualized solicitation of each prospective contributor is necessary to produce adequate giving; (d) programs of interpretation and information are necessary to the maintenance of interest and confidence of contributors; and (e) the solicitation of contributions most appropriately is accom-plished by volunteers who ask the gifts of their neighbors and occupational associates.

Only the large United Funds can actually afford a year-round staff for this costly process. Naturally, therefore, commercial firms are often employed to carry on the painstaking, and not service-oriented, task of fund-raising. This procedure is employed by many other philanthropic, educational, religious, and political organizations, and can therefore be dismissed as a particular social work technique. More pertinent is the process of distribution of funds to constituent agencies. However, here, also, service-oriented techniques have little ultimate weight. It is the service, agencies that have to prepare budg-ets, and these must be determined by the cost of service, direct and indirect. Logically, the service agency would estimate cost of a unit of service (as an average) and multiply it by the number of units to be served. But units of cost are different in the different services: economic assistance, foster care, personality adjustment, recreation, clinic or hospital, etc. More important still, the number of units to be served should be equivalent to the extent of need. But how is that to be determined, by whom, by what means? It is not part of fund-raising; it is not part of fund-distribution. And the problem there-fore is no different, if different at all, from the tasks facing legislatures, federal, state, and local. For they also must choose between more or less to schools, health, police, roads, parks, and other sectors of public life and public service. Nor is there a very great difference in the nature of power pressures in central financing and budgeting of voluntary service agencies and those in political life. The techniques are universal.

Logically it would seem that this is where the Welfare Council function would come in. In the councils we find agencies and individuals, informed and interested in services to be given to those in need. Inasmuch as school systems, courts, public health authorities, and other distinct government agencies have separate, if related, spheres of operation of their own, the central group of agencies included in welfare councils would be those with the more strictly social service programs. Before the thirties it was not very difficult to define these, and councils did, therefore, spring up with the membership more or less uniformly determined. Within councils, therefore, community organization might well have been thought of as appropriate and possible. To some extent this has, in fact, been the case. How far, and how successfully, depended on the extent to which certain major problems could be handled with professional independence. These major problems have included relation to central financing structure; relation, more and more significantly, with public welfare authorities; rivalry for funds among agencies; rivalry among agencies and their spokesman for power and influence, and relation to fact-finding for service and financing.

The relation of welfare councils to local fund-raising structures is one of the curious phenomena of the field for which no simple logical explanation can be given. Central financing came first. Coordination and planning seemed a natural next step, in order to determine, chiefly, the relative budgetary claims of agencies to resultant dollars. But increasingly the power of the chests as against coordinating councils grew, because the power of allocation resided in them, even though it was the agencies that knew needs, had inaugurated services, had paid in sweat and blood for funds they needed. It might have been logical for them to determine allocation through conference, arbitration, committee assignments. But the inevitable rivalry for funds and status defeated this logic, and the dispenser of funds came to be the distributor as well as the raiser of funds. Strength flowed to the chests and away from the councils. This tendency became more pronounced as councils themselves drew their operating funds more and more from the chests and less and less from direct membership contributions by agencies. Even this development was not a clear tendency, for other interferences also came into being. In one large city, for example (and this was not a unique occurrence), the large, old, well-established agencies were reluctant to yield leadership to this new apparatus and its new personnel. No overt break took place, but agency interest often lay athwart coordination and leadership needs. Another difficulty—also having no foundation in the needs of clients or in the desirability of greater coordination—has been due to the existence of sectarian groupings of agencies. These had diverse roots: sectarian group consciousness is one; religious interest is another; fund-raising machinery within the sectarian organization still another. No technique could apply to these difficulties any more than to life itself.

From the point of view of technique, community organization never did claim the acceptance that was given it in the academic system. The increasing and pivotal importance of public agencies had never been adequately incorporated in the total functioning of the council programs. Its use of fact-finding and research was probably far above that of casework agencies, and more community-oriented, but remained secondary, and consistently emphasized the agency rather than the client. Nevertheless, research is one of the areas in which its contribution was palpable and important. It has a place in the historical perspectives of social welfare as a whole.[16]

Community organization as a technique is clearly secondary in importance to community organization as program-making. Program-making is a very realistic part of normal community life, and it occurs in all the phases of social activity, from mutual help in farm operations or repelling locust plagues to music, dancing, pageantry, church functions, politics, and vendettas. It is because community organization takes place on the entire front of cultural life

---

[16] On many of the facets of this subject, the interested reader may wish to consult the "Social Study of Pittsburgh," by Philip Klein and associates, Columbia University Press, 1938.

that it also has made its appearance in the operations of charitable agencies. And as these operations expanded into an increasing network of welfare services, community organization tended to be thought of as welfare activity. For that reason also it became a highly developed area of program-making in the voluntary agency field. For decades this organizational activity built up an identifiable body of techniques and for that reason entered into the curricular structure of schools of social work. The fact that similar activities were to be found in other community interests, like chambers of commerce, American Legion, housing developments, mothers' clubs, and neighborhood theaters did not interfere with the gradual conscious community organization specifics in the welfare field. The complications of our day arise from the fact that the definition of what is "welfare" is changing perhaps more swiftly than the nature of "organization," and consequently "community organization" becomes a more conscious and more varied presence in the cultural life of the community.

There are, indeed, some older and more picturesque examples of this type of community action even though we rarely think of them as related to present-day events. Peasant revolts in the history of Europe, revolutions through the centuries and in our own day as well, and the Crusades, give a bit of historical perspective. A little closer to our time and place are the organizations of the unemployed in the early 1930's. These were effective and militant bodies and they emerged from the realities of mass destitution of those days, the destitution growing faster than the organized mechanism of economic assistance. With the effective organization of state and federal relief administrations, the imaginative and creative activities of the WPA under federal auspices, and the eventual economic recovery of the nation, the reason for the unemployment committees, and with it the committees, disappeared.

But life does not stand still. Within the past half-dozen years new occasions for what may in part at least be designated as community organization have come into being. Some of it may hark back to the march of war veterans to Washington to press their demands for action by Congress. More recent and more significant, particularly from the point of view of community life, and quantitatively far more important, have been the demonstrations for equal rights for Negroes and in general for civil rights. At the moment these community-based demonstrations have become part of our national life.[17] Perhaps different in detail, and based on larger foundations so far as the economic life of the nation is concerned, are the thousands of community-structured operations that have become part of the Organization for Economic Opportunity (OEO, or War on Poverty). As indicated elsewhere in these pages, the total operations within this national program and its related state and local coordinates are still in the formative stage. In any case, the extent and variety of the operations is far beyond the scope of practical presentation here. Perhaps if this book were written five years from now a totally different picture would emerge. For the present, while it may affect the curricular structure of the schools of social work, the character of the student body, and the technical concepts of community organization, this development must remain part of a perspective only.

⌇ RESEARCH AS A SOCIAL WORK TECHNIQUE

Research in the physical sciences justly holds its position of prominence. In chemistry, physics, astronomy, biology, or in the ancillary science of mathematics, there would have been no progress without research, important as imagination and intuition have been. Conversion of scientific research into practical utility has reinforced its importance and supported its claims. In the social sciences also, though with less justification, research has attained a place of honor. And here, too, its entry into the field of application has advanced its progress, as in economics, sociology, and anthropology, and later in social work. In this latter field it gained a place in the academic spectrum of major divisions, as a fourth category, joining those designated as casework, group work, and community organization.

Techniques and function of research in general, and specific research conducted in any given field, are often confused. "General

---

[17] The fact that the techniques are employed by reactionary bodies does not alter the nature of the phenomenon, any more than its resemblance to picketing in the trade union organizations' armory of weapons.

technique of research" is simply another way of designating the scientific method of investigation—and that is universal. Researches in any field are but the universal method applied to the specific materials of that field, and for purposes inherent in the goals of the field: so we have test tubes and telescopes for some, descriptive fact-gathering in others; all testing hypotheses, seeking generalizations, and, so far as suitable, applying quantitative methods and the laws of probability. The purpose of research in any field is to learn something not yet known, or to test presumed knowledge to make it certain rather than presumed. What to research, and why, are questions inherent in the nature of each particular field; and the motivation may be pure curiosity, or practical utility, or the urge to know more because that is in the nature of the human animal. The one great difference between research in the physical sciences and that in the social sciences is that in the latter it is difficult to be merely curious; there is almost always a purpose, and the purpose is almost always determined by what for lack of a better term has been called "values." And values are tricky things, for they cannot be proven or tested; they are arbitrary, deliberate, arising from "cultural" sources. The methods of research may, and even *must,* be scientific or else they are not research, while the purposes may be ethical or capricious, or even antisocial.

When research techniques are carried over to social work (or social welfare), therefore, a difficulty arises that is well-nigh insuperable, for the selection of value-determined facts or purposes tends to become an operation for proving or disproving previously identified "values." These in turn come dangerously near to defending vested interests, whether these be organizational, intellectual, or power-oriented. It is not appropriate in this place to review and to judge all research within the field of welfare, even if the writer could be quite certain of freedom from prejudice himself. Since research is still being thought of as a distinct technique in the welfare field, it may be useful to illustrate a few typical research tendencies or categories. Research commonly encountered in this field may be roughly classified as coming in the following areas:

1. Problem identification and measurement, mainly akin to sociological studies.

2. Quasi-diagnostic studies of community situations, problems, programs—usually designated as social surveys.
3. Quasi-diagnostic studies of single agencies or groups of agencies.
4. Studies of results of technical operations either with respect to community problems dealt with or with respect to clients served.
5. Studies of the validity of techniques and of their components.

As in all scientific research, generalizations to be arrived at must be supported both by validity and pertinence of the data and by the method of their organization; items to be quantified must be clearly definable and identifiable; findings must be unconditionally separated from recommendations or proposals. But since value judgments are inescapable in the social sciences (or, as some prefer to call them, the "behavioral sciences"), no eternal truths need be expected; the temptation to apply mathematical formulae of statistical probability and their conversion into established generalizations have to be religiously guarded against. The following examples of research in the welfare field do not in themselves justify the status of research as a fourth major technique in the field; they illustrate, however, identifiable types of materials pertinent to objectives for research in the field.

. 1. *Problem identification and measurement.* Examples of this type would be *West Side Studies* in New York City by Pauline Goldmark,[18] and the study of delinquency in Chicago by Shaw.[19] The first of these concerned itself with problems of poverty, poor housing, ethnic-cultural isolation, and apparent concentration of criminal activity. It could well have been a piece of research undertaken by a sociologist, as was the study of Middletown by Robert S. and Mrs. Helen Lynd,[20] or the one of a New England community by Warner and Lunt.[21] The major difference lay in the fact that in

[18] Published by the Russell Sage Foundation, 1914.
[19] Clifford R. Shaw and others, *Delinquency Areas in Chicago* (Chicago University Press, 1929).
[20] *Middletown—A study of contemporary American culture* (Harcourt, 1929).
[21] *The Status System of a Modern Community* by Lloyd Warner and P. S. Lunt (Yale University Press, 1942).

West Side Studies action programs were sought because of welfare sponsorship or community discomfort with the behavior symptoms. The West Side Studies were actually conducted by a Bureau of Research, at that time an integral part of the New York School of Philanthropy, under the administrative direction of Professor Samuel McCune Lindsay of Columbia University, who was Director of that School. This sponsorship was further emphasized by the interest of the Russell Sage Foundation, which largely financed the enterprise. The delinquency study by Clifford R. Shaw in Chicago, dealing with delinquency areas in that city, was associated with urban studies in Chicago University. Both these studies could well have been undertaken by purely sociological sponsors and could have been no different in the methods employed or the nature of the findings.

2. *Social Surveys,* though originating in what may be called sociological interests, of which Booth's *Survey of London* and other English enterprises are leading examples,[22] became in this country one of the most frequent and best-known undertakings, usually classed as research and often included in curricular discussions in schools of social work. In appraising this particular brand of scientific inquiry it is well to differentiate among three components: fact-finding, which is almost akin to investigation; diagnostic judgment, residing primarily in the experience of the staff; and research of the more strictly scientific type incorporated in the survey as an essential but partial component. These studies, more closely allied with welfare interest than with sociology, have usually been a first phase in planning specific action on particular matters in a particular locality. Rarely has it been possible to keep out of focus the concatenation of forces to be dealt with when action is called for. The importance, therefore, of practical experience of the survey staff in the given subject becomes paramount. For facts, as such, hardly exist in the applied field of social study, except as they are so construed in the diagnostic judgment of the surveyor. So the findings are construed as facts subsumed under generalizations previously established as applying to similar situations.

[22] See below, Chapter Fourteen.

The task becomes more difficult when findings, though intended to be scientific research, are combined after diagnosis, for the purpose of defining practicable action.[23] These surveys have been, in fact, almost universally instituted as a means for promoting action. The English studies mentioned were relatively free of any commitment to action, and so their research methods were more amenable to the rigor of scientific research. Large portions of the classic Pittsburgh survey[24] were also conducted on a scientific level, although the intention was clearly for social action. It was thought, however, that the scientifically impartial organization of collected data would prove persuasive enough to render subsequent action acceptable and inevitable. In this respect, however, the hopes of the survey staff were sadly shattered by the reaction of the power structure involved.

In another social survey in Pittsburgh and its surrounding industrial-rural county some thirty years later, the problem again presented itself of supplementing the diagnostically and experientially competent staff and its equally important advisory body with a strictly scientific analysis of the basic problems of livelihood (and poverty) in the area, a problem more clearly amenable to strict research, and less subject to diagnostic competence. Arrangements were therefore made with the independent Bureau of Business Research of the local university to undertake that part of the assignment. This was within the shadow of the great depression and after the first major federal-state relief measures had begun to operate. After nearly a year's work by a considerable statistical staff of the Bureau, one of the rare gems of that type of inquiry was produced. It was then to be drawn upon for the survey staff's final report.[25] Needless to say, this extensive and inclusive survey fared not much

[23] This troublesome fact has given rise to a pattern dubbed "action research," which tries to combine fact-finding with tested action based upon the facts, in a simulacrum of converting fluid, normal, social behavior into an experimental laboratory. The difficulties, both conceptual and practical, have not yet been frankly appraised by the proponents of this pattern.

[24] *The Pittsburgh Survey,* in six volumes, published by the Russell Sage Foundation in 1907.

[25] *Economic Backgrounds of the Relief Problem in Allegheny County* by J. P. Watson, Bureau of Business Research, University of Pittsburgh, 1937.

better than its predecessor at the hands of the same vested power interests of the community.

3. *Studies of single agencies or groups of agencies to discover effectiveness of administration.* These are the types of studies that are numerically perhaps the most frequent in the welfare agency field, and to which the technique of research is usually considered applicable. They are often conducted by national agencies, such as those concerned with community chests and councils, with family service or child welfare programs. They are also occasionally undertaken by arrangement with appropriate university departments or with free enterprise firms engaged in that field of work. It is in this type of study that the problem of true research becomes particularly crucial and where a research technique peculiar to welfare agencies may more appropriately be considered as existing. When a local agency is studied by the appropriate national agency there is always the possibility that impartial analysis is obscured by the vested interest of one or another of the parties. Often, standards of practice are not clearly defined or accepted, so that findings may be opinion more than fact. Sometimes such studies are undertaken by contract with a business firm, entered into either by agencies or by legislative bodies, or state or municipal governments. In these cases, a free application of research methods has a better chance, no matter what ultimate disposition may be made of the findings. Usually free enterprise firms which, as a matter of course, employ competent personnel on particular assignments, are available for any part of the field.

In considerable degree these studies have helped to emphasize the importance of comprehensive, regular, well-formulated quantitative reports by agencies, public and voluntary. Such quantitative data are not only an indispensable source for fact-gathering, but may occasionally offer legitimate use of mathematically sound probability calculations and creative combinations. Among important sources of such data are various annual and special reports of the Department of Health, Education, and Welfare and its various subdivisions, and particularly the Public Health Service. Many state departments also have admirable quantitative data that are serviceable beyond the bookkeeping and auditing function for which they are primarily intended.

4. *Study of results of technical operations.* If there were some high court of research, above suspicion, free of the atmosphere of vested interests, even free of ethical commitments (which, after all, involve human values and emotions), this is where it would have its most important, and perhaps its most rewarding, field of service. For the temptations of compromising with the iron laws of logic and of scientific method just a little bit to make a good case, for a goal which is ethically and socially valid, may lead at first to only a small misstep, or may lead eventually to intellectually slipshod methods and to misleading generalizations of serious dimensions. A small example is a study made some years ago by a well-known child guidance clinic, a pioneer in many ways in dealing with children presenting emotional disturbances, with a prominent group of psychiatrists to give the work direction and leadership. It was natural for the agency to wish to test its results, even though it had no doubts of its successful operations. Since the demand for the agency's services exceeded the manpower at its disposal, those on the waiting list not receiving service constituted a natural control group for the study based on those under treatment. But statistical handling of the resultant data, whether due to defensive short cuts or to failure to obtain unbiased advice, resulted in conclusions not justified by the data and serving no useful purpose.[26]

A more serious failure to apply the rigorous research standards that are imperative in the physical sciences but equally desirable in behavioral studies is illustrated by the work of Eleanor and Sheldon Glueck of Harvard in their long list of research publications in the field of delinquency extending over many years, and in the much publicized prediction tables they originated and promoted. Their data-gathering was of unusually high standard and called for enormous effort, patience, and persistence. As fact-gathering and organization, it might very well have qualified almost as the fourth technique in social work. But when examined as premises and conclusions in the light of logic, the conclusions repeatedly failed to be supported by the data. By contrast, the seeker after techniques for

[26] *Success and Failure in the Treatment of Children in a Child Guidance Clinic,* Jewish Board of Guardians, New York City, Monograph, 1949.

judging the results of service might well examine the Herculean efforts to determine them, again in the field of care of disturbed children, by Luton Ackerson of the Illinois Institute for Juvenile Research.[27] After the most meticulous and ingenious analysis of the problems, treatment, and results of some 5,000 cases, that agency did not hesitate to confess exceedingly modest results for the efforts expended, finding that perhaps only IQ and aging could be credited with dependable effects.

5. *Study of validity of a social work technique.* The most impressive and painstaking effort in this phase of welfare research deals with the question of the effectiveness of casework, which by general agreement has been regarded as the very heart of social work, its chief "professional" symbol. We are turning one presumed technique, research, on another technique, casework.

The Community Service Society of New York—formerly the Charity Organization Society—established within its structure an Institute of Welfare Research, with a committee of the organization instructed to take special interest in its operations. In 1942 that committee addressed itself to what seemed a logical task, since its operations were chiefly in the area of casework: "to determine and express how casework is carried on, at what cost and with what success." Quite properly the committee did not ask its Family Service Department, which was responsible for the operation of that service, to conduct the research, but engaged a staff experienced in general methods of research in the social sciences to carry on the task, with appropriate organizational participation of the operational casework staff.[28] The administrative staff responsible for the study were drawn primarily from the fields of sociology and social psychology. The plan was to answer the questions in the committee's assignment and,

---

[27] *Children's Behavior Problems* (University of Chicago Press, 1942).

[28] The cost of the enterprise was estimated at about a quarter of a million dollars; the casework staff, while under obligation to do its share, and without whose assistance the study could not have been conducted, were drawn reluctantly into the enterprise: first because they were deeply committed to validity of casework and its goals, and sincerely regarded such a study by uninitiated scientists as probably futile if not destructive; and secondly, because their habits of operation had not prepared them for the type of rigorous intellectual exercise demanded by research.

if successful, to make its practical results accessible to the entire field of casework and more particularly to the "family service" field.

Actual techniques were drawn from the field of social psychology—though the materials were drawn from casework in the Community Service Society—and refined by the less accurate techniques of setting up scales, by the employment of mathematical formulae for establishing reliability, etc.[29] The first concept attempted, using case records as a base, was that of "Discomfort-Relief Quotient." This experiment did not prove too promising,[30] even with the aid of a judgment scale and the appropriate reliability correlations. The next, and eventually chosen, concept, derived from the experience of caseworkers, and defined as "movement" in the course of casework service, then became the foundation of the study. Granting the identifiability and realism applied to the term, the study then proceeded in the best tradition of such psychological inquiries. A further refinement was introduced by designating "movement" (as a variable) as movement per se, rather than movement for which casework is responsible. The next step was to set up a movement rating, which would then be applied to a number of case records, as judged separately by a selected group of trained and experienced caseworkers, whose judgments would then be correlated to establish their statistical reliability. Unfortunately, even with maximum reliability as to judgment by the examining staff, there are at least two serious pitfalls in this design: one is the verbalization of steps on the scale (of movement, in this case), and the other their numerical conversion. The verbalized scale of movement ascended from *none, slight, moderate, considerable,* to *great,* and was converted into numerical values *1–5.*

The verbalization then underwent a further refinement which may have enhanced or diminished the accuracy of the scale items before numerical conversion. These were the listing of types of explicit evidence in support of judgment of movement as having taken place:

---

[29] The item of cost, as included in the committee's instructions, apparently was never tackled, and may be omitted from this summary.

[30] Reported on by John Dollard and D. Hobart Mowrer.

1. Changes in *adaptive capacity*
2. Changes in *disabling habits and conditions*
3. Changes in *attitude or understanding as evidenced from the client's verbalizations*
4. Changes in the *environmental situation*
5. *Prevention of expected deterioration* in behavior or circumstances
6. *The estimated permanence of changes*

After the major task had been completed, including a follow-up of (geographically) widely distributed clients, a manual was prepared with detailed description of methods of using the movement scale and methods of training caseworkers in their use. The authors of the study report, who were also chief architects of the enterprise, did not claim that they had succeeded in what they had hoped to achieve. "At the present stage of development of the Movement Scale," they sum up, "there has not yet been demonstrated the degree to which movement scores can be attributed to the casework services which has been rendered in the client's behalf. One may justifiably state that a given movement score is associated with the casework process, but it is inappropriate to conclude that the amount of movement is caused by the casework process."[31] A less delicate way of saying it is that the results of the enterprise contributed little that proved useful.

Needless to say, the research proved of no practical value to the field and its results are, in fact, not being put to use. The intellectual integrity of its staff, however, cannot be questioned. Nor does the study support, as yet, the legitimacy of including research as a fourth category of social work technique.

---

[31] The published reports on the enterprise as a whole include: *Measuring Results in Social Case Work* by J. M. Hunt and Leonard S. Kogan (Family Service Association of America). "A Method of Measuring Tension in Written Documents" by John Dollard and O. Hobart Mowrer. *Journal of Abnormal and Social Psychology*, Vol. 42, No. 1, 1947. *A Follow-up Study of the Results of Social Case Work* by L. Kogan, T. McV. Hunt, and Phyllis F. Bartelmy, Family Service Association of America, 1953). "Use of Judgments as Data in Social Work Research," *Proceedings* of Conference, Research Section, National Association of Social Workers, 1958.

⅊ SUMMARY

It would seem, then, that a half century of commitment to establishing a cluster of technical specialties has hardly produced a clear-cut, self-contained professional entity. We can lay no special claim to community organization or research as indigenous to social work. Nor can we claim to have done better in these areas than have other fields of social endeavor. Casework had a good start to becoming a realm of competence, supported by practice and by wisdom drawn from the social sciences, had it not lost its major commitment to helping the destitute and to dramatize the residual evil of poverty. The high competence that it did attain thus lost much of its social significance, even before it ceded its area of operation to relationship therapy in the vineyards of psychoanalysis. In a way, group work has had a more consistent and sustained identity over the years, for it maintained its core of activity, skills in recreation and leisure-time occupations. Though seduced by psychoanalytic and sociological concepts, it maintained a recognizable status of useful social work and added some value to experiments in group therapy and institutional management.

Chapter XII

✠

Personnel in Social Welfare Services

Whose responsibility is the conduct of welfare services in the United States today? Who are the persons that actually operate them? What is their competence and preparation for tasks they are expected to perform? Quantitatively, tax-supported and publicly administered operations are far greater than those under voluntary management. These operations are, moreover, of comparatively recent origin and structure, few dating back farther than the early thirties of this century. Exceptions are chiefly psychiatric services for veterans and some visiting teacher operations in public schools. The voluntary agency system by contrast goes back more than a hundred years, and in some aspects centuries. At this point we consider mainly the voluntary segment of the field, the oldest and best known.

This group consists of three major components:

Lay managerial personnel

The profession of social work

Training schools for social work

⤷ *LAY MANAGERIAL PERSONNEL* ⤶

Several types of important and extensive managerial sponsorship may well be omitted from consideration here, for they represent interests of primarily a different nature, though for their own purposes they have conducted operations clearly in the field of welfare. The various sectarian bodies within the Christian and Jewish tradition are a major example. There are orphanages, homes for the aged, a variety of leisure-time programs, institutional provisions for unmarried mothers, relief and casework organizations, schools for delinquents and many others under Catholic, Protestant, and Jewish communal bodies. Related but different sponsorship conducts Boy Scout, Girl Scout, and a host of other activities. Many of the typical settlement house activities also came into existence under sponsorship of this type. Similarly, fraternal organizations and ethnic minority groups, and, as of today, labor unions, may come within this general category.

The typical agency for economic assistance to the destitute, and later for child guidance and psychiatric clinic services, has been chiefly under geographic community sponsorship. These community voluntary agencies follow time-honored patterns of the general cultural climate in which they live. Directly or indirectly they carry out established ethical and esthetic precepts. Active members of the community who take on managerial tasks in these agencies have for many generations belonged to the social class defined by wealth and status, with a sprinkling of representatives of the ministry and the medical, legal, and teaching professions.

The usual pattern of management is that of the nonprofit corporation, enjoying the rights and privileges of such legal status. The organization is usually incorporated by a state authority, after approval of its nonprofit status and purposes, with a board of directors carrying responsibility. The board of directors elects officers, and both officers and board members serve for whatever duration may be provided in the bylaws. In some cases, there is a membership at large in addition to directors, but this is usually of little importance in the managerial structure, though useful in public education and for financial support. Except in the case of sectarian or fraternally controlled agencies there are no formal restrictions either as to general membership or places on the board of directors. This managerial structure is, however, only the formal framework. The actual process is quite different. There is a conscious sense of unity in our civilization among the socially prominent members of a community; and there is facility in communication, because they know one another through manifold activities in business and leisure-time occupations; they rarely know or have natural contact to any appreciable extent with members of classes representing a lower economic and social status. It would take enormous effort, perhaps an impossible one, for them to have a broad acquaintance with other layers of the social structure, who in any case would be far more numerous and in that sense less accessible. There are, also, subgroups within the community's socially prominent membership, usually influenced, if not determined, by religious affiliation, or by membership in a minority group, whether of race, church affiliation, ethnic, or other comparable factor. There is, therefore, a cluster of social aristocracies, largely sealed off from one another, and contributing the raw material from which managerial leadership is chosen.

There are also extraneous factors that enter into the eligibility for inclusion in this managerial personnel. In the first place, members of the group usually have more leisure and more sense of leisure than the mass of workers and their wives or husbands. What leisure these do have is likely to be used for their own relaxation and for such social activities as are provided by church, neighborhood, or other natural grouping. Moreover, charitable and related activities are, in our culture, a source of social prestige, and occasionally an auxiliary means of access to the power structure. Though many leaders of social welfare management have real, deep-seated interest and conviction with respect to these activities, this interest primarily concerns their willingness to labor and to contribute funds to those activities. Some research has been conducted from time to time on this almost-closed-society status of managerial administration of voluntary social welfare, including the tendency to draw on members of the same families generation after generation. Sociologically such research is fascinating, but it has only slight relationship to the essential characteristics of program development in welfare.

Like the nervous taxpayer who fears that all these public welfare activities are an unjustified drain on his energies and successes in favor of shiftless and self-indulgent "paupers," so the middle and upper economic classes as a whole have for many generations resented the claims on their resources of the hordes of poor. The friction between the economic classes is no new discovery. It has been known, though only reluctantly admitted. The needs and demands of the poor have been a festering discomfort to the "haves." Conviction that the poor should be held to standards of their "station of life" has been both a realistic defense of property rights that our culture has never denied and a less overt determination to assert the fundamental superiority of these classes over the client. Once, during the discussion of a proposed research enterprise in one of the training schools, the director of the casework services of a large family service agency described the reaction of a leading board member of the agency to the "preposterous" allotment of $50 a month to a dependent family. Without going into the merits of the particular case, he thought so large an amount to be indefensible. He was a highly respected person, who merely expressed the implicit reaction of his class to the level of living "reasonable" for a relief family. This simple episode illustrates the general point of view in the minds of this management group that sees no relation between the economic deprivation of their particular clients and poverty as a general problem of our civilization. There was, indeed, no perceptible inclination in that management group as a group to take part in the larger movements for economic improvement of the masses of the population. And, as proved to be the case, they remained entirely outside the varied efforts to establish a public system of prevention or economic assistance.

It is debatable whether this general disinclination to be drawn into the problems of economic justice, or into any plan for redistribution of wealth short of or including socialism, is in any way related to the enthusiasm of the board group for psychiatric orientation in casework. It would at least be logical to speculate that, since this new outlook in casework sidestepped the problem of economic thinking, it was a welcome new accent. It enabled the group, as it has enabled many people, to avoid also the moral issue, and to come closer to what appeared to be a respectable scientific way of thinking, and moreover one that had a titillating atmosphere about it. Actually the greatest receptivity for the new look at life created by psychoanalytic concepts was indeed found in the middle and upper middle classes. It is also this class that can afford the expensive luxury of psychoanalysis, which often extends over years of the patient's time. In a way this cultural flood of psychoanalytic thought which has swept through a large area of the behavioral sciences has created a more sympathetic attitude to the woes of clients among many of the managerial personnel, for a new common feeling of being part of the same frail species seemed to counteract class separation from the lowly client. But it tended to enhance psychological kinship rather than to create concern over economic deprivation.

A less important but not negligible effect of the new psychologically oriented social work took the form of temptation on the part of members of the management group to join the rank of professionals, for now there seemed to come into focus a common bond between professional practitioner and management representative. Not a few of the management group actually undertook the exhausting and in many ways depressing task of becoming full-time students in schools of social work. It is hard to avoid the conclusion that the gradual, and by now overwhelming, withdrawal of family casework agencies from the field of economic assistance to clients is due, in part at least, to the effects of the new psychological outlook of management personnel as well as of employed staff. Whether this particular conclusion is valid or not, the fact remains that the managerial personnel of voluntary agencies typified by the local family agency, and with them the casework staff personnel as well, have remained nonparticipants in social plans for aiding the destitute, preventing destitution, or diminishing the portion of the population generally described as poor.

If this aloofness reflected merely an absence of interest and of participation in efforts for the more equitable distribution of the wealth of the nation, it would be regrettable but not too serious. It leaves the problem of poverty in its various phases to the arena of politics, of the press, and of social science literature. Unfortunately, however, the absence of recognized leadership stemming from this social and economic caste deprives the movement of a potentially powerful body of support. Lack of audible interest of this group in the major struggle against poverty is like the minus sign in a column of addition: it pulls down the totals. Over and over again in local and state programs of assistance, where public opinion for the support of public welfare operation is needed and might be significantly helpful, the management group of the voluntary agencies has remained silent. And curiously enough, on occasions when it would almost seem as if the plight of the poor were still a major concern of these voluntary agencies, a closer look proves this to be a mirage. For example, that famous annual journalistic fund-raising pageant known as the "Hundred Neediest Cases" in New York City is a sort of joint partnership enterprise of a small number of voluntary agencies who benefit from the magnificent public relations effort of the *New York Times*. But it in no way promotes public understanding of the gigantic effort constantly being made by public welfare agencies at a cost in comparison with which the total funds raised for the "Hundred Neediest Cases" is but a paltry penny.

Finally, we have that curious distortion of social welfare promotion that goes by the name of "Community Chest," "United Fund," or some similar designation. It is, like the "Hundred Neediest Cases," an annual event. It provides annual budgets for its member agencies, usually confined to one community or metropolitan area or a group of neighboring areas served by the voluntary agencies involved. Full reports are issued by the national organization with which these local united fund-raising set-ups are affiliated. The impression usually created by the highly developed public relations apparatus is that the needy and suffering depend on the activi-

ties of the member voluntary agencies, without whose financial resources the poor and underprivileged would be in hopeless distress.
The lay managerial body, usually drawn from the same stratum of
wealth and social status as the general board membership of the
voluntary agencies, actually comprises the very cream of that
stratum, and the prestige of charitable activity is annually enhanced
by active participation of the leaders. In Suburbia, peopled predominantly by middle and upper middle class, the citizen is drawn
into house-to-house canvassing operations, and social status may
benefit this larger circle of participants. It has been customary to
ask the president of the United States to make an address or issue a
statement extolling the importance of the work of these United Fund
agencies. Rarely, if ever, is there a strong appeal by them for recognition of the great task performed by the public agencies which, of
course, do not receive any of the funds raised. Nor is the public informed of what a small part of the total welfare work is actually
carried out by the various United Funds, and still less is said about
how small a portion of the nation's welfare activities are derived
from and financed by this source. Most disconcerting perhaps is the
fact that so little is said, either at the time of the annual fund campaigns or at other times, of how the preponderant proportion of the
budgets of these very member agencies is derived from tax funds. In
child welfare agencies and institutions particularly, the share of the
cost borne by voluntary funds is relatively negligible, though the
managerial and administrative authority is maximal.[1] In hospitals
also, the usual share of private contributions is lower than the general public realizes or is told. Much of hospital construction and
some maintenance are covered by endowments; directly or through
Blue Cross or other insurance systems, patients probably pay the
bulk of the cost; and again public authorities in many communities
pay a substantial share of the cost of medical care for indigent
patients.

All that has been said in these pages about lay management

---

[1] Usually the governmental bodies pay per capita subsidies. There
is little question that public support is legitimate, but information as to the
fact is not much publicized by the voluntary agencies.

pertains only to cultural and social aspects of their function in the formalized structure of voluntary agencies and their relation to the general pattern of welfare in our civilization. It does not judge either the motivation of members of the management group or their success in enabling the agencies to perform their chosen tasks. One must remember that as long as the welfare services had to depend upon the individual initiative of the benevolent members of the community and could not depend on the officially enforced tax income of government bodies, it was up to charitable and community-minded persons to devise ways and means to supply needed services. And persons who had the time and resources and access to other resources were almost exclusively those in the comfortable and prestigious economic class. Even with these advantages the services could not be inaugurated by members of that group, and certainly not continued year after year, if these people had not also possessed devotion, often to the point of dedication, and been willing and able to work. Work meant two things at least: efforts to raise funds, and willingness to perform a great variety of voluntary tasks requiring great energy and understanding.

Nor were these demands upon them removed when Community Chests and United Funds came into the scene. For many, indeed, the new system created additional chores: participation in United Fund solicitations, over and above continued demands upon their services by the particular voluntary agencies on whose boards of directors they remained active. Only in a relatively small number of instances did the "rank and file" of board members—if they may be so designated—have the advantage of serving with outstanding leaders who started new enterprises, and were able also to continue their share in management. That list is very small compared with the number of persons who had to continue the prosaic task of management and financial worry in the agencies. It is interesting to recall the names of some of those notable leaders who were also available to management: Stanton Coit, Dorothea Dix, Dr. Richard C. Cabot, Clara Barton, Julius Rosenwald, Robert W. De Forest, Paul Baerwald, Adele Levy, Margaret Sanger, John M. Glenn, Judge Harvey H. Baker, Clifford W. Beers, Mrs. Russell Sage. There were a host of others.

One should not leave this subject without mentioning the founders of such outstanding and socially important foundations in the field of education, medicine, public health, and research as Duke, Girard, Carnegie, Rockefeller, Harkness, Ford. However, they touch the subject under discussion only tangentially.

Chapter XIII

✠

The Profession of Social Work

The existence of "professions" has a peculiar and interesting history in our culture. The concept involves assertions of intellectual pursuit, protection of the public against malpractice, social status, the assumption of economic prosperity of the practitioner, and a tacit obligation to serve general human welfare. It is assumed that a place in a profession is preceded by systematic training in specialized subject matter. It is not clear when, in any particular pursuit, professional status was formally achieved, nor what inherent characteristics all professions must possess.[1] In theological areas one is generally

[1] See Abraham Flexner's *Is Social Work A Profession* (National Conference of Social Work Procedures, 1915).

201

"ordained." In medicine formal acquisition of the degree of "Doctor of Medicine" and a license issued by the state is required for the right to practice. We are accustomed to "bar examinations" for lawyers as a precondition of practicing law and, having passed the examinations successfully, the lawyer gains formal status in the judicial apparatus. A "registered nurse" must be a graduate of an accredited school of nursing. Teachers, on the other hand, regardless of what they teach as long as it is in the intellectual realm, are also recognized as professional persons. In various ways, engineers, architects, and a baker's dozen other occupations are in that loosely defined brotherhood. In some but not all professions, a license is required for practice, the license constituting governmental approval after proof of competence. It is difficult to know to what extent recognition of professional status is a way of protecting the public or of elevating the self-esteem of the practitioner.

Whatever may be the legal and caste definition of profession, there has been added, with various degrees of authority and importance, another badge of recognition, that of membership in a "professional organization."[2] There are, accordingly, medical associations, bar associations, associations of nurses, architects, and so on. Similarly, social work also built up a professional organization, whose functions are:

1. to protect the interests and status of the practitioner;[3]
2. to protect the persons or public to be served;
3. to advance the competence of the worker and his usefulness to general welfare.

Since the personnel of the social services is by definition expected primarily to promote the public interest, it would follow that the first of the functions listed above would be least important, while the other two are sometimes indistinguishable from each other.

---

[2] It should be noted that in one of the most important professional fields of our culture, politics, none of the kind of recognition or for that matter systematic formal training contained in these observations applies.

[3] There is serious question whether those interests of the practitioner that relate to his security of tenure or appropriate compensation have been effectively advanced by the professional organization. This has become chiefly the concern of the labor unions in the field, covering personnel in both the voluntary and the public agencies.

How far does the professional organization in social work address itself to these purposes?

In a formal sense, the profession of social work came into existence in 1921–22 when the American Association of Social Workers was organized. In a less formal but perhaps more significant sense, the profession "was born" in 1898, when the first brief training course was initiated by the Charity Organization Society of New York. This course soon became the New York School of Philanthropy, a departmental activity in that organization.

Another, on the face of it totally independent, factor in bringing about establishment of the new professional association was the growing momentum in the economic emancipation of women. While probably no profession was legally closed to women in this country, not even that of the ministry, there were few of that sex in medicine, law, finance, or the ministry. Women's occupations, other than factory jobs and domestic participation in family farming, were chiefly teaching, secretarial work, and nursing. Social work suddenly came over the horizon as another, although not yet very large, area of occupation particularly suitable for and favored by women. An employment service intended to widen this new field of potential employment came to accelerate the trend.

The parent body of the Association of Social Workers was the National Social Workers Exchange, which in turn was a Department of Social Work of the Intercollegiate Bureau of Occupations, an employment agency. The Exchange came into being some time in 1916. From the very beginning it involved not only the handful of administrative and intellectual leaders of the field, but also the pioneer philanthropic foundation that had come into being somewhat earlier to advance the interests of social work, the Russell Sage Foundation. Especial importance attaches to the fact that Porter R. Lee, who had a few years earlier become the Director of the New York School of Philanthropy, joined the group of promoters. The schools for training social workers were from the very beginning the spiritual soil on which the profession and early professional standards were built. From the beginning of the existence of the National Social Workers' Exchange its plans, programs, and interests revolved around the concept of a new profession, and of specialized training in schools of social work as the chief badge of such professional status. Even though employment in a social agency of "recognized standing" was also a condition of professional standing, school training was probably the central moving concept. By the end of 1920, discussions had reached the stage of a "Constitution" for the Exchange, with an unmistakable commitment of rendering it a professional body. While its chief function was still that of an employment service, the name of the organization was changed to the American Association of Social Workers. By this time the first school of social work was nearly a quarter of a century old and had been offering a two-year sequence of training for nearly ten years. The conceptual consanguinity of formal training and professional status had been well established.

In light of the occupational impulse that had been so important a factor in bringing about creation of the professional organization, it is not surprising that a placement service became an essential component of its operations and that the personnel of that service exercised considerable leadership and influence. Parallel with this interest came a profound sense of dedication to the ideals of social work and a pride in the creative activities of the new organization. Its officers and directors included persons of distinction in the field who, in addition to their own leading roles in the practice of welfare work, were among intellectual leaders in the ground swell of democratic commitment and social reform. Child labor opponents and exponents of the protection of women in industry, of labor legislation, of the settlement movement, were among them.

This group was committed to the ideal of improved service and of social reform, and to advancement of the competence of social workers. Their dedication inspired them to liberate the association from dependence on philanthropic support for their operations and to accept the risk of financing by membership fees alone.[4] The internal factional strife that accompanied this new venture in self-confidence had no lasting effect on the vitality and purpose of

---

[4] The fact that the chief outside support came from a leading philanthropic foundation particularly committed to the service of this field, the Russell Sage Foundation, did not alter this determination.

the fledgling profession after the transitional pains had passed. The Association's "vocational bureau" remained for years an essential activity, while expansion of membership and specific professional activities increasingly occupied the center of interest.

From the time of this new orientation the attention of the Association was directed to:

1. organizational technique;
2. concern with the larger problems of social welfare;
3. protective and self-promotive interests of the membership.

The first of these activities was naturally crucial for survival, vitality, and growth. The more extensive the other activities are, the more it is incumbent on the organizational structure to develop a large membership, financial resources, influence, loyalty, and sufficient status possibilities for members to stimulate normal ambitions and pride.

So a system of local chapters was developed, as foci for all activities of the organization. To the same end regional groupings were gradually set up as the increasing membership and its geographic distribution seemed to warrant it. A variety of committees was created to discuss matters of concern to special groups in the membership, as for example research, personnel practices, welfare councils, ethics, and various subcategories of practice. The Association took an active interest in the *Social Work Year Book* publication, and had a responsible place among social science groups in sponsorship of the *Encyclopedia of the Social Sciences,* both on administrative and on advisory levels. It undertook publication of several technical monographs, issued periodic newsletters and a *Journal of Social Work.* Some of these activities were marginal to the second of the functions listed, namely an active role in promoting larger plans of social welfare. To this end, officers or members of the Association gave testimony at congressional committee hearings. As resources became available, a lobbying and information service was set up in an office of the Association in Washington. What was never seriously undertaken was any responsibility for, or active leadership in, attacking poverty as a major pathology in the current civilization. Nor did it face the problems of destitution as constituting a primary obligation of the personnel of the Association, though it had been claiming special competence, skill, and historical continuity in the field.

As a result, the profession lost some of its potential function as a promoter of social engineering in an age in which successful creation of wealth and know-how was accompanied by a large incidence of new poverty and new massive destitution.

Instead, the organized machinery of the professional association devoted an increasing amount of energy and commitment to its own status development, its own security, and the exterior trappings of its claim to special skills and formal recognition. It was quite natural for the new organization, at its inception, to construct some tenable definition of a social worker, one that would reasonably stimulate ambitions for competence, and differentiate them both from the managerial group and from genteel but untrained amateurs and clerical workers. It was equally natural to emphasize higher education and attendance in schools of social work. These were rapidly increasing in numbers and developing subject matter of both technical character and social science content. The actual job market was, moreover, in the early stages, not too far removed from what schools of social work might reasonably expect to be able to supply. Students tended to be attracted to schools and to the profession in part because it seemed to offer a new and exciting field for women (there were only a handful of men at first). In part they reacted to the new academic interest in the political and philosophic approach to social justice, in democratic ideals and a sense of personal responsibility to labor for a better world. It was to be another quarter of a century before the sweep of public welfare operations altered extensively the complexion of the market for workers. And in the interim, entrance of the psychiatric and psychoanalytic factor heightened the special status and limited the supply of qualified workers in relation to jobs available.

The size of the membership grew apace, especially after the change of name to NASW (National Association of Social Workers) and with it the expansion of both financial resources and activity program. An increasing number of members could be drawn into the administrative and committee structure. What, if anything, went wrong then with what was originally a promising force for advancing the interests of the beneficiaries of social welfare—the interests that so largely inspired Jane Addams, Jacob Riis, Margaret Sanger, Lillian Wald, Owen R. Lovejoy, Florence Kelly, Homer Folks, Grace and Edith Abbott—the pioneers? Opinions will differ. Prejudices or different philosophies may distort judgment. Part of what has happened or has not happened is inherent in the changed social outlook, in occupational distribution, and in the professional expression of the social outlook. The following characteristics appear significant:

> *Persons formally qualified for membership in the professional association are a minority of the persons engaged in welfare services.*
>
> *A diminishing proportion is engaged in what was in the earlier period the settlement field with its active role in social reform and neighborhood service.*
>
> *The casework membership has become a self-conscious elite, and within that group the psychiatric technique of casework has become predominant.*
>
> *Interest in destitution and poverty has become less and less, and the influence of the group in that field has declined.*
>
> *Activities on the organizational level of the association have veered toward advancing and preserving interests of the worker as against those of the client, in a manner often verging on a caste-like trend, and the worker is increasingly being defined as "member of the NASW."*

Several specific items come under this last heading—not all of them of equally dubious benefit to the client, but all of them somehow reminiscent of the protective mechanisms of the American Medical Association.[5] State and local public assistance bodies are forced, for lack of available trained personnel willing to enter this service, to hire investigators (sometimes designated caseworkers) with no specific training for their jobs, who receive only a very imperfect system of indoctrination after employment. Yet the NASW has made no attempt to gather this army of workers into the fold of

[5] See Chapter Four, Medical Care.

the profession by lowering the barrier of formal eligibility for membership, and so to encourage in others a pride in their supremely important social service. As a body they remain outside the professional association, only a small fraction being drawn into training by scholarships and special course offerings. This major fault is shared by the training schools, which insist on the now traditional two-year course of preparation, usually required by them in candicacy for a Master's degree.[6]

In one of the largest states in the Union, for example, a recent inquiry disclosed that, among nearly 2,100 "caseworkers" and supervisors in its public assistance program, only a negligible number would be "eligible" to membership in the professional association. Any sense of "belonging" to the social service profession was therefore automatically denied them. Such staff members as had had some formal training were with few exceptions among the supervisory personnel of some 360 persons, who necessarily had minimal, if any, contact with clients. And since the whole program of public assistance was geared to establishment of eligibility for relief and calculation of permissible relief grants—the very foundation of public assistance—it followed automatically that this service was denied any stimulation and incentive that might have come from being part of the recognized profession.[7] Since this group is also the one on the lowest level of the salary scale in the assistance service, and therefore presumably most in need of any protective services offered by the professional organization, its members are the ones most clearly denied that sort of benefit. Yet the various protective services for members of the professional organization are admittedly among the dominant reasons for social workers to seek membership in that organization.

In a recent (August 1964) official publication of the National Association of Social Workers dealing with the question of

[6] On this point, see the next chapter, and the Epilogue, Perspectives for the Future.

[7] This is the state that ruefully, but frankly, includes in its successive annual reports the statement that the rate of assistance actually provided in all but its old age cases is more than two thirds of the minimum standard (the standard itself being far below common labor budgetary calculations).

possible admission of workers not now eligible to membership, an illuminating passage occurs on this last point:

> Here it is well to remember that *only slightly better than half the persons fully eligible for NASW joined until specific tangible inducements in the form of insurance plans, the directory, and ACSW were offered.* Some of these tangible inducements would be available to the new persons covered in this proposal, the main exception being the ACSW which has been the most potent force in securing and building NASW members. . . .[8]

This quotation is part of the text of a statement submitted to the membership for study in connection with a "proposal to involve all social workers in the program of NASW." The entire text is almost devoid of any sign that a dedication to interests of service might be a fundamental purpose of the organization, and that a "Master's degree" was not the *summum bonum* of professional outlook. This deplorable lowering of the ideals of welfare service extrudes in other parts of the document and of the organization's structure as well. Not surprisingly, a recent "delegates" meeting of the organization declined to make any decision on the proposal to liberalize its membership qualifications.

The importance of the idea that the major obligation of economic assistance still is or should be the concern of social work becomes highlighted also in some of the statistics cited in the same memorandum. For example, quoting a manpower study conducted in 1960,[9] and in an effort to show the potential financial benefits to the organization from *some sort* of membership status being offered to the presently ineligible group, the memorandum says:

> There were approximately 115,800 individuals covered in the social welfare manpower study of 1960 . . . [and only] 17 per cent or about 20,000 had a Master's degree . . .

---

[8] *NASW News*, August 1964, p. 43. As to ACSW, see below.

[9] *Salaries and Working Conditions of Social Welfare Manpower in 1960*, U.S. Bureau of Labor Statistics, National Social Welfare Assembly, Inc., and U.S. Department of Health, Education, and Welfare.

Various conclusions are drawn from these and some further analyses of the manpower data, but all of them bear on how many additional members could be drawn into the organization and what kind of limited membership might be devised for those not now possessing the formal qualifications, rather than on the importance of recognizing this army of public servants as the major operational staff in what is the major obligation of social work. Evidently the members already entrenched in the protective envelope of the Association are not eager to dilute their special status by admitting a group who, no matter how important their work, would not decorate the image established for the present incumbents of the membership. The title "social worker" is made to seem more important than the substance of the services: They would, of course, be fully justified in this point of view if they boldly proclaimed that public assistance is not social work and that beneficiaries of that service are the less important part of social welfare.

The lack of vision and social philosophy of the Association and its inability to recognize the significant findings of the Manpower Study are reflected in some other citations. For example:[10]

> In 1960, approximately 116,000 social welfare workers were employed in social welfare settings in the United States. Of these 73,550 (65%) were employed in Federal, State or local government agencies, compared with 42,250 in national, State or local voluntary agencies.

Elsewhere in the report[11] it is shown that, of all these workers, 30 per cent were in public assistance, and 21 per cent were in public child welfare services, or, when converted into numbers, some 59,000 such workers were in these two categories of welfare service.

Occasionally the impression is given that public assistance investigators, now almost totally outside the organization membership, lack basic general education. But the data of this study show that there is little difference in the percentage holding the Bachelor's degree in the major grouping: 71 per cent over-all, 75 per cent

[10] Page 3.
[11] Page 7.

among federal, 70 per cent among state and local, and 72 per cent among employees of voluntary agencies.

There are almost no turnover statistics for the field as a whole, although these might be very illuminating. A recent piece of information on the subject from records in one of the states shows that of 705 caseworkers (the term used by tradition) in the beginner's classification on July 1, 1961, the ensuing year showed a 43 per cent turnover.[12] It means that 303 of them left their employment during the year. That, in turn, meant that somewhere in the neighborhood of 40,000 to 50,000 cases had to change hands, as it were. The next higher grade of caseworkers, of whom there were 1,003, lost only 120, a turnover of 12 per cent. By further contrast, there was a turnover among the supervisors (363) of only 3.6 per cent. Rough arithmetic would seem to indicate that, excluding supervisors, a working body of some 1,285 caseworkers were steadily occupied at their chosen task, and almost none of them would have been eligible or admitted to membership in the professional organization. This discouraging turnover indirectly testifies to the failure of the profession as a whole and of its professional association (and of its training schools) to address themselves seriously to this situation.

Perhaps the most regrettable factor in the status- and security-seeking aspects of the professional association's program is its commitment to "licensing" for practice, by legal procedures, in the several states, with the title of "Social Worker" protected by trade mark provisions as in commercial commodity protection, and the creation of the so-called "Academy of Certified Social Workers" a major activity of the organization in the past five years. Both of these items reflect the NASW in one of its most narcissistic aspects stimulated also by the prospect of financial benefits. One of the members of the association has referred to the "Academy" as the instrument for "professional monopoly." The responsible leaders evidently had been mesmerized, and in turn had mesmerized the rank and file, into thinking that the establishment of this impressive sounding title, de-

---

[12] Data from Philadelphia. Similar information for New York City is reported in the *New York Times* Jan. 29, 1967, quoting Lawrence Podell of the Welfare Department to the effect that in 1964 there was a turnover of "caseworkers" of 44.6 per cent.

spite its hollow substance, was a sound and forward-looking step. Development of competent workmanship in any field, manual or professional, is a legitimate and highly desirable objective, but it is important to make certain that that purpose be clearly kept in focus. Among the first objectives of this profession would be to make certain who its beneficiaries should be, what kind of service they require and in what amounts; and to make certain that persons in need of help would receive that help in some reasonable relation to need. These purposes are being subverted by the obvious shifting of emphasis to the benefits to the employed worker rather than to the client, and by the persistent disregard of the fact that the meeting of primary client needs has been accepted by governmental bodies and their employes.

Certainly if licensing were seriously thought of and were practicable, a minimum requirement would be that the nature of the practice to be licensed and certified would be clear. On the contrary, however, the trend has been in the other direction. Witness, for example, the mumbo-jumbo definition of social work offered as the basis of the thirteen-volume report on the social work curriculum of the future as presented by the Council on Social Work Education:[13]

> *Social work seeks to enhance the social functioning of individuals, singly and in groups, by activities focused upon their social relationships which constitute the interaction between man and his environment. These activities can be grouped into three functions: restoration of impaired capacity, provision of individual and social resources, and prevention of social dysfunction.*

A course of study that would enable the social worker to do these things calls, according to the same report, for "an appropriate combination of undergraduate, graduate and in-service training curricula which would provide (1) pertinent knowledge about man, society and their interaction; (2) appropriate attitudes toward man, society and their relationships; and (3) skills for carrying out the activities required by the functions of social work." If such a defini-

[13] Published by the Council on Social Work Education, 1959, Vol. I, p. 54.

tion made any sense and if the resultant activity were sufficiently clear-cut, it might legitimately be a basis for granting or refusing a state license to practice. But the proponents of licensing recognize the difficulty of describing intelligibly the nature of social work as a whole and so they have recourse to a time-honored method of circumvention: first by repetition of the term, then by listing undefined components. So they submit, in the draft of the law for licensing (in New York), the following qualifications:[14]

> A person . . . who engages in the practice of social casework, social group work, community organization, administration of social work program, social work education, social work research, or any combination of these *in accordance with social work principles and methods.*[15] This practice of social work is for the purpose of helping individuals, families, groups and communities to prevent or to resolve problems caused by social or emotional stress.

No mention is made of destitution, poverty, illness, and there is a curious absence of the realities faced by people who need help. Cross reference, as it were, is to the employing agencies. The proposal, now a law of the state, then reiterates the matter of Master's degree or Certificate as described in the accreditation parlance of training schools, and this is followed by reference to an examination to be passed. Various alternatives are also suggested for elimination of the requirement for passing an examination for an introductory period following enactment of the law and on various conditions involving among other things work experience of from three to fifteen years in combination with other factors.[16]

There are differences of opinion about a number of aspects

[14] Proposed legislation for Legal Certification of Social Workers in New York State, New York State Council of Chapters, drafted May 1961, revised January 1964. The law was eventually passed.

[15] Italics added.

[16] Compare the very illuminating discussion of the entire "licensing" episode as it took place in California, in *Welfare in America* by Vaughn Davis Bornet (Oklahoma University Press, 1960), particularly Chapters XI and XII, pp. 226–244.

of this proposed licensing system. But it is difficult to condone the attitude that to give or to offer help to a fellow human being there is only one path: formalized state licensing, involving a specified sort of training in an especially accredited school, and that after such a course of training and by virtue of it a person can handle any of the complicated human problems that may beset a man of his family —and without it, he cannot. By implication also, though this is not overtly stated, such a practitioner should be a member of the NASW, and by deliberate pressure within that association he would hardly avoid being an ACSW, that is, a member of the "Academy" of Certified Social Workers. Even in medical practice not all physicians are, or care to be, members of the American Medical Association. But in this field of social work, where free enterprise is a minimal factor, all employment would practically be restricted to licensed social workers, whether in public or voluntary agency. And would the employing agency be free to employ an unlicensed person?[17] If not, the staffs of many public assistance bodies would be automatically reduced by half or more.

As to the value of licensing, there is only a simulacrum of analogy to conditions for practice of law, medicine, or nursing. More comparable is the authorization of teaching in the public schools, where the term "license" is in vogue, although the predominant feature in that field is that most teaching is in public schools, where elaborate systems of checking on the performance of the teacher are in effect. The Association does not propose that licensing of social workers be placed in the category with licensing of cab drivers, plumbers, electricians, undertakers, engineers, pharmacists, and a host of others. Yet in these areas, there are some tangible procedures for judging success or failure of results. It would be interesting to speculate how licensing of lawyers or ministers would affect their ethical performance, their successful litigation, or dependable intercession with the divine powers.

Licensing of social workers, as proposed, would result in the automatic exclusion of the host of workers in public assistance from the closed, licensed ranks and their equally automatic designation as

---

[17] On this point, also, consult Bornet, *Welfare in America*.

inferior, unqualified workers. Conceivably this would not have to happen, if state and local governments employed only "trained workers" as that term is now used. But neither the professional organization nor the intricately interlocked Council on Social Work Education have made any serious attempt over the past decades to help set up suitable training plans, and to promote appropriate salary scales for workers in public assistance.[18] For that matter they have paid little heed, except in pious position papers and occasional lobbying in legislatures, to the whole field of public assistance and associated public services.

In view of the tremendous, and quantitatively as well as philosophically predominant, importance of public assistance and social security in our welfare structure today, it would seem that both those engaged in the field and the general public as well should be aware of the way in which the professional association and the training schools for social work have deviated from that path of service. The activities of the NASW in pursuing a legal licensing system and a deceptively defined self-certification in its "Academy of Certified Social Workers" call, therefore, for some further comments, especially since both these developments have led to a curious "merchandising" quality in its public relation practices and something resembling "personal cult" aspirations of its leadership.

The initial large-scale campaign of the professional association for "licensing" and for the Academy of Certified Social Workers promotion appears to have opened in 1959 and 1960.[19] The movement sprang, it seems, from the successful efforts of social workers in California to provide legal licensing in that State.

The claim of the proponents of licensing—to take that pursuit first—was that *"regulation* was needed to protect the public

---

[18] It is interesting to note, incidentally, how little influence the professional organization had in the serious work stoppage adjustments in connection with the strike of workers in the Welfare Union in New York City in 1965.

[19] See successive issues of the *NASW News,* the periodical organizational issue, as distinct from the more professional *Journal of Social Work.* The California licensing law was enacted in that state in 1945. Cf. Bornet, *Welfare in America.*

against abuses and incompetence from would-be practitioners."[20] But there is not a scintilla of evidence that such abuses were occurring except as they might occur in any field, and there is no indication of what a "would-be practitioner" might be. The argument then continues:

> Social work has certain additional reasons . . . for needing regulation. These are:
> 1. To establish a true and dignified public image of social work.
> 2. To obtain formal societal sanction for social work.
> 3. To increase public confidence and understanding of social work.

These are curious arguments indeed for licensing. But the same NASW report includes some further revealing comments (p. 16):

> The progress NASW has made, particularly in relation to social work practice, has made us aware of the extent of our ignorance concerning our own practice. The difficulties experienced by the national commission on Social Work Practice [of the NASW] . . . underline the impossibility of social work's defining practice for the purpose of legal regulation at this time . . .

The conclusion then is arrived at, through a process difficult to understand, that since admittedly there is some difficulty in defining practice, and consequently the title of "social worker," by legislation, resort is to be had to "voluntary certification" as an alternative method for the protection of the title of "social worker."[21]

The voluntary certification attained by the NASW prior to the achievement of a nation-wide licensing system was thus glorified into that impressive creation, the Academy of Certified Social Workers. In brief, the plan provided that:[22]

[20] NASW News, February 1960, pp. 14ff.

[21] Periodical publication of the New York City Chapter of NASW, entitled Currents, April 30, 1964.

[22] NASW News, February 1960, p. 17. Also, NASW News, February 1959; p. 24.

1. The full members of the NASW shall receive the title of "certi- fied social worker," on satisfying certain incidental require- ments.
2. After a member obtains the title *"certified social worker"* the right to this title shall be renewable annually on an automatic basis so long as the individual remains a member in *good standing.*

The proposal continued to specify the purchasable aspect of the title by the following undisguised provision for the plan to help fill the coffers of the Association:

A non-refundable application fee shall be charged for the initial application, and an annual fee shall be charged for the annual recertification. . . . A *certified social worker* whose membership in the National Association of Social Workers is terminated loses his certification, but regains it upon reinstatement.

It is difficult to imagine a more disingenuous assertion that the title is but a money-making device, that it has little if any relation to com- petence, that it does not protect the public from abuse; and it is cer- tainly difficult to see how "it establishes a true and dignified public image of social work." A final giveaway occurs in the resolution that the NASW protect this title "by federal copyright."

The opposition [to the proposal] focused on the monopolistic aspects of the plan, its attempts to create the illusion of public protection in the face of eligibility requirements barely above NASW membership itself, and the deceptive aura around the Academy device . . . We now face the test of implementing and interpreting a plan which is inherently defective in both intent and application. Its defects may be summed up as follows:
1. As presently constituted, the plan provides certification re- quirements which bear almost no relation to standards of competence . . .
2. We are deliberately offering the public the illusion of pro- tection where there is none. . . . This is misleading and— the only suitable word is a harsh one—unethical. It is a terrible price to pay for professional prestige, even if one is

foolish enough to believe that any lasting prestige can be
built on so shaky a base. . . .

5. The plan must necessarily create the effect of further con-
centrating the location of the new MSW (Master of Social
Work degree) in the larger cities . . .

6. The same consequences will accrue to the public agencies
which are having even now a difficult time recruiting and
holding trained workers. This move will tend to freeze them
in their present status. . . . The argument that these
agencies—as well as those, public and private, in the smaller
communities, have but to "raise their standards" to compete
is more than slightly arrogant on our part, and unworthy of
our understanding of how changes come about . . .

7. . . . as far as the public is concerned, we have twice during
the past six years "blanketed in" many thousands of workers
with little or no professional training at all, offering them
first the NASW designation, and now the ACSW symbol
of advanced competence. . . . The second . . . is more
serious in its consequences: it creates a huge pool of unqualified but "certified" supervisors . . .

If Dr. Abraham Flexner were now to discuss whether social
work is a profession, in the light of his standards, he would hesitate
less than ever to come to the conclusion that it had missed the boat,
and is slowly, though loudly, paddling backward.

Admittedly, it is a "registered trade-mark."

On December 1, 1961, the "Academy of Certified Social
Workers" (trade-mark *ACSW*) was "officially" established, and
some 18,500 members[23]—more than half of the membership of
NASW—signed up, with an initial resulting income to the Association of some $129,500.

The reaction among responsible members was not universally
favorable, but the proposal was rushed through at record speed, and
all that the disenchanted individual members could do was to sor-
row, and not to sign up. No appreciable consideration was given to
the point of view of the dissidents except the publication of one
article in the Association's *Journal of Social Work*. The author of

[23] *NASW News*, February 1962.

that article[24] is a member of the faculty of the Columbia University School of Social Work.[25]

Dr Schwartz wrote:

. . . in its six years of publication from January, 1956 through December, 1961, the Journal has in fact produced exactly two articles on the subject of regulation, four letters to the editor and one peripheral comment . . .

. . . by restricting eligibility to members of the Association NASW had laid itself open to charges of illegal monopoly. Therefore, a legal fiction had been devised, namely another "organization," the Academy of Certified Social Workers . . . That the fiction was specifically designed to circumvent certain legal and ethical requirements drawn up to protect the public evidently held no horrors for the sponsors; in any event, it was not discussed by them . . .[26] The debate was long and heated. Its most striking feature, to this participant, was that *no arguments were advanced to show that this was a measure designed to protect the public* . . .

[24] July 1962 issue of the *Journal*.
[25] Dr. William Schwartz, Associate Professor of Social Work.
[26] Reference is to a meeting of the administrative body in 1960.

Chapter XIV

✤

Training Schools of Social Work

By far the most important factor in the definition and growth of social work has been the creation of schools of training. As educational institutions they have been the means of rendering the field respectable in the same way that universities have, over the centuries, the study of theology, philosophy, economics, the humanities, sciences, mathematics. The formal framework of higher education has tremendously expanded opportunities for integrating daily practice with scientific advancement and discovery. This has been the case with medicine, law, engineering, architecture, and, in later periods, for example, agricultural and business administration methods. The chief difference between these other practical pursuits and social work in entering the field of higher education has been that, by definition, social work was to be a pursuit of service, motivated by benevolent interest in society's less fortunate members. It would follow, therefore, that within the setting of higher education, theoretical foundations, specific technical practice, and in no less degree the altruistic or social purpose would be emphasized. It is in the light of this triple objective that the work of schools of social work has to be examined.

The field of social work for which these schools were to train personnel underwent a confused incubation period. There was relief to the destitute, but it was hit or miss. It responded to individual good will and multiple agency resources, including the local systems of relief. Many well-intentioned persons felt that they were being exploited by unscrupulous beggars, who had attained some expertise in drawing upon more than one source of beneficence. Informed and public-spirited leaders in this country were impressed with the English charity organization movement, which combined efficiency with sympathy and philosophical perspective. The settlement movement was making a deep impression on the minds of American philanthropic leaders. Yet they feared pauperization of the beneficiary; they thought that denial of relief might be more useful in the long run than the threat of pauperization. Charity Organization Societies had sprung up in several American cities, notably Buffalo, Baltimore, Boston, and New York, but their goals were curiously entangled: large views of general social order combined with distrust of the clients asking for help, an assurance that efficient handling would bring maximum results—that "friendly visiting" was a potent helper.

There were bold disturbing cross-currents also. Leaders like Jacob Riis and Jane Addams were not generals in the armies of charity organizations. Amos Warner,[1] an economist before he entered the service of the charity organization movement, seemed to find lack of employment and sickness larger causes of poverty than all

[1] Amos Warner, author of *American Charities* (published by T. Y. Crowell, 1894 and numerous revisions), still the great classic in the field.

other causes put together. He quoted Professor Edwin Seligman,[2] a leading economist of the day as saying (1905):

> . . . modern poverty is bound up with the facts of modern economic life, and modern economic life is a complex product. . . . Density of population, private property, competition, government, speculation, and money have each been absent at various stages of history without exempting society from the curse of poverty. Each stage has had a poverty of its own. . . . The causes of poverty are as complex as the causes of civilization and the growth of wealth itself. . . .

One of the early directors of the New York School of Social Work, who had previously served as general director of the Charity Organization Society of New York, Professor Edward T. Devine[3] says, in the same vein:

> England was saved from pauperization, revolution and other unforeseen disasters not by deciding to distribute less relief, or by deciding that the able-bodied poor, if assisted at all, should be assisted only in the workhouse, wise as these decisions were, but by the rise of religious and political liberty, by introducing in advance of other countries modern forms of agriculture and industry, by developing her commerce and trade, by the adoption of a more nearly democratic organization of society, and by listening to the voice of humane and public spirited counsel: *The lessening of the poor rates was made practicable by and was not the principal cause of the progress of the period.*[4]

It is a curious fact that, throughout the period which just preceded the first steps toward setting up a school of social work in America, there appears to have been little interest in finding out how serious and how extensive were poverty and destitution, how many families lived on the brink of starvation. Aside from the few prophets

---

[2] See Edwin Seligman (previously administrator of the Baltimore Charity Organization Society), *Principles of Economics,* p. 591, as quoted by Warner.

[3] Edward T. Devine, *Principles of Relief* (Macmillan, 1914).

[4] Italics added.

like Jacob Riis, any thought given to the problem was in the channel and mold of charity organizations. It was quasi-scientific and efficiency-minded. Without quite saying so, it categorized the beneficiaries as a sort of small permanent layer of helpless people, not too important except as a field for charitable, sympathetic, clear-headed, earnest philanthropists, but not for militant action. When Mary Richmond first proposed a "training school in applied philanthropy"[5] she was pondering the question "how to get educated young men and women to make a life vocation of charity organization work." "In these days of specialization," she said, "when we train our cooks, our apothecaries, our engineers, our librarians, our nurses, . . . we have yet to establish our first training school for charity workers . . ." Her suggestion appealed to the charity organization leaders, and in 1898 Robert W. DeForest, president of the Charity Organization Society of New York, announced the inauguration of the first training program, a six-week course within the Society's structure. In 1904 the new School of Philanthropy inaugurated its full year's program of theoretical and practical instruction. In 1910 it formalized a two-year sequence, which became and still is the standard training period for social work.[6] Other schools were soon established in Boston, Philadelphia, Chicago, New Orleans, and other large cities.

The phase of the social work movement that remained in closer touch with the general field of reform, and with the development of civic, political, and recreational programs, was centered in the settlement houses. It had only indirect and informal relations with the growing body of schools of social work, chiefly in certain limited areas of the curriculum, and it supplied some of the instructional personnel. As a sector of the field and as a factor in the professional commitment of schools, the settlement houses were a "junior partner."

[5] In a paper read before the National Conference of Charities and Correction in 1897.

[6] For a detailed history of the New York School of Social Work, two documents are available, both replete with pertinent data: Saul Bernstein, *New York School of Social Work, 1898–1941;* and Elizabeth G. Meyer, *A History of the New York School of Social Work,* in the *Bicentennial History of Columbia University,* 1954.

With few exceptions, schools of social work training have remained within the sphere of influence of the charity organization movement. They have concentrated on the training of caseworkers with some growing attention to preparation of administrative as well as rank-and-file and supervisory personnel; they have, with few exceptions, remained within the palisades of voluntary agency employment, although public agencies have drawn on their graduates for supervisory and administrative appointments. The schools have nurtured, reinforced, and provided foundations for "professionalization of the field." Lastly, like the professional association itself, the schools have permitted themselves to be drawn into vested-interest temptations and bureaucratic practice patterns that cater to administrative interests rather than goals, operations rather than social purposes, techniques rather than social policy.

This has been true ever since the first dominant appearance on the scene of Mary Richmond. Her irresistibly persuasive and incomparably well-documented mind and presentation gave its character to all that the charity organization movement and its loyal followers carried on. The assumption of the unquestioned superiority of the worker over the client in attitude, knowledge, and influence created a sort of narcissistic frame for the worker, and a psychological rather than material and environmental setting for the work. A remarkably clear statement of the point of view held in the early days of this century by the family casework agencies is contained in the *Annual Report* of the Charity Organization Society of New York for 1903–04 (page 17), quoted by Miss Meyer:

It is increasingly apparent that goods, clothing and money are not relief but only the instruments of relief; that experienced skill and good judgment and personal sympathy with which the necessary inquiries are made, cooperation of the family which is in need secured, and the cause of the destitution gradually removed, are more important than the material means of relief, though the latter is, of course, also essential.

It will be recalled that by this time the pioneer school of social work in this country was a department of that family casework agency. Its curriculum was dominated by casework courses. A comparative summary of the courses in that curriculum is given in Bernstein's study, for four separate years, approximately ten years apart.

Unfortunately no comparable data are available for later periods, nor does the major distinction between technical and nontechnical throw a great deal of light on the subject. For example, 18 out of 86 "nontechnical courses" as reported by Bernstein, are "orientation to social work," which is hardly in the same class with

Sections of Courses (outside study requirements) :[7]

	1914–15	1924–25	1934–35	1940–41
Total courses (as sections)	29	100	168	214
Nontechnical	17	47	57	86
Technical Subdivided as follows:	12	53	111	128
Casework	6	31	64	73
Group work and community organization	6	14	21	32
Administration in public welfare	0	0	16	14
Psychiatric and psychological	0	8	10	9

such nontechnical courses as socio-economic and political backgrounds, for example. Even so, 73 out of 214 courses in 1941–42 are clearly in casework, with no other group approximating that proportion. If "technical courses" are used as a base, which is more realistic in view of the field practice components of the curriculum, the ratio is 73 out of 145, or almost exactly half. Even more indicative of this progressively casework-oriented trend of the School are data on field-work training and the field of employment of graduates. The field-work placement of students on which data were reported by Professor Bernstein is as follows:

[7] These are figures at periods ten years apart, ending in 1940–41. Full tables will be found in Professor Bernstein's report, pp. 130–157. They are interspersed with comments and summaries, but no general conclusions are offered.

Field-work placement
Percentages

	1927–28	1934–35	1941–42
Casework	87.6	95.6	85.5
Community organization and group work	6.6	2.4	6.3
Public welfare administration	—	.5	—

These figures on field-work placement have a special significance, of greater importance in many ways than the ones pertaining to course units. They spell out, as course units cannot do, the ultimate employment orientation, and the associated activity interests served. These figures happen to come from just one school, but one that has reflected the characteristics of the entire group. The occupational flow of graduates is similarly mirrored in the statistics cited in the following tabulation:

	Two-year Graduates			
	January 1931		August 1941	
		%		%
Total in Social Work	208	100	1,018	100
Casework	125	60.1	841	82.6
Community organization and group work	49	23.5	91	8.9

In judging the full significance of these figures, and of just one additional tabulation to come, it is well to recall the function of field-training assignments and of their weight in the credit points of the academic system. Perhaps no other professional training curriculum, unless it be medicine, places as much emphasis on field practice as the schools of social work. If then that field practice is so overwhelmingly concentrated in casework as these figures show, it is prima-facie evidence of the preponderant concern of the schools with that segment of the social work field. Laboratory components in the instruction in the physical sciences are not analogous. There the laboratory is part of teaching method, rather than occupational practice. But field assignment in a social work school is more than a variant of teaching method; it is an introduction into practice almost at the very start of the training, before the intellectual components of the curriculum have been assimilated. In a way, it corresponds more to internship in medicine, except that internship in medicine comes after the basic course of instruction. This fact, however, is not necessarily a negative judgment. It may, in fact, be one of the ingenious inventions of social work training for which some laurels are due. The point under discussion here, however, is not the pedagogic inventiveness displayed, but the specialized orientation indicated in the practice.

The rationale of field-work practice in a social welfare curriculum—especially when directed to economic or related problems of service—lies in the unavoidable Janus-like task of the worker. His job is under constant pressure to serve two purposes, inherently opposed if not actually contradictory. When he faces the problem of a person or family, unless he is a bureaucratic robot, he must first see the problem with the eyes of the client. The client has difficulties; he is trying to deal with them; he has his own interests, desires, objectives, and hopes. These interests and hopes are just as legitimate for the client as are the ones in the worker's own life. That is the basic fact, and if the worker cannot sympathetically understand it he misses the perspective for helpfulness. As to the client's outlook, *he, the client, is the only one in trouble,* and the worker's job is to help *him,* not a hundred or a thousand others. Unless the worker can to an appreciable extent identify himself with the client in that outlook, he is only an outsider with power and resources but no concern.

But the worker, by definition, is an instrument in the apparatus of the agency which has sent him to the client; that is his other face. To the agency, this client is one of many, and not necessarily the most important one. The agency, in turn, is not only the instrument of its sponsors; it is also part of the apparatus of society, a society whose obligations also include schooling the young, preventing epidemics, curing the sick, supporting higher education—and also the armed forces, the police, the water supply, the roads, etc.—all parts of organized social life. All these must be seen as parts of a whole; each is contained within that total structure, and the client is but one tiny unit in this enormous surrounding universe. It is not so much a question of how much can be given him in dollars and cents; it is rather how the function of helping him can be integrated in the entire task of social management. To be sure that that perspective, together with the ethical and moral demands of the existing culture, serves as guide, the agency establishes policies, regulations, theoretical concepts, a pattern of service in which the many clients are at the same time equal, even though all different from one another.

It is not easy to acquire such a perspective. To learn it takes time, thought, worry, and trial and error. The extended time allotment in a social work curriculum to achieve this degree of intellectual and emotional apparatus would seem legitimate. The details of assignment are, however, quite a different matter. Bearing in mind the relative weight of economic and noneconomic components in the client's distress, neither the actual distribution of field-work assignment nor the occupational flow of graduates would seem automatically to reflect social purposes. Nor, considering the quantitative responsibilities of tax-supported and voluntary agencies, does the following table seem to show that the purposes of society are judiciously served:

Distribution of Graduates of the School as of
February 1936* and May 1941

	1936		1941	
	Number	Per cent	Number	Per cent
Total in Social Work	458	100	1,017	100
Voluntary agencies	278	60.7	740	92.8
Tax-supported agencies	180	39.3	277	27.2

* This is within the shadow of social security legislation, 1935.

These figures relate, of course, to one of the schools only, the oldest and probably the largest in student body. Figures in other schools would undoubtedly be different in detail, though for the schools as a group hardly different in totals.[8] Figures could conceiv-

---

[8] Particularly significant in this connection is the analysis of certain

ably vary also, if brought up to date. Nothing in the writer's experience would justify a guess that the situation has changed substantially. And as indicated elsewhere, data relating both to casework and to community organization and group work apply to an overwhelming extent to voluntary rather than to public welfare agencies. In fact, if there is one major sin attributable to the training schools, it is that they have, with few exceptions,[9] failed to rise to the fact that social work is no longer the task of a select group of voluntary charitable agencies, but a major component of "social engineering," that is, the adaptation of governmental functions to the nature of the needs of the citizenry. These needs have not remained the same and, more important, the ways of meeting them have not remained the same, as technology, productivity, education, and democratic will have changed the culture in the nation.[10] Public education

---

data relating to the graduates of the "accredited schools of social work" who had gained their Master's degree in 1963. A total of 2,505 such graduates were contacted, and 1,685 returned the questionnaires as requested. A variety of interesting data were reported (by Mignon Sauber, author of the article based on these data—in "Personnel Information," National Association of Social Workers, January 1965). The item of particular interest here lists the field of employment of these graduates. They may be grouped as follows (in percentages of the total):

Public Assistance		10
	Child Welfare—all fields	31
"Casework"	Family Services (voluntary)	12
	Psychiatric Social Work (public and voluntary)	22	.. 72
	Medical Social Work	7
Other, varying from 2% to 5%		15
Unknown		3
Total		100

The clearly "casework" group would be roughly 72 per cent, with some exceptions and modifications in Child Welfare and "Other."

[9] Notably, the Chicago University School.

[10] Some change and progress with respect to this particular item may be represented by the following rough tabulation, supplied to the writer by the field-work administration of the Columbia University School of Social Work, as of November 23, 1964:

early entered the arena of planned social engineering. Public health followed, including medical services to all who needed them—and, as of now, mental hygiene and care of the mentally ill and retarded. Social work would have been still another such field if the appeal of its early leaders had been heeded. When in the early 1930's political leaders, economists, and a mere handful of individual social workers opened the way, with social security and public assistance as normal components of the postdepression realignment, the bulk of training school leaders and faculty members were not ready either to show the way or to put their shoulders to the wheel. Part of the explanation may be in the extent to which the schools were almost compulsively committed to the professional status of workers and of themselves as the principal exponents of professionalization. Part may be the extreme specialization in casework. But a substantial part of the explanation lies also in the early defensive and vested-interest nature of the group of schools, intent like the profession itself on recognized status. The vehicle of this particular vested-interest component has been the Association of Schools of Social Work, now the Council on Social Work Education, started as far back as 1919.

In 1915, less than twenty years since the first six-week course of instruction for Charity Workers was inaugurated, and while some

---

Students in field work as of this date covering those designated as *"casework"* placements:

			Per cent
Total casework placements		170	100
In voluntary agencies		119	70
Family societies	69		
Child welfare	50		
In public agencies		51	30
Economic assistance	69		
Child welfare	24		
A cross-calculation indicates that			
Child welfare placements were	74		
Family and public assistance	96		

The public agency placements in these two major categories are therefore: 33 per cent in child welfare, and 28 per cent in family and economic assistance.

leaders of social work still labored on arousing interest and action for social improvement tasks in child labor, social legislation, public health, infant mortality, insurance, and related fields of social reform, the schools were already pressing for professional status and recognition. A committee of school representatives met and presented papers and discussion on the project. Dr. Abraham Flexner, who had some time earlier made an epoch-making study of medical education, was requested to read a paper entitled, "Is Social Work a Profession," and the members of the committee addressed themselves to this discussion.[11] After an analysis of factors which he regarded as pertinent to the question, Dr. Flexner came to a negative conclusion:

> At the moment, therefore, it may be—observe that I am not endeavoring to be very positive—it may be that social work will gain if it becomes uncomfortably conscious that it is not a profession in the sense in which medicine and engineering are professions; that if medicine and engineering have cause to proceed with critical care, social work has even more . . .

In his discussion of the problem he says, for example (and this is long before the claims for casework had become so decisive):

> . . . the social worker is at times perhaps too self-confident; social work has suffered to some extent from one of the vices associated with journalism, excessive facility in speech . . .

The importance of Dr. Flexner's opinions lies not so much in what he said, but rather in his competence to pass judgment and in the very sympathetic approach to the problem in his paper. Needless to say, his opinions were discussed for years, but not noticeably heeded. Within four years of that meeting (1919), some fifteen schools of social-work training by then in existence established an Association of Training Schools for Professional Social Work. By 1929, the membership had risen to twenty-eight, and the name slightly changed. Under the present Council on Social Work Education, suc-

[11] *Proceedings* of the Conference of Charities and Corrections, 1915, pp. 576–626, included Dr. Flexner's paper and those of the discussants.

cessor to the Association, there are now some seventy-five Graduate Professional Schools of Social Work in Canada and the United States, with an affiliated group of nearly 209 undergraduate departments of colleges and universities, "offering courses with social work content."

These bare facts do not tell the whole story. They emphasize the extent to which the schools, together with the professional organization, have intensified the concept of professionalism. Together the two have succeeded in designating professional maturity in terms of a Master's degree. The schools are, in addition, responsible to a large extent for the numerical limitation of training workers for jobs in public welfare by making no effective efforts to create a training program suitable, in a realistic way, to the requirements of the large mass of workers engaged in public welfare services. They have not as yet emerged from the defensive stance that created the Association of Schools in 1919.

The occasion for setting up that vested-interest machinery was the indirect result of events in World War I. The American Red Cross, as part of its stupendous operations in connection with war needs, had introduced worker training operations in all or most of its regional offices, each of which covered some half-dozen states. It was instrumental in introducing some *ad hoc* training in colleges and state universities;[12] a director of this program was appointed in the national office of the American Red Cross, to promote and advise on this pressing need for workers and for some continuing plan to assure provision of workers to help in problems in families of servicemen and in the lives of the men themselves. This sudden proliferation of training programs brought about the defensive mechanism resulting in the Association of Schools. From that time on a sort of cold war appears to have been waged between established schools on

---

[12] In one such regional office, located in Atlanta, Georgia, Professor Howard Odum had requested substantial help for a school to be established in the University of North Carolina. The regional Red Cross director of training, with the help of the venerable Joe Logan, obtained a grant of $20,000 to establish that school in Chapel Hill. In this enterprise the present writer was associated with Professor Odum, representing the American Red Cross, in all the activities involved.

the one hand, and state universities, land grant colleges, and other educational institutions eager to enter that field. The battle to "keep out" and to "come in" is still in progress, and a few of the details are cited at the end of this chapter. Since, however, the weapons and goals of the cold war are too complicated, and the details not always important, it is well to point out in what way the existing association of schools of social work (the Council on Social Work Education), its predecessors, and individual schools have failed to face the central problem and the central challenge:

1. They have built up an assumption by no means supported by adequate proof that a two-year graduate training in a school of social work actually does, or that it is *the only thing* that does, prepare a competent social worker.

2. They have, without saying it in so many words, acted on the major premise that social work is casework, and as seen from the statistical data quoted on graduates and on courses offered, the extent of other technical training has been relatively small.

3. They have accustomed themselves, the field, and civil service authorities to the concept that "professional training" or "professional worker" is some basic and indisputable concept.

4. They have failed to recognize the importance of public welfare even after the federal-state program had produced the largest establishments of service and the greatest demand for workers.[13]

5. They have, as part of all this, allowed themselves to be engulfed in the psychoanalytic conceptual world, paying relatively little attention to the social sciences, particularly economics, labor relations, and political science.

6. They have promulgated the concept of accreditation in the operations of their organization to the point where it reads like Talmudic text or some esoteric code, and with far less flexi-

[13] Note the fruitless attempts to swerve the training course in that direction by some members of the faculty of the New York School of Social Work in the early 1930's: Elizabeth Meyer's *History of the New York School,* p. 87. Note also the estimate in the annual report of the U.S. Department of Health, Education, and Welfare for 1963 of a probable number of public assistance workers to be employed in state systems by 1970, approximately 65,000.

bility than applies, for example, to hospitals in the medical field.

At last, in 1963, after more than three decades of fencing about the exclusive competence of orthodox social work schools, there appears—or appeared in 1963—an analysis of some pertinent facts about the nature of the field as it relates to training and at least something more than a half-hearted attempt to relate the function of training to realities of the field. This analysis, and the proposals arising from it, came after some thirty years of the intraschool cold war and was still far from acceptance by member schools of the council. It is coterminous with what must be seen as a condescending and, as it proved, unsuccessful proposal in the National Association of Social Workers to recognize and admit into the professional association, on a sort of second-class citizenship, a group not presenting the outer symbols of "two-year graduate trainee" with Master's degree. In the annual "program meeting" of the Council on Social Work Education in 1963, the opening address of its executive director, Dr. Ernest Witte, dealt with "Training Social Work Associates." As the title indicates, the address was still a grudging proposal, but at least it faced some of the facts, if it did not marshal behind them a militant intent. In his first paragraph the author attempts:

> . . . to convey the urgency and the necessity for the initiation of a beginning but substantial experiment, under educational auspices, which offers a reasonable expectation of contributing to a solution of the *increasingly critical shortage of the personnel needed to staff welfare services.*[14] . . . We have lived with their problem for so long that we have come to accept it as we do the weather. The *image ideal we have created for ourselves of fully prepared social workers staffing the social service programs has inhibited us from facing the realities of the present staffing situation.*[14]

Among the quotations offered by Dr. Witte in support of the proposal for a major effort to rectify the situation, one is from a letter

[14] Italics added.

from Professor Charles N. Lebeaux of the School of Social Work of Wayne University (dated September 1962):

> I am in a state of continuous amazement at our inability to face up to the problem of the fact that only one or two per cent of the workers in public assistance agencies have adequate social work training. The fact is that we are not, in the next 100 or 200 years, going to supply *so-called trained workers*[15] to the public assistance agencies. But the problem of service to public assistance clients remains, and it seems to me that it is our bounden duty to up-train these people at a non-professional level. Somehow it must appear to social workers that to undertake such a project must be unprofessional. The facts are quite the contrary. . . .

The details of the Council's proposals are still timid and inadequate, but even so they have not been accepted or begun to be implemented.

What then should be the future of schools for training of welfare personnel?

Perhaps this question should be framed differently: What is the future complexion of welfare services for which personnel should be trained? In a sense this entire document is addressed to this larger question. The problem of future training can be examined within such perspectives as are available now, while bearing in mind the direction of the necessary and even probable future of welfare.

As in many or most systems of preparation devised for professional personnel, whether in engineering, law, medicine, nursing, or whatever, there is a twofold problem facing the educator's curriculum-building task. He must provide for the student trainee two things:

A. The Conceptual and Factual Foundation of the Subject, and

B. The Operational Practice.

As components of the educational subject matter these areas of training can be considered independently of academic hierarchical

---

[15] Italics added.

categories, whether these be "courses," hours, credits, titles, or "sequences." These things are but gadgets. The faculty of a school organized for this purpose must include in its personnel a combination of competencies in both divisions of training.

✑ THE CONCEPTUAL-FACTUAL FOUNDATIONS OF THE CURRICULUM

Unlike the physical sciences and unlike perhaps some other professional fields, the worker in the welfare services must have an eclectic, even if necessarily superficial, horizon covering diverse specialties and orientations. He will have to be content with what may seem fragmented but authentic portions of contiguous areas of knowledge, a vernacular, as it were, of social and environmental sciences. And certainly the curriculum must resemble a university tapestry rather than a set of theoretical positions drawn from operational practice. More specifically, the following components are suggested for this part of the curriculum (without reference to priorities, dosages, or other aspects).

1. *The economic structure as seen in the United States.* The selection of items within this topic is likely to be difficult. It is bound to deal to some extent with the general, chiefly technological aspects of the American economy. But equally or more so it has to be directed to the economic pattern of family and person in his task of combining income with consumption and security. On the borderline between the self-maintaining economic unit, including dependents and provision for contingencies of all kinds, the prospective possibility of dependency must also be envisioned. It affects standards of living and their cultural components. All this has to be related to the capital-taxation-wage-investment-national product-occupational distribution-distribution of per capita and per family income—a complex conceptual world in which the welfare worker cannot be illiterate any more than the service agency can plan in an ivory tower.

2. *Political science and government.* The subject is hardly less important for the welfare service worker than are economics and its major subdivisions. Moreover, the concepts and facts of economic structure and of government are becoming inextricably enmeshed in

an increasing number of governmental service and budget operations in a way that the time-honored charitable activity planners of the past could hardly have dreamt.

3. *Power structures.* Politics, labor, sectarian, bodies, organizations of financial, manufacturing, and commercial enterprises, the press and other communication industries, all this constitutes a conceptual-factual area of major proportions in the setting of welfare services as well as in the general cultural and political environment of the citizen. This subject is not to be confused with the preceding topic of political science and government, even though the two are tangential at many points.

4. *Cultural realities in American life.* If it were merely sociological curiosity or a matter of interest in a comparative study of cultures, the topic would have little justification in a curriculum designed for welfare service workers. The importance of the topic lies in the fact that it affects the daily task and quality of welfare services as established, and also, or even more, the growth, past and future, of their scope. There are controversial aspects of this subject, as for example:

The meaning and socio-political power of the concept of democracy—far more realistic than the word alone;

Unyielding dedication to the "sancity" of property rights, and militant rejection of assaults upon it by ideologies of any kind;

The deep-seated mutual exclusiveness in varying degrees of sects, churches, and ethnic groups;

The nature, function, and operational patterns of community life;

The explosive changes in attitudes toward extramarital sex, birth control, social control of marital relations.

This list is not a compendium; it is suggestive of the realities of our culture that must be seriously examined and adequately handled in such a curriculum.

5. *Psychology.* This, the most ponderous part of the present curriculum of social work training, will undoubtedly be the most difficult to fit into a future conceptual tapestry. It will require imagination, courage, and reorientation of purpose. It will have to be divorced from the commitment to treatment to which it has had a spurious and unreal attachment ever since the psychoanalytic en-

lightenment and the growing surrender of social work to psychiatry. The invaluable contributions of psychoanalytic discovery and its inundation of psychiatry have seduced the field of social work to psychological theory and treatment; they have become the center of professional interest to the near-exclusion of the relevance of economic insufficiency and distress. There has been a distortion not only of professional services to client and a recognition of who was the legitimate client, but also, and equally serious, of the nature of psychology as a subdivision of the biological sciences and of the elusive but imperative field of social science.

How then handle psychology in the curriclum? The answer will require a painful reappraisal. Normal human psychology will have to be reinstated as the dominant and regnant subject matter, illuminated by all relevant discoveries of deviation. It will have to enfold client, worker, and all others in the same world of reality, differentiated only by factors of health, culture, tradition, and technological status. Understanding the client will have to be seen as no different from understanding anyone except for the incidence of the same external or pathologically deviant factors that may affect anyone. Understanding and sympathy would become the goal in concepts and motivation.

6. *Other conceptual-factual subjects.* There is no sacrosanct, inclusive body of additional areas that would logically and realistically constitute the remaining components of this part of the curriculum. Nor do they represent problems as difficult for a rejuvenated curriculum as those listed above. They would seem to comprise, for example, material such as laws and legal concepts, both in the "civil" and the "criminal" divisions of the subject, and including procedure; biological and medical fields, which, important as they have always been, and occasionally included in curricula under medical designation, will take on unprecedented importance with the federal Medicare program, state legislation relating, for example, to Title XIX of the Medicare law, and some newly ascendant emphases on chemotherapy and gerontology; and resources.

It is difficult to say with any assurance how much of the subject of resources had best be subsumed under the conceptual-factual phase of curriculum planning, and how much under operational practice. It partakes sufficiently of both categories to justify some diversified experimentation, and should provide an important field for controlled study. Certainly no operation of services can be conceived without knowledge of resources. It is true on the other hand that resources are not evenly distributed over the land, over urban and rural areas, over areas with diverse occupational, climatic, and cultural regions. Yet a fundamental and generic conception of the nature, availability, and state of development of resources should have a solid unified physiognomy, just as the practice of medicine requires a universal perspective beyond immediately ready resources.

Administration has been a typical "advanced" course in some of the schools, at various levels of the student's progress. It is of debatable validity standing by itself. Perhaps the most practicable way would be to work it into the pedagogical guidance of field practice. There it is essential for effective and acceptable internship; probably all that is necessary for the student to know can be, and in a sense, must be integrated with his field practice. In a restructuring of the curricula for welfare service workers, no competent faculty can fail to find an adequate bridge between theory or concept and successful operation.

➤ OPERATIONAL PRACTICE IN THE CURRICULUM ➤

The procedure in the past has been roughly a traditional combination of "agency policy" in the organizations providing field placement for student practice, and "professional techniques" as gradually calcified in the accepted techniques of the field: casework, group work, community organization, and research. Whatever fresh new life can be pumped into the settled traditions of the field will depend in part on the extent to which leaders are ready to redirect their outlook; to a larger extent, however, it will be determined by the massive development in public assistance, Medicare, education, and diversification of institutions. There are only a few recommendations that would seem to be worth submitting at this point to a forward-looking body of educators in this field of operations.

First, all students should have field practice assignments in public assistance agencies dealing primarily with the economically disadvantaged population (this does not include social security administration except on the administrative level, for obvious reasons). Second, specialization should be provided as the requirements of the field and a socio-political conception of welfare services may permit, provided that this specialization does not perturb the priority in quantitative planning of service to the destitute.

Examples of fields of specialization would be:

child welfare, in its varied aspects;

family cohesion problems, including broken families, disturbed marital complications, unmarried mothers with children;

psychological deviations and problems they create, and cooperation with psychiatric services;

nonindividualized services to groups of various ages and in various institutionalized categories;

community agency services, as in housing, and settlement types of community activities.

A general redirection of future curricula along the lines suggested would have desirable counterparts in the formal academic aspects of the work of training schools and in the associated problems of professional organization. The academic stages as usually related to the progress of the student, and as formalized in the generally current academic designations of progress, would need redefinement as relating to this field of endeavor. The following tentative structure and the implicit changes from the present are suggested.

(a) *Basic education,* for which the Bachelor's degree is a convenient symbol, should be continued but the title not "worshipped";

(b) The spurious standard of a *Master's degree* as an imperative proof of competence and as defined for the present purposes of social work is ready for dethronement. Certainly the requirement of a Master's thesis is an almost meaningless nuisance and rarely useful. Perhaps the degree might automatically be granted after a year's employment or practice or upon some other formalized condition;

(c) *Postgraduate advanced study* as an avenue for enriched perspective and scholarship may well be retained as in other fields.

If this is to be associated with a Ph.D. degree it may properly bring this field into useful comradeship with other scholarly pursuits. The Ph.D. has, through the centuries, become a symbol of scholarly attainments, and surely philosophy in the social work field is no less appropriate than where applied to chemistry, literature, or economics. But there seems little justification for the new-fangled escape into "doctor of social welfare";

(d) Finally, the retention of *field practice* associated with conceptual-factual practice is as important in this field as in the physical sciences or medicine, with the additional benefit of unavoidable indoctrination into the demands of administration, and the testing-out of the student's temperamental suitability for this nonclassical field of operation.

At this point it is well to return to the crucial question, fundamental to the legitimacy of training: What is the complexion of welfare services for which the educational and training school serves merely as a provider of competent personnel?

Perhaps the simplest way to examine the question is by analogy to economic concepts. And these, in turn, must be looked at in the light of modern science and technology. We recognize in the first place the beneficiary (or client) as the consumer, and what he consumes is welfare services. The agency (community, nation, organized society) is then seen as the producing apparatus, and the service worker as part of the personnel in that apparatus. The items of consumption consist of services to meet ascertained needs of the consumer, as defined in part by the nature of the service required. This in turn takes the form, in its simplest categories, of economic assistance, hospital, foster home, institution, and more recently pension, vocational rehabilitation, and a score of others. There is inevitably a quantitative aspect of consumer demand and a qualitative aspect in designing the appropriate service. Underlying this pattern of need and corresponding service is cost of production and distribution. The analogy might be pursued further, but to no immediate purpose. Up to the present we have not troubled to ascertain the extent of consumer demand or, in more appropriate language, the incidence of need. This then becomes an inescapable obligation for assuring quantitatively the extent and qualitatively the character of services to be performed. This is a major task of research in a fundamental social engineering approach.

That dependable motivating factor in the economic world, the search for profit, is evidently not pertinent at this point. What then is to be the nature of the motivation for defining service to be given, and quantitative estimate of its production? Before the present system in industrial cultures, the motivations were, in the main, the impulses of the donor, the religious otherworld compensation, and a variety of cultural mores. These provided little inducement for quantitative estimates of need or concern with results. We may assume that present motivation is more clearly a social philosophy, social engineering, and the effective demand of the potential consumer. For our own day the specific facts of incidence, study of the nature of appropriate services, and an administrative apparatus of laws, financing, and provision of operating personnel are imperative. Psychological motivations of mercy, salvation become irrelevant, though the lurking, ever-present search for power remains. Ultimately, the character of operational personnel, its size, its administrative structure, its competence, and its social motivation will inevitably be associated with facts of incidence, and that implies appropriate research, and testing the suitability and results of services calls for more research. With imaginative patterns of training, that may call for more than research. They call for hard-headed dedication, scientific pedagogy, and the minimization of vested-interest determinism.

PART FOUR

HISTORICAL
PERSPECTIVES

Chapter XV

శ్రీ

Social Welfare in
Western Culture

History could very well be pure indulgence, like the arts or music, or wild life. It is exciting to those that like it, as antique furniture or the cathedrals of France and England are exciting to those whose enjoyment of life and of living is enhanced by them. Why historical perspectives in a treatise whose purpose is to promote social values and examine welfare practices as they exist today or as they might be improved for the morrow? In contemplating the present scene one cannot fail to be aware of certain satisfying facts of life today— in the United States at least—and certainly in some other countries as well—that in their totality are far superior to the historically identifiable stages through which Western culture has passed.

There are greater resources, substantive and technological than ever before.

In the main, power rests with the majority, not with an oligarchic few, or a dictator and his henchmen.

Political liberty and democratic equality are regarded as paramount despite many unwholesome spots.

Respect for human dignity as residing in all men is in undisputed ascendancy.

Solutions for residual evils are being sought and worked out in technological and social engineering.

But our present-day mores, motivations, and procedures are a complex tapestry of theories, motives, and aftereffects of the events of countless centuries; and these are still alive like the germs in the cells of biological entities with all their cross-fertilizations and environmental changes. It would seem difficult to devise and to establish a perfect and logical social structure, or within such a structure to build an effective social welfare system, without recognizing and counting with the inherited ways of thinking and feeling of the generation in which we work. Men carry the history of their culture in the activities of daily life and in quick reactions which they are rarely aware of. Any plan of action or proposed theory must pay its respects to and purchase its authorization from the accumulated impress of the past. Certainly that is the case in the field of welfare. A pertinent and functioning historical perspective would therefore seem realistically inescapable. Much of this historical background has been touched upon in earlier pages when it seemed relevant or necessary. It may be desirable, nevertheless, to recapitulate in more organized fashion the principal items of importance.

Some of the events touched upon here might not, at first, seem to bear too directly upon the emergence of present-day "welfare." Who, for example, can prove that the French Revolution was a powerful factor in the history of democracy, or that democracy, if so influenced, had anything to do with the development of social welfare systems? And how would we disentangle the French Revolution from the American one which preceded it and which is certainly nearer home? The effects of the French Revolution may very well have been quite different in England during the opening period of the nineteenth century, when we were still drawing upon England for our basic culture, from what it was in those same years in the United States. It was more direct and massive, even more mixed, and more sharply resisted there than in this country. And its influence here was largely indirect, through our political leaders, pro and con, Jefferson and Madison or John Adams and Hamilton and Sam Adams. Even so, it would be difficult to be certain that, for example, the elimination of capital punishment for a number of crimes, traceable to that period here, could have been influenced by the wholesale murderous indulgence of the leaders of the French Revolution. Nevertheless, through Jefferson and his group, and Tom Paine and others, the effective influence of that even on one version of democracy is easily seen, and its indirect but dominant long-range effect would seem to have prepared the way for the majority of our eventual social welfare plans. Perhaps it was the militancy of the exponents that carried weight and made converts—as well as enemies —for democracy rather than their logic and persuasion. There certainly was little of the gentle teacher or persuader in Tom Paine and nothing meticulous about Sam Adams in attacking the seats of power.

Whether stormy 1848 in Europe had any appreciable effect in feeling and thought on the "proletariat" in the United States a superficial scanning of history does not disclose. But the immigration from several European countries that followed that popular movement on the Continent brought into this country many persons whose impulses were actively on the side of democracy rather than on maintenance of the European status quo. But by that time American movements and action had attained a momentum of their own distinct from the ways of Western Europe.

A rough and uneven list of events and of factors other and later than the French and American Revolutions would probably include the following as somehow pertinent to the emergence of social welfare here:

1. The Rise and Growth of Trade Unionism
2. The Socialist Movement in Europe and Its Reverberations in America
3. The Discovery of "Poverty" by Charles Booth and His Contemporaries
4. The First World War
5. Sigmund Freud and the New Psychology
6. The Beveridge Report
7. The Great Depression of 1930–33 and Its Operational Results

In various ways that follow no easily discernible pattern, all these events and persons have contributed to the coming of age of social welfare in the United States.

ꙮ THE RISE OF TRADE UNIONISM

There cannot be much question that this is the most important single factor in the list, despite the many ways in which trade unions have occasionally displayed a lack of that state of grace so difficult to retain with the acquisition of power. The early days of trade unionism in England were bitter, harrowing, and dangerous to the life and limb of its active promoters. Unions were legally designated conspiracies and as such could be and were subject to criminal prosecution. In the long history of trade unions in the United States there are weird byways. Unions are responsible for the original exclusion of Chinese from immigration; they have often held the color line; and the narrow interests of separate crafts have time and again led them to forget that the less fortunate worker also has to live and support his family. For a time before World War I there was little interest on the part of labor leaders to extend their protective mechanism to the larger circle of labor and to attack on a grand scale the condition of the poor. Nor, in those days, did they seek to interest themselves in the wider fields of social legislation or in the protection of women and children. But today there is only a residue of that narrow preoccupation with the interest of a labor aristocracy. The important relevance, however, of the labor movement to our present concern lies in the fact that it elevated "the poor and the worker" from their historical low status to the place that their preponderant numbers deserve; that it increased wage income and the accompanying level of living, job security, and general economic security of the masses to levels undreamed of a generation ago. It has given self-respect and assurance to the worker and so eliminated the low-caste status consciousness which he had for millennia accepted. The organized strength of the movement has contributed to building a solid foundation for welfare services under public administration and extending far forward the outer edges of over-all economic security. Equally important, also, is recognition by labor, with only occasional lapses, that government, whether central or local, is the paramount means and responsible instrument for an inclusive welfare system—already far advanced and with places still to go. Far less important, therefore, are the special provisions for a variety of welfare resources for members within the trade union structure as distinct from their status as people of the nation. They are now a "plus" to a national system and should be publicized for the benefit of less-well-organized and less-well-provided-for segments of the population.

One can speak of the trade union movement, therefore, not only as a happy provision of a fortunately militant large sector of the population, but also as a force pressing for engineered social structure and planned social welfare. The fact that in some countries this process may have gone further, and achieved a philosophical foundation of more impressive grandeur, than in the United States is important perhaps more for mankind as a whole than for American social welfare. This is true of Great Britain, of some other members of the British Commonwealth, and of some of the Scandinavian countries. It is more debatable whether the Communist countries may, in that respect, be grouped in this company. The major and incalculably important contribution of trade unionism is, of course, its primary objective, namely the increase of wages to levels that finally should obliterate the age-old identification in Western civilization of poverty with destitution.

To have eliminated the crude universality of poverty in the wage-earning majority would seem hardly less important than liberation of the masses of people from feudal and arbitrary subjection whether as wage-slaves or serfs. And this has happened in the United States. Poverty is indeed still with us. But it is no longer the condition of the majority of workers and their families. The abolition of poverty has come to be regarded as a major task of politics, government, and organized labor. There is still, as we have seen, destitution with its accompanying evils, especially in the minority groups. But destitution as such has become manageable within the administrative structure of government to a point where one can see its virtual disappearance in this country in a not too distant future. That this task is being carried into execution chiefly under leadership of the federal government is hard for many to accept, but until all states and local governments attain the level of interest of the central government it is likely to continue so. At any rate, up to now organized labor has been a powerful factor in promoting democracy as the foundation of social welfare, and in securing specific benefits to the worker and his family by governmental responsibility for insurance against unemployment, illness, death or absence of the breadwinner, disability, and superannuation.

There are some lesser aspects of the history of the labor movement where it meets on more intimate terms the operations of social welfare. For example, despite some attempts at different times to integrate the interests of unionism with social work professionalism, there is little progress to report. Some persons are conscious of their dual status: union members and professionals. In the former, a legitimate primary function and accent is centered on the protective purposes vis-à-vis the employing agency; in the latter, the identification of professional status is paramount as carrying out the stated policy of the employing agency. These two faces of the same person have not easily coalesced. And it has been the relatively rare agency that has been able to achieve a sympathetic acceptance in its professional purposes of the labor aspect of the employee. There have, in fact, been not infrequent occasions when the client became victim of the conflict between union activities and agency operations. In a sense, there is logic in that situation, for the employer, as in all fields, and an employee, equally, is just that. In many instances, also, where the managers of employing agencies are representatives of wealth and privilege, they may have prior loyalties to their social status and economic beliefs, and these may conflict with the agency's prior obligation to serve its clients.

While trade union interests and professional interests are not necessarily in conflict, they have not in fact been successfully integrated. There was, for instance, a bold proposal at one time by union representatives in one of the large municipal social agencies that at the application or intake points clients be seen by social workers as persons in need and be referred to the appropriate agency without regard to its sponsorship or its character as a voluntary or public organization. So far as any record exists this eminently logical proposal did not receive a hearing either by the professional body or by the employing agencies. In another instance—in a voluntary agency—the professional employees had over a long period of time been attempting to organize as part of the union of social service personnel. They were opposed both by the professional administrative staff and also, logically, by the employing body. There was a very close relationship between the administrative personnel of that agency and the professional training school—a leading institution of its kind in the country—in leadership and outlook and in organizational structure. The school at that time had an active union membership in the faculty. The controversy in the agency grew, and at one point the union member faculty group went out in good old union picketing style, demonstrating on the street at the agency's offices. But no "integration" of outlook or action ensued.[1]

Important as these picturesque examples may be within the organized agency structure of social welfare, the major accent lies not there but in the contribution of the labor movement in emancipating the worker, including also the welfare worker, in raising his income and employment security in the entire field of working for a livelihood.

[1] A far more challenging situation arose early in 1965 when members of the union working in the public assistance service in New York City went on strike. No visible common interest of the union and of the profession emerged.

❧ THE SOCIALIST MOVEMENT AS A FACTOR FOR SOCIAL WELFARE

Within the general perspective of social welfare in this country, the socialist movement in Western Europe may appear to be of minor significance. Nor are we here concerned with, or in position to assay, its importance on the structure of Western civilization or of world civilization. It is of specific importance, however, even in our more limited historical scene, for it has had a perceptible effect on the ideological development of our social welfare system. Here again, as in many other aspects of the American social scene, the major influence came more by way of English developments than directly from events in the United States. This influence does not appear to have been very strong. The reasons seem to lie chiefly in the different cultural characteristics of the two countries. It was, for example, the intelligentsia in England that studied with sympathy and understanding the socialist movements in Europe; and this English intelligentsia was so close to the personnel of social and political leadership there that what it thought was discussed and absorbed by that political leadership.

Perhaps an underlying general religious attachment to Christian tenets also helped. In his excellent study, *England's Road to Social Security,* Karl de Schweinitz quotes a revealing statement by Clement R. Attlee, one of the best-known leaders of the British Labour Party, who said in 1937: "Here one sees a feature which distinguishes the British movement from most of those abroad. In no other country has Christianity become converted to socialism to such an extent as in Britain. In no other socialist movement has Christian thought had such a powerful leavening influence."[2] But more conspicuous is the fact that the intellectual leadership, which also possessed social status and political influence, took an active part in propagation of the socialistically colored, progressive, labor-oriented philosophical literature of the day. This was particularly true of the Fabian Society, uniquely English in origin and ways. The accents then became either conservative or labor; political parties became

[2] Karl de Schweinitz, *England's Road to Social Security* (University of Pennsylvania Press, 1943), p. 173.

thus aligned, and programs could be discussed on levels legitimately political. And since the Poor Laws and their administration had been for many years one of the most uncomfortable areas of governmental responsibility, it was possible for the interests of labor and those of the destitute to coalesce in part at least and to be promoted by the same leaders. Increasingly the Labour Party became frankly socialistic. But its progress in the field of labor relations was not matched by its success in revamping Poor Law administration.

In the United States the intellectual and political influence of English (and of European) socialist movements turned up as specific programs rather than as social philosophies. The ways in which these programs took form were either through promotion of social insurance, or, in the minds and plans of political leaders, in the legislation effected in the administration of President Franklin D. Roosevelt. For the men who became his creative brain trust were social scientists fully conversant with English experience and skilled in transforming theoretical concepts into legislative and administrative format.

As a political movement socialism in the United States has had a scant history and even less influence. Robert Owen was better known in England than in America, and any influence he had in the long run was there rather than here. With the incomparably large and speedy development of capitalist production, the enormous concentration of financial resources, the lack of political interest in the early leadership of labor, the close interweaving of financial and political power, and the absence of the long and bitter history of poverty as it had festered in England, socialism had little chance for calm analysis in the United States. Owen, Marx, Engels, were practically unknown, and membership in socialist parties was numerically insignificant. These parties were, moreover, early divided into factions. They rarely appealed to the farmer, and the power of industrial giants was too great for them to buck. When at last socialism in the form of communism seemed mature enough for the American public to recognize, enough hostility had been engendered to make its appeal purely negative. Only when democracy seemed untainted by any relationship to socialism or communism did it continue to be a powerful force for dealing with problems of poverty or

destitution. It may be fair to say, then, that insofar as socialism may
have seeped into the conscious intent of the American public or law-
maker, it was only in disguise, and the only explanation for accepting any program for improving the income of the poor or destitute
lies in the unconscious practice of the democratic dogma. Moreover,
public relief never constituted here the drain on public resources
that it did, relatively, in England. Also when the major provisions
for public assistance and social security came into being the general
public saw it somewhat as a disaster-relief measure rather than as a
permanent piece of social engineering.

⚶ THE DISCOVERY OF POVERTY

Here again, as in the case of socialism, historical perspective
must recognize the influence, of enormous dimensions, of British
scholars and political thinkers. Poverty in one form or another had
been the subject of political controversy, of a welter of legislation,
pamphlets, books, rebellions, philosophical debates, of accusations
and exhortations, for some six hundred years of English history before an attempt was made to gauge its extent and form in a factual,
scholarly way. Sir Frederick M. Eden's *State of the Poor* was the
first such attempt, and his study, published in 1797, was unique,
almost a prophetic book, in the place it holds in this phase of English
history. It was detailed, descriptive, inclusive, and covered a considerable area of England. Charles Booth's study, *Life and Labor of
the People of London,* might have remained but a monument for
the antiquarian to contemplate had it not been for the Fabian Society of which he was a member, and which from its inception in
1884 became an activist force, combining propaganda for the socialist and labor cause with intellectual leadership in the economic-
political field. In the peculiar way of England its members also had
connections and social acceptance in the "palaces" of both aristocracy and the business world. Booth himself was not a socialist and
not really an activist in the field of welfare. But he was puzzled by
what he saw, and his curiosity was aroused. For some four years or
more he labored collecting data and writing, using his considerable

personal resources to engage staff and for other necessary expenses.[3]
The result was some seventeen volumes published by 1903.

What may have been the influence of Booth's work in England is not something that can be evaluated in this book, except insofar as it was the first of a series of related studies which continue to make it an invaluable part of the historical perspective relating to poverty. Even before it was completed it had inspired B. Seebohm Rountree, a wealthy chocolate manufacturer of York, to undertake a similar study covering the entire city of York. Other studies followed, and by 1935 a remarkable series had been published, covering nearly ten municipal areas.[4]

Perhaps the most tangible influence in the United States of Booth's masterpiece stems from the fact that it was the first scientifically conducted "social survey" in Western history. It was replete with suggestive concepts and stimulated a spate of local social surveys in this country, large and small, sociological in outlook or pro-

[3] A most enlightening biography of Charles Booth was recently published by Professor T. S. Simey of Liverpool.

[4] These further studies represented conditions in additional areas in England, but were also increasingly more sophisticated in techniques; together they constitute an incomparable achievement, combining scholarship with devotion to public interest in the problems of poverty. They may well be classed with Eden's *State of the Poor,* the Hammonds' studies of the village and town laborer, and with the monumental work of the Webbs on the history of the English Poor Law. More specifically, in view of their combined importance, the following should be listed:

B. Seebohm Rountree. *Poverty, A Study of Town Life* (1901), dealing with the City of York, and its sequel, *Poverty and Progress,* by the same author, published in 1932.

A. L. Bowley and A. P. Burnett-Hurst. *Livelihood and Poverty,* G. Bell (1915), covering five selected towns in England, the general intent similar to Booth's but along statistically expert lines of sampling. Followed ten years later by a restudy of the same areas, *Has Poverty Diminished* (P. S. King & Son, 1925), by Bowley and Margaret H. Hogg.

London School of Economics and Political Science, under the leadership of Sir Hubert Llewellyn Smith, with advisory committee that included Sir William Beveridge and Sidney Webb (Lord Parsfield). *New Survey of London Life and Labor,* in several volumes (London School of Economics, 1932).

D. Caradog Jones. *Social Survey of Mersey Side,* the area surrounding Liverpool (Liverpool University Press, 1939).

grammatic in intent. In the field of social work these surveys became increasingly associated with plans for community action for the disadvantaged. The first and most significant of these, the "Pittsburgh Survey" (1907) was almost wholly financed by the Russell Sage Foundation. While a classic in its own right and initiated by an outstanding American leader in social welfare, Paul U. Kellogg, it certainly was stimulated by the impact of Booth's work on social welfare perspectives. The interest taken in the Pittsburgh Survey by the Russell Sage Foundation was in turn responsible for a considerable number of other social surveys and similar enterprises sponsored over several decades by that Foundation[5] and subsequently by other bodies, both local and national. Since there existed no counterpart in the United States of the Fabian Society, the influence of the Booth study[6] was indirect, and it was little known or discussed in this country. There were indeed a great many surveys undertaken after the Pittsburgh Survey, and a number of these were actually conducted or financed by the Russell Sage Foundation and by lesser similar organizations. But after "Pittsburgh" the accent on poverty was lost. The range of interest of the Russell Sage Foundation extended over the entire field of social welfare. Not until the great

[5] In the history of the Russell Sage Foundation, published in 1947, the Pittsburgh Survey is referred to as "the most important and best known of the studies made possible by the Foundation in its early days." A footnote to this modest statement indicates that one source for this suggested survey was a suggestion submitted to the Trustees of the Foundation by Henry R. Seager, an outstanding American economist of that day, for a study of "the life and labor of the people of New York City comparable with Charles Booth's study of London."

[6] The writer's first awareness of this great work came when he was a student in the New York School of Philanthropy in 1911. The faculty member charged with instruction in research at that time, Edward Ewing Pratt, used the Booth study as partial text material. When this writer himself became responsible for that subject in the same school nearly two decades later, the follow-up survey of the London inquiry, conducted by the London School of Economics, had already been published and the state of poverty could be surveyed across thirty years. It was, for teaching purposes, even more suitable, especially since the more sophisticated statistical methods could then be applied. In the writer's recollection, however, it all seems to have been to the students in this country more esoteric and foreign than it should have been.

depression of the 1930's did problems of poverty and destitution come into focus again here, and the emergency nature of that situation made any continuity with the poverty of vast portions of the population as shown by Booth and his successors unreal and irrelevant.

What made the English studies so significant was the fact that the poverty they discovered, measured, and identified was not some single occurrence or emergency like the catastrophic Black Death (or our own depression), but a persistent characteristic of Western civilization. For that reason a few outstanding items from at least the original London study may be worth recalling. In the first place, Booth introduced, for the first time, the concept of a "poverty line," constituting a minimum consumption standard of food, clothing, lodging, etc., adjusted to size and composition of the family. To obtain the components of this minimum he and his staff made a careful analysis of the income and occupations of a number of families, their habitual expenditures for various items of consumption, and their relation to each other. But while the "poverty line" was, in a sense, the great divider of those above and below, he did not content himself with simple statistics of incidence of the two, but on the basis of painstaking study arrived at a classification of the total population into a series of economic classes (they happened to come to eight), leaving a fluid interpretation possible, rather than a rigid division into two: above and below. Yet the four lower groups were the poor and distressed, shading from distressed and in want to poor and—though he did not use the term—statistically vulnerable. Moreover, while keeping constantly in focus the quantitative relation between income and necessary expenditures, he never lost sight of the psychological and cultural elements involved. His terminology from the habits of today may seem archaic, his moralistic outlook constantly recurring in description and definition, but there was little of the repressive and impatient upper-class attitude in evidence. He introduced a large number of striking and original ideas, not the least of which was the construction of maps for various parts of London based on extent of poverty in the population of streets surveyed. The seventeen volumes of the great study are by now of only historical value, and particularly so for London. But when considered as the foundation of the significant studies that followed, of the changed attitudes engendered, and of the numberless acute and original observations included, it is still a pertinent modern scientific entity.

⌦ WORLD WAR I AND THE APPEARANCE OF FREUDIAN PSYCHOLOGY

Perhaps the only good reason for including these two items under one heading may be one of chronology. The dates of World War I are 1914–18; Freud's works were first noticed in America about 1914. *The Interpretation of Dreams* may be the first of his works that came to the attention of the general public. On the clinical side of the subject, it will be recalled that in recruitment and in discharge, and later in determining combat fitness, the psychological element quickly became an important concern of those responsible for the enormous number of persons drawn into the armed services. This concern was reinforced by the mounting task of caring for discharged veterans under federal sponsorship and at federal expense. It is likely that the entry of psychoanalytic thought into acceptable social welfare planning may have been one of the important results of World War I operations. While the full weight of the relevance of psychological factors, both for men in the service and for those discharged, showed up only in World War II, a sense of responsibility on the part of government for those in any way disabled, physically or emotionally, emerged even in the earlier war. There was also a new sense of common concern by civil and military authorities for the welfare of servicemen during and after active service. Still another element was added by items in draftee classification with respect to family responsibilities of the men called up for service. This in turn drew into the organizational set-up the Red Cross, particularly in its civilian responsibilities. The economic factors of families became a military concern, and this soon brought in psychological considerations in part at least, a common area for a casework approach in and out of the field of active service. By the end of World War II psychiatry and psychiatric casework were organically related to the problems of military personnel both for the armed forces and for veterans. An enormous demand therefore developed for psychiatrically competent medical, nursing, and casework staff. In the market for caseworkers the military and veterans' service became a great competitor and tended to draw them away from civilian agencies. The employment market had undergone an enormous change.

The effect of psychoanalytic psychology on the orientation of caseworkers, on their training, and on their massive withdrawal from service in the field of economic assistance in favor of "relationship therapy" has been commented on in earlier chapters. In historical perspective, the importance of the Freudian conceptual flood goes beyond the competition for trained workers in the several services. The new psychology affected the workers' sense of identification both with the client and with the sponsoring personnel of voluntary agencies. At the same time, also, it tended to diminish the workers' interest in the economic and environmental aspect of the social system.

So far as client relationship is concerned, the effect of the commitment to psychoanalytic thought, reinforced as it was by the indirect effect of its new place in the sphere of military personnel, has made, in a sense, for an egalitarian attitude comparable to the democratic dogma in the socio-political field. For now worker and client were sisters or brothers under the skin. The condescending and perhaps impatient judging of the client as inferior, shiftless, or incompetent and immoral gave way to recognizing a fellow-being beset by the same kind of emotional problems and drives, all legitimized, for client and worker alike in a "scientifically established" and universally operative network of pressures within the psyche. One could understand, accept, and forgive the frailties of the client, for they were, except in detail or in severity, the same as those of the worker. On the positive side, therefore, an affect-conditioned democratic feeling was created that was far easier to bear than the external democratic dogma to which many of the values of centuries of caste system were attached. The worker knew, moreover, that the new psychology had a far greater and culturally more equalizing quality than either political theory or theological tenet. In a sense, therefore, it seems that a certain deeply democratic acceptance of the client was achieved as both fellow actor and fellow audience in the complicated ballet in which id, ego, and superego performed.

There has been much evidence, also, that something of the same kind of egalitarian atmosphere has grown up between the board-member personnel of the sponsoring voluntary agency, particularly in the casework field, and the social worker engaged in that agency. For cultural infiltration of the new psychology among members of board personnel resembled its counterpart among workers. A considerable number had witnessed psychoanalytic therapy in their own families, or had obtained help in marital problems or problems with their children, or had themselves undergone psychoanalytic therapy. Since not a few students in schools of social work also entered formal therapy, there grew up a sense of considerable fellowship among workers and sponsors. For concepts of psychoanalytic psychology appear to have become part of the culture of the "educated" American in a more intimate and living way than theories of economic, sociological, or perhaps even political philosophy. Its importance is visible in both technical and operational aspects of welfare.

≥ THE BEVERIDGE REPORT AND SOCIAL SECURITY

The Beveridge Report,[7] so called, was published in England in 1942. It has come to be recognized as the Magna Charta of inclusive systems of social security and economic assistance. The Social Security Act of the United States was signed by President Roosevelt on August 14, 1935, and the Social Security Board began its operations on October 1, 1935. Judging by these dates alone the movement that resulted in that legislation preceded the English by some seven years. Nothing could be further from the truth. The epoch-making American legislation is the high point of this country's achievements in social welfare, but it came as the immediate result of the near-catastrophe that followed the Wall Street crash of 1929, not as the logical effect of mature public opinion. The road for the

[7] *Social Insurance and Allied Services* by Sir William Beveridge (Macmillan, 1942; American Edition).

American security system (other than the financial debacle that preceded it) was built and paved by political and social leadership in Britain, and we are in that sense its beneficiary.

Why this country did not in its own right think through and experiment with a social security system until its depression following 1929 is a matter for speculation. England is a small country, with a compact history, with one Parliament, and with a national outlook. It also has its local differences, its local governments, its notions as to what is voluntary and what is public concern, but insofar as major economic, political, and social issues are discussed, they become a matter of national concern. We, on the other hand, have fifty state parliaments, with all the accompanying power rivalries and special interests, and fifty variables as to financial resources, all these watchfully and jealously viewing the single national parliament and its potentially abundant resources. It has always been a difficult thing in our political system to think as a nation first, and as a group of sovereign states second. But basic economy and basic problems are national in fact, though it is against the grain for political and special interests so to view them. Through the mediation of economists and political scientists in the brain trust under President Roosevelt we did have a chance to observe the English developments. Before identifying high points in the story of social security in this country, it is therefore appropriate to mention the milestones on the English road to that goal, bearing in mind that England had not waited for a near-catastrophe. De Schweinitz, in his compact review of the English experience, recalls some of the more striking changes in English official points of view as presented by its leaders.[8] First, quoting David Lloyd George, speaking in 1906:

> Shame upon rich Britain that she should tolerate so much poverty among her people . . . There is plenty of wealth in this country to provide for all and to spare. What is wanted is a fairer distribution . . . I do not suggest that there should be a compulsory equal distribution of wealth of this country among its inhabitants,

[8] Karl de Schweinitz, *England's Road to Social Security,* Chapter XVIII.

but I do say that the law which protects those men in the enjoyment of their great possessions should first of all see that those whose labor alone produces that wealth are amply protected with their families from actual need, where they are unable to purchase the necessaries . . . I mean not that they should be referred to the scanty and humiliating fare of the pauper, but that the spare wealth of the country should, as a condition of its enjoyment by its possessors, be forced to contribute first towards the honorable maintenance of those who have ceased to be able to maintain themselves.

In a speech some two years later, the eloquent statesman of that era, Winston S. Churchill, speaking on unemployment, says more philosophically:

I do not agree with those who say that every man must look after himself, and that intervention by the State in such matters . . . will be fatal to his self-reliance, his foresight, and his thrift . . . If terror be an incentive to thrift, surely the penalties of the system which we have abandoned ought to have stimulated thrift as much as anything could have been stimulated in this world. The mass of the laboring poor have known that unless they made provision for their old age betimes they would perish miserably in the workhouse. Yet they have made no provision . . . It is a great mistake to suppose that thrift is caused only by fear; it springs from hope as well as from fear; where there is no hope, be sure there will be no thrift.

It is in the light of these new points of view (as persistently pressed by the Fabians) that we can understand the series of legislative acts listed by de Schweinitz, leading up to the great event, the National Insurance Act, as follows:

1907: Education Act, principally concerned with medical inspection in the public elementary schools

1908: Old Age Pension Act

1908: Coal Miner Act, concerned principally with the eight-hour day

1909: Labor Exchanges Act

1909: Trades Board Act, dealing with minimum wages

1909: Housing and Town Planning Act

1911: National Insurance Act, for health and unemployment insurance

This last piece of legislation marked the final commitment of Britain to a basic attack on destitution, on a national scale, and independently of such concern with poverty as remained within the realm of general political action and programs of organized labor. From this as a foundation came further specific legislative enactments, expanding, refining, and coordinating provisions which from various angles were intended to keep the wolf from the door or doors still accessible to inroads of destitution. One of the persistent difficulties that kept provisions in a turmoil was the bureaucratic dispersal of administrative responsibility, rooted in the long history of England, and in some ways producing the same inefficiencies and inequalities attributable in this country to the concept of "sovereign" states, to regional differences in a land 3,000 miles across, with contemporary ancestors sprinkled over longitudes and latitudes.

The Beveridge Report, which must have begun its incubation back in 1911 when Sir William worked closely with Churchill in the birthing of the National Insurance Act, is a landmark not by way of specific legislation enacted, but because it proposed two simple, but from the point of view of social engineering, nearly prophetic proposals: one to shake the multiple and unwieldy administrative maze into a logically integrated whole; the other to establish the theory of a national minimum—too low, apparently from every point of view—but of social significance beyond anything except perhaps the liberation of slaves and the enactment of universal adult suffrage.

THE GREAT DEPRESSION AND THE NEW DEAL

The foregoing components of the historical perspective may possibly be improperly weighted. Items may have been omitted that should be included. The reader may judge some things overemphasized, others too cavalierly treated. But except for dates and places, history is, after all, largely a matter of opinion and of individual values. Few informed persons would fail to recognize that the Social

Security System of the United States as enacted in 1935 and further developed and improved since that time is the most important act in the treatment and prevention of destitution in this country. And it is also the most essential accessory factor, aside from the trade union movement, industrial technology, and federal regulation of economic forces, to have made this country with its immense natural resources and its democratic commitment the inspiring civilization that it is.

There had been advocates of social insurance in the United States before this time, but they were voices in the wilderness. Here and there in the country there had been workmen's compensation laws enacted, but they were uneven and stray occurrences. They are still, at this time, within the realm of state legislative acts. The same is true in the main of unemployment insurance; but there had been no concerted movement of any substance for a comprehensive social security or social insurance program. Even the subject of widows' pensions enjoyed only desultory interest, and its appeal, such as it was, seemed limited largely to *ad hoc* efforts for child welfare or public assistance in general. There were two early American exponents of the general idea of social insurance to cover all forms of incidence of economic breakdown. The earliest was I. M. Rubinow, a physician and actuary, and later the executive of a sectarian family agency. His interest had been consistently in the field of economic assistance as well as in social insurance. He wrote, spoke, and taught,[9] and published the first comprehensive treatise on social insurance in this country in 1916, some five years after enactment of the British National Insurance system. He was followed by an equally scholarly, but even more militant spokesman, Abraham Epstein, whose comprehensive treatise, issued as a part of his organized efforts, was published in 1932,[10] after the Wall Street crash but before enactment of the Federal Social Security Act. This country had seen little or no effort up to that time to promote public responsibility for relief of the destitute on a national scale. On the

---

[9] At one time he gave a course on social insurance in the New York School of Philanthropy.

[10] *Insecurity, A Challenge to America* by Abraham Epstein (Random House, 1933), 939 pages.

contrary, those conducting relief for the destitute labored mightily to keep control within voluntary agencies and succeeded in several instances in effecting discontinuance of even local public relief. If there was some apparent excuse for so doing, on the theory that public relief tended to pauperize the recipient, voluntary agencies rarely if ever examined their performance to see whether all in need were actually helped and whether those that were helped received adequate assistance. Repressive habits persisted. There was no interest in insurance, and no studies were conducted to test adequacy of relief. Attention was increasingly on casework, with relief only as one of the tools in that service.

The great depression of 1929–33 concerns us here at this late date, because it combined—though not clearly—the unavoidable duty in this country to respond both to demands for large scale relief of destitution and, in the fullness of time, to face up to the call for social security. It is not feasible, of course, to cover all the events of those critical years but it may be possible to suggest, in rough, four stages:

1. Intensive efforts by voluntary agencies—chiefly what were still "family agencies"—and by community chests and councils, to study the situation and to raise emergency funds.

2. Setting up state emergency relief structures in the several states to deal with the immense number of incomeless families.

3. Setting up the Federal Emergency Relief Administration to subsidize, support, and standardize state and local emergency efforts and efforts to deal with the problem of transients and migrant labor.

4. Devising national legislation for a permanent program dealing with relief of destitution and with pragmatic efforts for prevention of its occurrence.

Everything about those events following the crash was sudden and unexpected. There were, it is true, some sophisticated members of the financial world who were nervous about the enormous inflation of security values, and here and there a cautious banker would advise his client to sell and make more liquid his investments in high-priced stocks—and they were virtually all high-priced—but these cautious souls were relatively few. Here it is important only to recall that social agencies were as much taken by surprise as the sanguine investor and enthusiastic banker and broker. It was not long, however, before relief agencies began to be flooded with applications, and their resources rapidly failed to meet demands made upon them. At first the situation looked merely like an emergency, comparable to a natural disaster, and efforts were made beyond anything precedented to raise funds for the emergency. Each community focused on its own immediate problem, and frantic efforts were made to meet the "disaster." In New York City, for example, successive city-wide drives were made under leadership of prominent citizens, and it took some time for operating agencies to recognize that something was happening for which not only were their funds inadequate, but also their habits of thought and their theories.[11]

Equally unprepared were state and federal governments. It took several years before governments and public realized that this was not only a temporary emergency, although it certainly was that also, but either a permanent debacle, or at least something in the nature of an economic earthquake, which might recur in some form more or less severe again and again, and that some permanent means would have to be devised to meet the situation. Voluntary family agencies and particularly the national organizations representing their points of view and habits of thought found it difficult to face the inevitable: that they were, and would continue to be, unequal to the task of supplying economic assistance to the large number in destitution or threatened with destitution. Even when the inevitable happened and relief measures had to be organized by state and federal governments, there were attempts and pressures toward designating existing family agencies, both sectarian and nonsectarian, as the distributing instrumentalities.[12] It was a bitter pill

[11] For example, in New York City it took the agencies some time to recognize that the center of interest had to be not their individual budgets but the distribution of the unemployed. It came as a bitter shock to some that the huge funds subscribed in the first frantic drives would have to be allotted to the agencies, not in accordance with their relative budgets, but with the geographic distribution of the unemployed in the city.

[12] A point of view still regnant in children's agencies and many health-care organizations. In this connection, a quotation from Miss Brown's

to swallow that thenceforth the frequently derided public relief departments might have to be entrusted with this preeminently important phase of welfare.

The actual sequence of events is both too long and too simple to require any detailed recitation. Its main features can be briefly stated in terms of the present program of the Federal Security Administration, its achievements, its "toothaches," and its probable lines of extension in the immediate future. Its history during the brief span of a generation since its inception is accessible to interested students.[13] Part of its basic present shortcomings are rooted chiefly in events preceding its establishment. State emergency administrations came into being before the Federal Emergency Relief Administration was created or the Social Insurance System established. As a result, state administration of public assistance programs appears irrevocably established, not only as an administrative method —which is quite reasonable—but also as the standard-setting and regulation-making instrument. It is in this latter aspect of their functioning that parsimonious, repressive, punitive, and archaic theories about the poor and destitute live on. And too often, match-

---

volume on *Public Relief* mentioned earlier is of particular interest. She quotes part of Mr. Gifford's testimony before the Senate Committee on Manufactures. (Mr. Gifford was director of the President's Committee on Unemployed Relief, appointed by President Herbert Hoover; he had been for many years, while an executive of the American Telephone and Telegraph Company, chairman of the Charity Organization Society of New York, and a thoughtful leader in the field of voluntary family agencies.) The quotation reads (p. 88): "In theory, I like the tax resources better. We have, however, built up the system the other way. We have in normal years, community chest campaigns and a great to-do about it, and in view of the grave situation we are in today, I think it is a dangerous thing to change the practice, whatever the final evolution may be."

[13] See, for example, *The Big Change* by Frederick Lewis Allen (Harper, 1952). See also, as an example of the way in which the federal government seeks to raise standards by a combination of scheduled escalation of demands upon state systems and seductive offering of increased federal contributions as these standards are approached, *Annual Report* of the Department of Health, Education, and Welfare, 1963. pp. 54–59. A most helpful concise statement of the 1964 program of the federal provisions is contained in *Social Security Programs in the United States* by Ida C. Merriam, Director of Research, Division of Research and Statistics, Department of Health, Education, and Welfare, 61 pp. (Government Printing Office).

ing contributions of the federal government for the aged and for mothers with children are used as a way of stinting in the states' own financial responsibilities and as nostalgic reaching for judgment against the poor and needy. Fortunately, the states cannot reach the insurance systems (except perhaps to some extent the unemployment insurance provisions). Eloquent testimony to this local and ungenerous commitment exudes in many spots in statistics annually reported by the Department of Health, Education, and Welfare. This is, alas, the less inspiring aspect of the American road to social security and to the democratic life.

In all this development, through their boards or their employed personnel, voluntary agencies did not as a group or through their national associations crowd the halls of legislative and executive offices to offer enthusiastic support toward making the new day in social welfare a shining one. After the first intensive activity of voluntary agencies at the outbreak of the depression, and the initial flocking of trained personnel to assist the new public enterprise in its heartbreaking task, the tendency was for personnel to ooze back into voluntary agencies and to programs more enticing in content, and away from "Operation Public Assistance."

In the formal process of setting up the plan for the inclusive Social Security Act there was an interesting similarity between the steps taken here and those recorded in Britain. A Cabinet committee was entrusted with the task of designing the new system, so that it became an executive task for quick decisive action, in view of the desperateness of the situation. The Congress did, indeed, exercise its final power in passing the necessary legislation. But unlike many other measures in the gradual evolution of a system—such as had been the case in the Tennessee Valley project—it had a crisp executive plan, approved by the legislative body and then enacted into the basic governmental structure of American social welfare.

Chapter XVI

⧉⧈

Theoretical-Philosophic Foundations

There are two rather distinct, though not totally separable, sources of our present social welfare system. One might be called the bio-logical-anthropological source; the other, the institutional or or-ganizational source. Family cohesion, clan solidarity, tribal unity, would seem to have arisen from a combination of animal need to perpetuate the species; group or social organization in a more in-direct way serves the same purpose. Cultural anthropology has identified various patterns in primitive society that provide this social structure. The essential characteristics of this social organization are with us today, and they are as much part of our habits—almost

269

instincts—as feeding, procreation, self-preservation. They have become emotions, concepts, mores, compulsions. Part of them enter into what we have called compassion, mercy, good will, charity, loyalty, group cohesion.

Distinct from these internalized psychological foundations of social welfare are the procedural means of implementing communal intentions. These have taken an incredible number of forms. To illustrate the institutional or procedural designs of helping the less competent members of society one need only sample a list which would include: systems of providing for parentless children of the clan; cities of refuge as defined in the Old Testament; the right of the poor to glean edges of fields; formalized provisions for traveler and stranger; "bread and circuses"; monasteries and hospitals; orphanages, almshouses, indenture; parish relief, endowed charity; settlement laws, tithes, poor-rates. And now we would add social security, unemployment insurance, Medicare, public assistance, aid to families with dependent children, rehabilitation and vocational education, and so on.

☙ THE JUDEO-CHRISTIAN TRADITION

In a very practical sense the Judeo-Christian tradition has been the foundation of charitable activities from the beginning of post-Roman Western civilization. It should, in fact, be called the Christian tradition, for the Old Testament and the post-Biblical Jewish precepts were restricted to the Jewish communities as a minority group, whereas the vast Christian population received the Judean precepts via the New Testament and the great Christian theorists like St. Augustine and Thomas Aquinas. But the church as an organization took over the task of interpreting Biblical guidance on charity as a duty and as an organized practice. The extent to which the church became the law and guide is aptly expressed by the Webbs[1] in the very first paragraph of their monumental study of the English poor law:

[1] *History of the English Poor Law* by Sidney and Beatrice Webb, which is part of *English Local Government* (Longmans, 1927–29), is not only the most remarkable and complete work on the subject, bringing it up to the Royal Commission report of 1909, but also contains footnote references

Throughout all Christendom the responsibility for the relief of destitution was, in the Middle Ages, assumed and accepted, individually and collectively, by the church. To give alms to all who were in need, to feed the hungry, to succor the widow and the fatherless, to visit the sick, were duties incumbent on every Christian, not wholly, and perhaps not even mainly, for the sake of those who were relieved, but for the salvation of the charitable. Almsgiving ranked with prayer and fasting as the outward and visible signs of the inward and spiritual grace, which it was the very purpose of religion to create and spread among all men, as it was its most noticeable effect.

There were, however, some aspects other than theological and organizational coverage by the church that determined the nature of the tradition of charity. It is highly doubtful that the Judeo-Christian precepts on charity would have succeeded through Christendom if there had not been, from primitive times, long antedating any written history, the basic pattern for members of the human group to aid one another. It was perhaps a question of how the group was defined, and what form the aid would take. It is safer to assume, therefore, that the Judeo-Christian tradition mainly conceptualized ageless customs and formalized them, then spread them into the organized mores and practices of the increased masses in Western civilization who first accepted and then were largely ruled by the church or churches over Christendom. More important for our practical perspective is the question: What, aside from Christian tenets, were the realistic traditions that controlled the operations of charity in the Western civilization of which we are heirs and present parts? Roughly they might be summed up as follows: moralistic precepts that were intended to control behavior; power concepts associated with these precepts; and *ad hoc* regulations imposed by changing external conditions. These traditions were not always in harmony with one another, either in theory or in practice.[2]

---

that constitute an invaluable bibliography of practically all authoritative material. If there is a bibliographic "must" on the subject, it is this work.

[2] The reader will find some repetition, hopefully held to a minimum,

Insofar as charitable activity was proclaimed a Christian or a social virtue, and also insurance for afterlife, the act of charity was its own reward. It had no bearing necessarily on the nature and extent of relief extended. This became a fact with respect to individual charity, and to organized practices of parish, monastery, endowment, and public relief. It had, however, unintended effects on behavior that tarnished both theory and practice. For the donor developed self-righteousness, pride, and a sense of moral superiority over those aided. To the natural sense of superiority of those in possession of material and social advantages, regardless of whether earned or inherited, was easily added this sense of moral superiority. Nor did possession by inheritance rather than by personnel effort reduce that sense, rather the reverse, so that the aristocratic tradition gained reinforcement. This in itself might not have been harmful were it not for the converse: that the recipient was *ipso facto* of a lower moral order. Written history of these many centuries amply illustrates and supports this general thesis, and it is no less evident in colonial writings and in present-day resistance to realistic public relief measures. An additional support to this tradition was supplied by the absorption into Judeo-Christian precepts of a negative attitude to sex in general; and while those in possession of means and power could satisfy their sexual needs without being a Henry VIII or an urban Frenchman, infraction of sex morality by the poor or destitute added to the judgment of their "inferiority." In our own day in the United States, the most virulent attacks on aid to mothers of dependent children have managed to derive considerable momentum from emphasizing illegitimate children in addition to nonsupporting parents.

Nothing in the religious tenets of synagogue or of Christian church supports this assumption of the inferior moral worth of the poor. Any such tradition cannot, therefore, gain authority from theological sources. On the contrary, considerable adverse argument is recorded. That, however, has not prevented responsible leaders within the Judeo-Christian community, as individuals, legislators, and rulers, to combine power of possession with virtue in the pos-

in these chapters of comments and references made when they were pertinent in earlier pages.

sessor, even to the point in relatively modern times of making property qualifications a condition of suffrage. It was probably inevitable that power and possession in tandem would find support in economic theory and in socio-political organization. In retrospect it is clear that these twin guides of social behavior brought confusion into organized Christian practice as well. The power-plus-property pattern was reflected both in monarchic political structure and in the elaborate feudal design that ruled Europe for the better part of the Christian era, and it was given sanction by church machinery, albeit in a confused form. Bishops and archibshops became feudal lords, even though their legal power descended not by blood but by clerical title.

Charity retained its fundamental place of honor and its administrative machinery in parish and monastery. But there was no solution to the contradiction between indiscriminate benevolence to the beggar and the destitute and exploitation of the land-bound laborer in the feudal net. The history of many centuries of English life shows at one and the same time near bankruptcy of the parish weighed down by an impossible burden of poor relief and exploitation—within the law—of the tithe-paying citizen by the landholding church structure. So we witness "burghers in strife with monks," parish priests sympathizing with the villein farmer, John Ball preaching against the "Caesarian clergy"; we learn of the prior of Bury St. Edmonds murdered by his own serfs, and the Archbishop of Canterbury beheaded in London by Wat Tyler's men.[3] Yet the mores of Christian charity continue, by individuals and by parishes, through local relief, donations, and philanthropic endowments.

If all this were only a matter of historical interest, fascinating as it is, one could dismiss the whole thing from present consideration and turn to the practical problems of social welfare: purposes and administration. In at least three inescapable respects, however, it is important to disentangle the confused tradition and to evaluate its parts as they concern our present welfare tasks. One is the continuing association of Christian precepts of charity and ethical behavior flowing from other philosophical sources; another

[3] See G. M. Trevelyan, *English Social History* (Longmans, Green, 1943), Chapter I, on the rising in 1381.

is the residual operation of services under sectarian sponsorship; the third, the intricate ways in which property and power pressures, masquerading as ethics but operating through legal and governmental instruments, manage to retard acceptance of the fact that all members of the community are inextricably intertwined as both producers and consumers.

Except for those who regard all morals and ethics as having been derived from revelation in the Judeo-Christian tradition, it is clear that democratic concepts and social conscience existed before Greek, Roman, and Christian cultures spelled them out. And it is equally clear that the democratic principle in politics, economics, and social relations as we now know it has emerged as much from synagogue and church as it had from philosophical writings in Europe, from political tenets of the Puritan fathers, and from relentless preachings of such men as Tom Paine and Karl Marx. Granting that the main preoccupation of most religious observers is with their future salvation; granting even that charitable activities are part of a partial payment plan with that in mind, persistent reiteration of church precepts of charity, coupled with biological impulses of good will for others of their kind, has made charitable tendencies a reality. And while charitable intent may be, and often is, betrayed to serve prestige, vested interest, power, and social group life, it would seem that a vast proportion of those professing the Christian or Jewish faiths have built up as part of their faith a deep sense of true charity. It is not that those without church commitment have no ethical impulse toward charity. It is merely that faith as nurtured in organized religion has supported attitudes and practices of good will, both in individual and social activities.

In some instances, in fact, ethical demands of a formal sect appear to have overshadowed theological drives. It is so apparently in the Society of Friends, whose charitable services command enormous respect; and it is so with many missionary activities. But most important is that there is, or seems to be, a persistent layer of ethical feeling in those professing Christian and related faiths. It would seem also that some of the potentials for development of a democratic culture have been imbedded in the church, despite religious war, inqusition, Ku Kluxism, and prejudice. In much of the early gropings toward a democratic view and toward acceptance of one's fellowmen as equals, there seems indeed to be a quality that is akin to the less formal religious tenets of many sects. And it is hardly sound to assume that the very ones who practice prejudice, cruelty, and vindictiveness do not, alternately, sense the good will that is called Christian charity. It may be equally unsound to assume that those who profess, on philosophical grounds, a democratic and equalitarian philosophy are necessarily free of prejudice, insensitivity, and cruelty to their fellows.

Part of the Judeo-Christian tradition and an important part in this historical perspective has been the setting-up of institutions and organized practices for aiding the destitute and suffering. Types of institutions and institutions themselves were established as both organized and individual expressions of charity and good will. They then naturally came to be associated with the church or sectarian bodies that sponsored the institutions, reinforcing their status as vested interests and building up power structures of great variety and influence.[4] In the English pattern, and its American counterpart, the chief institutional exemplar was, first, the parish (sometimes township) as the universal local instrument for operating and financing charitable activities. The Webbs record that there were some 15,000 parishes in England—of all sizes and kinds—each with the obligation and authority to grant or to deny relief. That this parish system was eventually found to be economically an impossible burden, and for real "relief" an administrative defeat, was recognized only after centuries of trial and error. Independently of the parish structure as such came the brick-and-mortar institutions under religious auspices: monasteries and hospitals. These grew up without reference to local parish administration, generally related to formal church structure within the Catholic pattern and later under the Church of England. Still within the Christian tradition of charitable activity were orphanages and special institutions, and varied "endowments" and "foundations."

Significant for the system as a whole is the resultant group-

[4] This has been true particularly of nations and areas largely peopled by adherents of the Catholic church, like Spain, Portugal, Italy, France, South America, among others.

ing of welfare activities under sectarian leadership and in sectarian fragmentation: Catholic, Lutheran, Presbyterian, Protestant in general, Society of Friends, Jewish, and others. This sectarian grouping is responsible for several characteristics that have often posed obstacles to the development of an inclusive system of service. It has retarded planning by nature of need instead of by affiliation with sponsorship. With the development of types of united community financing, with the vested interest aspect of voluntary agencies in general and of sectarian groupings in particular, there has been a distortion of the Judeo-Christian tradition of charity and good will into group and power structure that may mask the reality of need and the truthful pattern of financial support. There are Catholic Charities, Protestant Unions, and Jewish Federations, with occasional variants like those of the Latter Day Saints; and all of them are reluctant to recognize social planning in which the need of the citizen—regardless of faith—is the center of concern. Major exceptions include the Salvation Army and the Society of Friends.

In economic assistance, where the public agency does not pay, there is great selectivity by religious affiliation. Family agencies (to the extent that they still give service to those in economic distress) tend to serve members, though with exceptions, of their own religious affiliation. This is particularly true of Jewish and Catholic agencies. In child care, where public payments are the chief source of support, sectarian lines are much more strictly drawn. This applies to institutions, to foster care, to adoption, often to guidance clinics, and to some extent to agencies serving handicapped children. The most consistent limitation of service along sectarian lines is in those providing recreation. In these agencies there is, in fact, little claim to the practice of Judeo-Christian tradition of charity. It is not a denial of that tradition, but rather an irrelevancy. For the agencies become promoters of sectarian and group cultures, instruments of group cohesion. Often sectarian specialization is reinforced by grouping of minority, ethnic, or racial preferences. There have been instances, as noted in an earlier chapter, of recreational and group activity services where the physical plant was actually abandoned and the services removed to areas more predominantly occupied by the sponsoring faith, sect, or minority.

There have been other, sometimes disingenuous instances of

sectarian retardation of welfare services. A regrettable instance was the move by the sectarian-voluntary group of agencies of one of our great cities in 1959. Its relevance to the present discussion rests in the fact that the move was sponsored by representatives of the three major sectarian groups of agencies together. The intent was not to expand services within the realm of charity as nurtured by the Christian and Jewish tradition, but to expand and further entrench vested interests of the sectarian-voluntary group, its sponsors, administrators, and financial backers. The incident has sufficient illustrative significance to justify quotation.

A report dated September 30, 1959, presents conclusions, recommendations, and supporting discussion of "The Mayor's Committee of Inquiry on the New York City Department of Welfare" (manned by representatives of the sectarian groups). A sort of preamble states: "A Department of Welfare should provide such services as are demonstrably necessary and otherwise lacking. No necessary welfare service is demonstrably lacking unless voluntary effort and every reasonable effort to stimulate voluntary services have failed. Before undertaking to establish a new public welfare service it should be ascertained that voluntary effort is unequal to the task and is unable to perform it with assistance from government. For example, before government itself expands its function, the purchase of services from voluntary agencies should be considered. The existence of financial need alone is not sufficient reason for a Department of Welfare to expand with its own staff, into services to an individual to the exclusion of voluntary agencies." It is pleasant to recall that the outdated and reactionary proposals of that group were clearly denounced by the professional social work organization of that city. At this point it is necessary to note only that the temptations of vested interests, even when operating under the banner of organized religion, may betray the fundamental Judeo-Christian tradition of charity as it has flowered in Western culture.

PUNITIVE PRESSURES—POLITICAL AND SOCIAL

It is difficult to know or to assess the relative importance in the mind of man of two staple requirements: goods to satisfy his physical needs and power and status to support his self-assurance. The history of poverty and destitution is obscured by the interplay of these two requirements, masked in form but brutal in realism; the instinctual drives behind both struggle for priority. Unequal availability of means for satisfying physical needs immediately becomes reflected in the distribution of power and status. We are dealing here primarily with pressures relating to relief of destitution and lessening of poverty. On the face of it, therefore, it would seem that "economic" should be added to "political and social" in the heading above. But while the substance of our concern is economic, pressures have taken the form of political and social measures.

In England's experience, it was often difficult to distinguish between the "poor" and the "laboring" classes. And as there were difficulties with the laboring masses that the ruling class was determined to handle its own way, so also it determined to handle the poor in the same way. And there was not always a clear distinction made between "pauper," "vagabond," and "poor." All this became reinforced and exacerbated as the catastrophic Black Death destroyed a very large portion of laboring men, leaving widows and helpless orphans; it enabled surviving laborers successfully to demand higher wages, seek employment of their choice, and gain a self-assurance from the new power that thus came their way. This eroded control by employer and landlord. Remedies attempted by the ruling class therefore sought legal control of wages, control of the place of employment, punishment by courts, and rigorous handling of dependents of the wage earners. The Black Death wielded a many-stranded whip over the economy and social relations in England. One can do no better than again to recall the general description of the situation as formulated by the Webbs, who amplified and illustrated their judgment with many literary and documentary data. So, for example,[5] "The King and his nobles were intent upon . . . the maintenance of the then existing order, based on social hierarchy of rulers and ruled, of landowners and those who belonged to the land. Thus for over seven hundred years, from Athelstan and Canute down to Henry VIII, the statute book abounds

[5] Webb, Part One, Chapter I, p. 23.

in laws of ever-increasing severity, against vagrants whether as sturdy beggars or rogues . . . or as laborers who abstracted themselves from their obligations to the manor or parish to which they belonged, as well as from the service of the 'master to whom it was assumed that they owed their labor . . .' " The Statute of Laborers of 1350, the Webbs further state, "required accordingly all persons able to labour and without other means of support, to serve any master *at the rates customary prior to the pestilence . . .*"[6] Suitable punishment was provided for infraction of the law, including branding on the forehead.

There are some data available on class distribution of population, and also some on levels of living in England among the poor in the centuries preceding this one. It is difficult to translate these into present-day concepts, even if it were possible to allow for differences in purchasing power over the years to say nothing of translating the English monetary system into dollars and cents). It becomes even more difficult when one recognizes that cultural traditions applying to food, clothing, shelter, sanitation, and social activities are almost beyond our grasp in present-day America.[7]

Roughly the pressures taking social, political, and subsequently legal form in English and colonial history—and continuing, though in less virulent form, in this country today—relate to cost of maintaining the poor, to fear of "vagabonds" and rebellious im-

[6] Webb, Part One, Chapter I, p. 25.

[7] Nevertheless it may be profitable for the reader to recapture some of the quality of the early period. In addition to the work of the Webbs already referred to, considerable light may be gained from G. D. Cole's *History of the British Common People,* and particularly from some of his citations from Sir Frederic Eden's *State of the Poor,* which describes in sober factual recital the mode of life of the poor in England. Some idea of the relative proportion of "laborers" and upper-class population may also be gained from these. It is, for example, probably shocking to the American reader to realize that the laborer with his average four or five children may have had meat at best once a month, cheese somewhat more often, milk but rarely, and even potatoes only after the earlier periods. Comparable material in many respects in reference to some of the less-developed countries today may be gained from the UN brochure on *Meeting Needs in Less-Developed Countries.* Wer― we able to cover the levels of living of the poor today, we might find that in many parts of the world seventeenth-century England is no stranger to the life of millions of its families.

pulses, and to danger of upsetting the caste structure of social life. In the theoretical rationale that justified repressive and even punitive measures against the poor it is not easy to disentangle moralist narcissism, economic defensiveness, and political intent. They combine and reinforce one another and take on an appearance of scholarly objectivity. In the introductory discussion dealing with circumstances that led to the appointment of the Royal Commission of 1832–34 (including the deterioration of the condition of wage earners), the Webbs quote expressions of opinion of some of the most influential writers on the Poor Laws. The general attitude of these writers as expressing the "New School of Thought" is summarized by the Webbs as follows:

> 1. That the public relief of destitution out of funds raised by taxation—as distinguished from the alms of the charitable—devitalized the recipients, degraded their character and induced in them general bad behavior.
> 2. That the operation of the Malthusian Law of Population, actuated by the Theory of the Wage Fund, rendered all such relief not only futile in diminishing the miseries of the poor, but actually harmful in the creation of a wider pool of destitution . . .

To illustrate more specifically the literary contribution of exponents of what they call the "New School of Thought" a number of selected passages are quoted from the Webbs. First,[8] "the Rev. Joseph Townsend (1739–1816), rector of Pewsey in Wiltshire and sometime chaplain to the Countess of Huntington and the Duchess of Atholl . . . in his famous *Dissertation on the Poor Law of 1785,* declares that:

> It seems to be a law of nature that the poor should be to a certain degree improvident, that there may always be some to fulfill the most servile, the most sordid, and the most ignoble offices in the community. The stock of human happiness is thereby much increased, while the more delicate are not only relieved from

[8] Webb, Part Two, Chapter I, p. 8, and Conclusions in Part One of the *History of the English Poor Law.*

drudgery and freed from those occasional employments which would make them miserable, but are left at liberty, without interruption, to pursue those callings which are suited to their various dispositions, and most useful to the State. As for the lowest of the poor, by custom they are reconciled to the meanest occupations, to the most laborious works, and to the most hazardous pursuits; whilst the hope of their reward makes them cheerful in the midst of all their dangers, and their toils. The fleets and armies of a state would soon be in want of soldiers and sailors, if sobriety and diligence universally prevailed; for what is it but distress and poverty which can prevail upon the lower classes of the people to encounter all the horrors which await them on the tempestuous ocean or in the field of battle? . . . When hunger is either felt or feared, the desire of obtaining bread will quietly dispose the mind to undergo the greatest hardships, and will sweeten the severest labors. The peasant with a sickle in his hand is happier than the prince upon his throne.

More intellectually sophisticated is the passage quoted from Dr. Patrick Colquhoun in *A Treatise on Indigence* (1806):[9]

Without a large proportion of poverty, there could be no riches, since riches are the offspring of labour, while labour can exist only from a state of poverty. Poverty is that state and condition in society where the individual has no surplus labour in store; or, in other words, no property or means of subsistence but what is derived from the constant exercise of industry in the various occupations of life. Poverty is, therefore a most necessary and indispensable ingredient in society without which nations and communities could not exist in a state of civilization. It is the lot of man. It is the source of wealth, since without poverty there could be no labour; there could be no riches, no refinement, no comfort, and no benefit to those who may be possessed of wealth . . .

While these and other examples of the late eighteenth and early nineteenth century would seem to be only literary antiquarianism, they must be seen in context of the effect they were intended to pro-

[9] Webb, Part Two, Chapter I, p. 9.

duce and did produce in the administration of public relief, and the effect they had on the smug assumption that individual charitable action was sufficient and that a strict regime should be imposed on the demands and behavior of "the poor." In view of the fact that the underlying philosophy behind these expressions of opinion and the subsequent recommendations of the Royal Commission of 1832–34 determined the way for American colonies and for the United States as well, these quotations are far more significant than if they were merely "interesting history." It is, for example, surprising at first that our own Benjamin Franklin fully shared the above points of view, and that Dr. Chalmers, often cited as the originator of modern scientific poor relief, strongly expressed similar sentiments. It should then be less surprising to see continuity between the attitudes expressed by leading spokesmen of English policy in the eighteenth and nineteenth centuries, and of much of the local public opinion in our own day, among businessmen, farmers, and even wage earners. Benjamin Franklin, visiting London in 1766, remarked that[10]

> There is no country in the world in which the poor are more idle, dissolute, drunken and insolent. The day you passed that act (of 43 Elizabeth) you took away from before their eyes the greatest of all inducements to industry, frugality and sobriety by giving them a dependence on somewhat else than a careful accumulation during youth and health for support in age and sickness . . . there is no country in the world where so many provisions are established for them, so many hospitals to receive them when they are sick or lame, founded and maintained by voluntary charities . . . together with a solemn general law made by the rich to subject their estates to a heavy tax for the support of the poor. . . . Repeal that law and you will soon see a change in their manners. St. Monday and St. Tuesday will soon cease to be holidays.

Finally, since the Rev. Thomas Chalmers holds so prominent a place in the history from which American relief principles have

[10] Webb, Part Two, Chapter I.

stemmed, and was recognized by some in his day as a political economist of distinction as well as being a Presbyterian minister honored by court and aristocracy, the following passage[11] may have special significance:

> Now it should be recollected that it has all along been our main object to show, that the poor laws of England are the result of a very bungling attempt on the part of the legislature, to do that which would have been better done had nature been left to her own free processes, and man to the unconstrained influence of such principles as Nature and Christianity have bestowed upon him. We affirm that the great and urgent law of self-preservation ought not to have been so impeded in their operation; that the sympathies and the attentions of neighborhood ought not to have been so superseded; that the powerful workings of generous and compassionate feeling ought not to have been so damped and discouraged, as they have in fact been by this artificial and un-called for process of interference.

It is not surprising then to see the general summary by the Webbs of the laws relating to the poor adopting an earlier writer's conclusions that they were designed "not so much to relieve 'the poor' as such, as to restrain the demands of manual workers from setting a higher price on their labour or insisting on greater luxury of life; and by savage punishments, to discipline the whole property-less class to the constrictions and regular service, in agriculture and manufactures, of those who were becoming their masters." And by this time it was clear that pressures to keep the laborer in his place—in essence largely economic, but also social—had become more puni-tive than charitable. Recommendations of the Royal Commission, aside from proposing an administrative reorganization of local and national functions, carried out the sentiments of the ruling classes. So far as a theoretical framework of the practice of poor relief is concerned, the Commission elevated the workhouse system for sup-port of able-bodied laborers and their families into top category; it spelled out as the "first and most essential of all conditions, that

[11] Webb, Part Two, Chapter I.

. . . [the able-bodied person's] situation on the whole shall not be made really or apparently so eligible as the situation of the independent laborer of the lowest class . . . that in proportion as the condition of any pauper class is elevated above the condition of the independent laborers, the condition of the class is depressed . . ." And to make the intent of the law dramatically clear, one official of the new regime suggested[12] that

> . . . new life, new energy is infused into the constitution of the pauper; he is aroused like one from sleep, his relation with all his neighbors, high and low, is changed, he surveys his former employers with new eyes. He begs a job—he will not take a denial— he discovers that everyone wants something to be done. He desires to make up this man's hedges, to clear out another man's ditches, to grub stumps out of hedge rows for a third . . .

and so on, in further detail.

The term "free enterprise" was not used in connection with these opinions, nor, except in the case of Dr. Chalmers, was emphasis on the spirit of the New Testament and the teachings of Christ the key argument. But the laissez-faire theory had been discussed, and the theoretical bent of that policy was clearly congenial to the natural desire for regimentation which was still the pattern of government. Whether by one name or another, the "less eligibility" concept was in harmony with the interests of the employer and the furtherance of what today we more generally designate the free-enterprise system.

If it is difficult to find a clear and smooth carry-over from English poor-law management to colonial ways, it may be due not to a difference in cultural tradition, but to a difference, beyond expectation, of the conditions of life. It is doubtful whether the habit of domination by those in positions of power as seen in England had disappeared. The Puritan colonists broke away from England chiefly because the specific domination by authorities committed to the theology and organization of the Church of England was repug-

---

[12] Webb, Part Two, Conclusions, p. 420.

nant to their own theological commitment. Authority was resented not because it was authority, but because it was predicated on religious observances not acceptable to the Puritans. But the habit of authority appears to have remained, if not in its pristine purity, hardly with less determination. In what way, then, was the "relief of the poor" different in the Colonies, considering the aristocratic and power domination reflected in the quotations of preceding pages? And in what way has it remained the same or similar? Only rough generalizations are possible, and these are not presented here as mathematically accurate scientific certainties.

There was a continuous need for manpower. The impulse to commandeer labor, and to determine the conditions under which it served, remained. But the feudal landowning pattern within which it had grown in England had largely disappeared in the Colonies. Land was available for anyone who wanted it and who chose to be his own employer. True, this was not the case with indentured labor, nor with slave labor; but it was true to a sufficient extent so that labor could often dictate its own terms. What to do then? Pass repressive laws to keep labor economically, politically, and socially "in its place" as long as possible. This was difficult, of course, for democratic ways were creeping into politics and government. But some successes could be achieved, and the habits of punitive administration did not have to be entirely abandoned. Nor was class distinction eliminated, whether based on property or on class. Farnam[13] quotes an early Massachusetts law "which humanely limited to forty stripes with which a man might be beaten, exempting from all whipping 'any true gentleman' and also 'any man equal to a gentleman, unless his crime be very shameful, and his course of life vicious and profligate.' " Laws were passed at different times and in the different Colonies. So, for example, servants would be punished if they married without consent of their masters. There were laws fixing wages of artisans, and laws against idleness. At one time law required that at harvest time, if labor was short, mechanics might be required in

[13] Henry W. Farnam, *Chapters in the History of Social Legislation in the United States to 1860* (The Carnegie Institution of Washington, 1938), p. 11, p. 23, p. 58.

each town to help in mowing, reaping, and other harvest operations.[14] (This in imitation of a statute of Richard II, passed in
1388.)

For a long time, in colonial America, attempts to regulate
wages—that is, to keep them down—continued, for the social-
economic caste system of England, and of the West in general, had
ripened over many centuries, and it could not be expected to evap-
orate from man's habit of thought and feeling merely because external conditions had changed. In Farnam's words, "The medieval
ideal of a static society, in which each individual had, and kept his
place, persisted long after the period in question. Society in its new
environment was exposed to sweeping changes, but it was the most
natural thing in the world for organized society, as represented in
the government, to resist these changes, and at the least to attempt
to moderate them . . ." But it seems that what government could
not do, individuals would continue to hope they could do, for that
is the way they felt.

The particular forms of punitive repression of the destitute
differed not only from those of the mother country, but also from
one colony or state to the next. Perhaps these differences were ac-
celebrated as the enormous growth of population proceeded, and as
immigration in combination with the industrial revolution brought
about an increase in the poor and destitute. For at first labor shortage held down the number of destitute, and repressive measures
were directed primarily toward insuring availability of labor and
maintaining the caste system. Only as economic conditions and employment changed and "paupers" multiplied was there need for
formal setting up of local relief instrumentalities. And these, in the
main, reproduced the administrative system of the mother country,
with little if any change in attitude. Any detailed picture of the way
in which it all functioned would have to be drawn from the history
of relief systems of the several states of the Union as they came into
existence. In some ways the most persistent and unpleasant phase of
the administration of relief has centered perhaps around the subject
of "settlement." For there we find, on the foundation of reasonable

[14] Farnam, *Chapters*, p. 58.

concern with the financial problems of the local unit, an easy outlet for the rejection of the destitute as generally undesirable.

A detailed history of the operation of the Settlement and Removal Laws of England is not in place here, even if a review of the enormous material on the subject were practicable. Nor is a review of the administrative innovations in dealing with the destitute as they occurred in various European countries pertinent to the general subject of repression dealt with here. Possibly the emphasis on settlement laws in general would be out of place, had they not been incorporated in the entire American system. In one respect perhaps, the question of settlement has a particular importance: it emphasized local responsibility, which had been the system for centuries and militated against a national concept of concern with destitution. Even today, with interstate reciprocal agreements on nonresident and nonsettled "poor," and with a tendency to develop state rather than local ultimate responsibility, and despite expanding federal financing, the defensive attitude about economic assistance still keeps up the barricades of geographical definition of proper relief service.

EMERGENCE OF THE DEMOCRATIC DOGMA

The concept of democracy concerns us here not from the point of view of its philosophical merits but as the third of the large opinion-making theories that have gone into the foundations of present American social welfare practice.

In his article on "Democracy" in the *Encyclopedia of Social Sciences,* Harold J. Laski offers some analysis of the concepts behind the term and some opinions as to the historical incidence of the function of democracy: in politics, government, power distribution. He sees no example of a full functioning of democracy at any time from before the city-states of Greece to our own day. Formal dissertations on the subject are, in fact, not very prominent until the period of the French and American revolutions at the end of the eighteenth century. In suggesting here the inclusion of the "democratic dogma" among the theoretical foundations of the modern social welfare systems, it is in fact not explicit formulations of democracy that we are concerned with but the activist assertion of the will of the many as they recognize that their hardships are imposed by the few. In that respect the French Revolution, though a decade or so later than the American, is far more significant, and probably had far greater influence on philosophical trends, even in America, than our own Revolution. For in America, despite the superb wording of the Declaration of Independence, that document reflected, chiefly, the determination of political entities and administrations representing power structure in the Colonies to liberate themselves from dictation by a superpower. The French Revolution on the other hand, involving some philosophical ideas as well, was the response of suppressed, exploited, and desperate masses, guided by philosophical leadership, to assert their right to life, food, and will. It was an action orientation of more significance for Western culture than the fight for independence of the American Colonies.

The corresponding action orientation in England came also from resentment and rebellion against limitations of individual economic survival, freedom, and social self-respect. That it is of direct concern with respect to destitution and poverty stems from the fact that the "poor" and the "laborer" were nearly synonymous, that the margin of economic survival was narrow, that the industrial revolution had altered the face of the nation's production, and that, despite the vitality of the caste system, political power of the masses was appreciably nearer reality than in the monolithic monarchy of France. As self-assertion of the masses of labor took shape, wages and labor relations were closely related to Poor Law and relief. It could well have happened, if the time and place had been some three thousand years ago in Judea, that some major prophets would have spoken out in fiery words. But no major prophet arose, and the minor prophets were either rebel leaders on destruction bent or men ahead of their time without effective power. Among the rebels were the Luddite leaders, the Chartist leaders, the nameless men who instinctively set up labor unions of infant size, and also literary and parliamentary gadflies like Cobden and Place. But despite slow and even inarticulate leadership the laboring poor increasingly made the government uncomfortable. Landowners and employers were attacked; houses, barns, manors, churches, were burned; hundreds of the rebels had to be prosecuted, executed, exiled, jailed. But the cowed acceptance of the system of power by rulers who had economic and political strength was giving way to something that in retrospect looks like the emergence of democratic self-consciousness. The Royal Commission to examine the Poor Laws anew made no democratic pronouncements, but it worked in the same place and time that produced the Reform Bill of 1832 which marked a great step in the direction of political democracy in England.

Specific recommendations of the Royal Commission, aside from its administrative proposals, were no great shakes in poor relief. Certainly it would seem that nothing striking was done before the report of the Royal Commission of 1905–09 and before total reorganization of service to the economically deficient, based on the Beveridge Report and its sequels. It is in the field of political thinking and political acting that democracy becomes visible, tangible, and effective. And it is in the trade union movement and in the growth of the Labour Party that its theoretical positions and its programs become explicit enough to eradicate the dominant accent of punitive-repressive orientation of poor relief that it had had for centuries. Actually, a final emancipation from the fight on the pauper preceded its American debut by several decades.

In this country the historical perspective and its component parts are not so clear and sharp as in England. Social acceptance of democracy has been older and more natural here, because the caste system has never been so rigid. Whether in the low years of employment and in the wholesale exploitation of labor by the galloping industrial revolution there was less destitution and less poverty than in England it is difficult to say with assurance. There is reason to believe that there was never the desperate and hopeless destitution and wide spread of poverty in the United States that depressed the English nation over much of the nineteenth century. Perhaps for the same reason there was never the consistent discussion and propaganda for measures to deal with it that there was in England. But in the attitude of the citizen at large, who was more rarely destitute and had less of the caste-cloud lying over him, there has grown up a lack of sympathy and lack of a sense of common fate with the poor. He had, perhaps, a lesser understanding of the meaning of poverty and destitution than his English counterpart. Perhaps also the waves of minorities with whom the earlier American felt no kinship afforded him little understanding of poverty, which tended to be greater among minorities whether ethnic or "racial."

What saved him from some of the bitter hostility to the poor has been the intangible atmosphere of "democracy" in the nation. It would be difficult to prove that the concept of democracy, or "the democratic dogma," is a legitimate major partner in the history of the theoretical foundations of American social welfare as it exists today. But it is certain that it is a major factor in the cultural structure itself. There have been thinkers and political leaders in the United States to whom the democratic concept was important and who without hesitation intended to incorporate that concept in operations of the government. It is less clear whether the general population, if it accepted that theory, did so because of intellectual conviction, or because real life in this country carried out that concept in ways only unconsciously recognized by the mores in their daily life. For, by the middle of the nineteenth century, there was little residual sense in America of the aristocratic caste culture or of the feudal heritage of English life. The only place where that caste system remained almost intact has been in the attitude toward the Negro.

There has been no lack of controversy in political, economic, and social discussions in the history of this country. But they tended to revolve around special interests rather than around the basic struggle between haves and have-nots as in England. It has been farmer against merchant, West against East, native against immigrant, ethnic group against ethnic group—but not poor and laborer against rich and upper class. Even if there were giants among the intellectual and political leaders—Sam Adams, Thomas Jefferson, Robert Owen, Henry George—they do not seem to have focalized partisanship along philosophical lines, and certainly not along the lines of massive poverty versus power of property. If, then, the democratic dogma remained in effect and grew in stature, it was hardly a dominant factor in the struggle for economic security before the events of the twentieth century opened the doors for debates on social welfare.

$\mathcal{E}pilogue$

ঌ PERSPECTIVES INTO THE FUTURE ঌ

In social planning, preferences have priority over probabilities. Preferences are the things one fights for. Probabilities are cautious evalua-
tions of expected success with respect to hoped-for happenings. In
this sense there would seem to be a fair probability, for example, of
the emergence of logical and effective planning for economic security
for all; there is also a fair probability of expanding suitable individualized services for those who, even though enjoying security of
livelihood, still need a helping hand to achieve a normal mode of
life.

What are the components of this "probable" economic security in the foreseeable future?

We already have increasingly adequate provision for old age and survivors insurance; for the disabled, the blind, and for a variety of custodial or permanent types of care. These are increasingly free of traces of the punitive past. We provide, at an increasing tempo, education at public expense on all levels of requirement and geographic location. We have increasingly satisfactory institutional provisions for those requiring intramural care, temporary or permanent.

We are approaching—if slowly—a pattern of administrative structure that retains the benefits of individual interest and creative imagination with public responsibility, financial and supervisory. Witness, for example, the agencies for children and adults with a variety of physical, mental, and emotional problems, such as cerebral palsy, muscular dystrophy, muteness, and deafness.

We are learning to retain the normal group interests within our culture which undertake to provide service facilities with diminishing prejudices of ethnic, racial, sectarian, or political origin.

Perhaps most important of all we have taken large strides toward the elimination both of destitution and of poverty—poverty in the sense of unacceptably low income levels for individuals and families—call it a "floor of income," or "guaranteed income," or "negative income tax." This we are able to do, and our economic-philosophical leaders have shown us the way.

Where, then, are we still failing? Where are preferences so little related to probabilities?

It would seem to be in the provision and structuring of required personnel for carrying on the necessary services. The pattern of training for this personnel still seems to be squeezed between promotion of the interests of the "profession" and the traditional mold of academic rigidities. As a result there is little of the purposeful planning for service personnel that would correspond to the demands of the field. Manpower provided for service corresponds less and less to recognized requirements for operating.

There is no organized study of the incidence of need (other than the social insurance and related provision already in the laws) and the relation of that incidence to required personnel. As a result, schools of social work turn out a minimal portion of the manpower required. And that minimum has little relation to the categories of personnel required. There is little organized information to differentiate both qualitatively and functionally among, for example:

1. Personnel for the vast demand for clerical and statistical labors,
2. Investigators (wrongly designated as caseworkers) in the public assistance programs,
3. Psychologically trained workers in services to children in institutions, foster care, and clinics,
4. Psychologically trained workers for service to the aged, to mentally or physically deprived persons,
5. Group leaders in a variety of organized services,
6. Executives and organizational personnel in the increasing fields defined and expanded in programs of the Organization for Economic Opportunity ranging from Head Start to vocational guidance.

Neither definitions nor studies of incidence are in the front line of endeavor. We are almost at dead center, almost immobile.

A vast number of clerical and administrative personnel is needed for social security measures, to operate, check, review the tasks. No type of agency, least of all schools of social work, is ready to venture into the requirements of this task, where the largest personnel may be required. What personnel is used receives no professional encouragement or recognition. Investigators and practitioners in public assistance, necessarily operating on local levels, receive no imaginatively and invitingly planned preparation. Psychologically and socially trained workers intended to give individualized and understanding service to children, the aged, or disoriented, delinquent, or deviant clients are indeed given preparation in schools of social work—full-fledged or limited—but the number forthcoming do not begin to meet the quantitative demand.

There is an unclear, undefined area, with inadequate job analysis for personnel, to manage group activities whether in recreation, housing, job corps, or community programs for activities such as those in the Organization for Economic Opportunity. Suitable persons are found by happy accident. And it has nothing to do with "hundred neediest cases" or the solicitors for "United Fund" campaigns.

With the probabilities of tackling the major tasks of personnel training so low, and the vision, originality, and courage in the major professional and academic centers so dim, one is again reduced to falling back on preferences if not hopes. One thing is certain: Until the extent and nature of client needs become the proper focus of planning, and the ambitions of professional personnel take their appropriate place as auxiliary motivations, the development of effective welfare programs will come increasingly from the leadership of economic and political thinkers in government, universities, and the press.

If we attain a sufficient degree of modesty to replace pride in our successful vested interest structure, we might again look at the road traveled by the people of Great Britain from whom we have learned so much, including their "career system" for national and local government employees. Because of its evident pertinence at this point, the following compressed presentation of the British system is drawn from a report published in 1956, particularly from Chapter I of the report by Arlien Johnson, an American social worker of long experience and formerly the dean of one of the American schools of social work.[1]

"The central government for the past 100 years," says Dr. Johnson, "has had a Civil Service which has become famous for the ability, integrity and devotion of its personnel. . . . Most appointments are on a permanent basis and promotion in the various classifications is from within the service . . . a number of Ministries, and in particular the Ministries of Health, Education, Labor,

---

[1] Selected from *Some Impressions of Social Services in Great Britain* by An American Social Work Team, published by United States Educational Commission in the United Kingdom. The group consisted of Frank T. Flynn, Elizabeth Goddard, Arlien Johnson, Jean Reynolds, and Theodore H. Soule. Chapter I of the report contains brief statements entitled: The British Attitude Towards Social Change; Voluntary Organizations and Voluntarism; Professionalization of Social Work; Education for Social Work.

Housing, Pensions and National Assistance . . . have important responsibilities in the social service field. . . . The main Civil Service grades [are] briefly outlined."

1. Clerical grade are recruited at 16–17 years of age . . . [they] may have considerable responsibilities as in National Assistance where they make home visits under the supervision of the executive officers.
2. Executive grade personnel are recruited at ages 17½ to 18½ . . .
3. Administrative grade are recruited at age 20½ to 25 from among the ablest university graduates with honours degrees . . .
4. Professional or technical staff are recruited at a later age and are people with relevant experience in their particular fields, such as inspectors of children's institutions; or doctors, lawyers, social workers etc. . . .

This is only part of the story. But to those who realize the wide margin between operating personnel in the American welfare services on all levels and the output of M.S. graduates of social work schools; to those whose interests are in the meeting of needs of masses of clients, more than in the image of the social workers, "licensed," "certified," or other, to those there is a choice for preferences to be militantly pursued, and the British pattern deserves a close and purposeful scrutiny.

⤳ THEN: WHAT TO DO—WHO TO DO IT ⤶

In ancient Greece it was the practice to consult the Oracle at Delphi when statesmen and generals were planning important moves. About 480 B.C., as the Persians were invading the territories of Athens and Sparta, the Oracle was asked to advise. If its opinion had been the guide for action, the great culture of Greece might well have been destroyed. Fortunately, after another consultation, a revised version, just in time, modified the Delphic opinion and the Greek states were saved, though at the price of the lives of Leonidas and his valiant Three Hundred at Thermopylae. The culture of Greece was more important than the fortunes of its professional warrior personnel.

We are here discussing American culture, or that part of it known as social welfare. There is no Delphic Oracle to guide us. But there have been pronouncements of oracular intent, some of them ancient of days, that until the recent past and even today seem to give direction to the welfare services. Revised versions of these guidelines are in the making, but the older oracular signposts are not yet removed. They may well lead us astray. We must take a close look at these still extant and functionally operative oracular entities if we are to redirect the course of social welfare to a system appropriate to our national wealth, democratic ethic, and technical competence. These entities may be roughly designated as:

1) Voluntary agencies and their several national organizations, comprising men and women of wealth, status, and political influence, and their power-wielding employed executives. These bodies guide policies, dispose of power, set up personnel in the charitable structure, and capitalize on the culture merits of centuries of philanthropic activity.

2) Professional associations, repositories of operational personnel claiming to possess special skills and techniques, cap-and-gown palisaded, "license"- and trademark-protected, theoretically dedicated to service but functionally vested-interest-oriented, and guardians of the "social worker image."

3) Training schools for social service personnel, mostly within college and university structures. They are either full-fledged and accredited M.S.-producing bodies, or one-year preparatory curricula accepting non-full-fledged status, having less of a vested interest within the training field but automatically participating in whatever vested interest may attach to their college or university matrix.

The assumption, rarely disputed, has been that the agencies in the nation serviced by these organizational entities exercise whatever oracular power they possess to advance the welfare of the disadvantaged persons and families within our economy. The various needs that bring the flood of troubled persons to social agencies in the hope of obtaining assistance have been discussed in the foregoing pages. The services designed in their interest are recognized as the social welfare service component of our culture. The tribulations of the needy have been chiefly economic in substance, even though often the presenting symptoms may appear as having many hues, and operations through which they are served may be simple or highly complex.

Rarely, with but few exceptions like the former National Child Labor Committee or the promoters of Planned Parenthood today, have these nation-wide bodies conducted militant battles for even such noneconomic reforms as, for example, child adoption, without the strangling limits of religious affiliation, or reform of abortion or divorce laws, or spelling out the constitutional (if not Constitutional) interest in "life, liberty and the pursuit of happiness" in place of a sex-defined concept of morality.

It is high time, therefore, that in the interest of a true social welfare culture the oracular content of the voluntary agency structure, of professional organizations, and of training schools to provide service personnel be revised if they would still serve as trustworthy oracles.

The following major reorientations are therefore suggested.

First. It should be recognized and unequivocally declared that the first and foremost obligation of a social welfare structure is the provision of economic assistance to the destitute on a culturally acceptable level, and then the prevention of destitution by methods already recognized and practices but not yet comprehensively developed. To this end:

a) It should be declared without reservation that government and its taxing power constitute the fundamental instrument for the maximum possible attainment of this purpose, and that it is even now the major resource and operational structure in that field. Voluntary agencies have given up the possibility of providing this security—at first reluctantly and with philosophic aversion, then happily, as one of their leading spokesmen has said, to "remove the albatross of relief from the neck of social service"—a curious heresy when seen in the light of Christian dogma and economic philosophy.

b) The voluntary agencies, including boards of directors and employed personnel, should make it their chief obligation and task as has already been done to some degree in education and public health) to assist government in its gigantic task, to help gain for it public approval and respect as has been done, for example, by leaders of education and mental health services. To this end the Community Fund-raising instrumentalities should proclaim loud and clear that they are but "junior partners" especially operating at the marginal task of specialized services. They should offer to give help to government programs in whatever way possible, as numerous foundations are already doing, and particularly to help improve the reality and the image of government services. That highly respected section of the press, the *New York Times,* should discontinue its unrealistic and, in essence though not in interest, reactionary publicity pageant of "100 Neediest Cases" appeal; its beneficiary families are a minuscule fraction of the needy in that city, and the beneficiary agencies a quantitative pigmy in the light of the millions expended by the public welfare lists.

Second. The National Association of Social Workers, the "professional association" of employed welfare service workers, should revise its policies, membership requirements, and program so that it may emerge from its archaic mold and practices. Particularly,

a) as to *policy,* that organization should, if it still would claim the social purposes it originally accepted, devote its labors clearly to advance the interests of clients, not the interests of a privileged group of social service employees. There are legitimate aspects of employee interest that are more logically within the functions of labor unions. Except when usurping technical functions under guise of professional interest, labor unions in this as in other areas are better suited to defend the economic status of employees. For these reasons, and for reasons that relate to membership qualifications, the organization should drop its elaborate and disingenuous strutting behind palisades of M.S. degrees, "licensed" social workers, and the spurious "Academy of Certified Social Workers."

b) as to *membership,* it is reasonable that all persons employed in social agencies public or voluntary, and having an interest in remaining in that field, should, after satisfactory performance during an initial period of six or twelve months, be eligible for membership in the professional association and promote its legitimate purposes. Probably in our kind of culture a basic standard of education as symbolized by the Bachelor's degree, should be, in any case, a condition of employment as well as of membership (though even this practice may well be modified in relation to workers trained in foreign countries). Under such a system of membership qualifications, public assistance and similar personnel would come to constitute a substantial proportion of the Association membership, and it might not hurt to drop such designations as "cabinet members." There might well be instituted a system of "honorary memberships" for nonemployed personnel, such as board members and "lay" activists.

c) as to *programs,* under such a system or structure they not only would not suffer but might well improve. One program development may indeed be expanded when a liberalized concept of membership and of purpose is created, namely legislative lobbying. It will then be easier to concentrate on client benefits rather than personnel. Lay, professional, and labor union interests might well be combined to battle the reactionary elements, whether tax-minded or infected with moral superiority.

Third. The schools for training of welfare service personnel, unless they are to be protected antiques and semi-alien entities in the university educational pattern, should and, whether they know it or not, will have to re-examine their function Medicine has done it, even if not perfectly. In that field, personnel comprises admittedly diverse types. There are not only physicians, but also nurses, laboratory technicians, public health service administrators, research workers, and specialists. Is the training of all this personnel the same? Curricula, duration of training, professional organization the same? Yet even in medicine shortage of personnel has not received adequate consideration in an over-all and geographically realistic design.

It would seem that the training schools are in a strategic position to trigger and guide a philosophic reorientation of the social service perspectives second only to the federal government and to the genius of intellectual adventures by philosophical leaders in the applied social sciences. If the schools can escape the bonds of their vested-interest shackles, if they find the leaders who will re-examine in bold perspective the labor market for social service and the curricular structure as well as the operational consumer body interests, then perhaps they will again lead the field of social service as part of national planning and as ethical goal. Any such re-examination and planning would have to go much farther than the more immediate proposals submitted in an earlier chapter. It would involve a retailored pedagogy in classroom and field, and a suitable modesty, willing to accept a secondary role for schools, professional associations, and voluntary agencies to the national program for all citizens.

If then we should discover what is to be done and who is to do it we may slowly come to recognize that we need no oracles—only dedication, wisdom, and, above all, common sense. For we will remember that without these qualities trained workers can be as cruel as the tax-opposed man of property or the sturdy laborer who regards the relief recipient as a parasite. Individual members of the affluent class are often no less sympathetic to the needy client than the polysyllabic graduate of a training school. It is the complex nature of our culture that determines the pattern of social services. That culture is heir to the tribal and feudal cruelties of scores of centuries. It is heir also to the ethical visions of the prophets of Judea and Christendom. It has not escaped the eloquent message of St. Francis any more than the pride and love of property of the privileged.

Today many of us see in the trend of democratic philosophy the promise of a mature system of social welfare. Ethics and modesty provide the color, and technical competence the tools. These can rise above the drag of bureaucracy whether in government or in other administrative machinery. Organization is an enabler as well as a killer. There have always been those who were intrigued by the promise of vested interest structure. But also there have been, in the history of social welfare as well as in the history of Western culture, leaders with vision and with courage. We need some of that now. They will know what to do and who should do it.

Index

ABBOTT, E., 207
ABBOTT, G., 207
ACKERSON, L., 188
Academy of Certified Social Workers (A.C.S.W.), 209, 211, 214, 215, 216, 218, 219, 298 (*See also* National Association of Social Workers)
ADDAMS, J., 115n, 117, 120, 122, 134, 207, 221
ALBEE, G. W., 101n, 105n

ALEXANDER, F., 155
ALLEN, F. A., 267n
American Association of Social Workers (A.A.S.W.), 203, 204 (*See also* N.A.S.W.)
American Medical Association (A.M.A.), 74, 75, 76, 110n, 207
American Red Cross, 232, 232n
"Appalachia," 23
Assistance: to aged, 50; to blind, 48, 50; categories, variations between, 61; to disabled, 48, 50; to families with dependent chil-